Codex 2/50

D1576992

Alfasud
Owners
Workshop
Manual

by J H Haynes
Member of the Guild of Motoring Writers
and Tim Parker

Models covered
Covers Alfasud 2- and 4-door saloons, 1186cc, from 1973 through 1976
Alfasud
Alfasud SE
Alfasud N
Alfusud L
Alfasud TI
Alfasud 5M
Does not cover the Estate or 1300 Sprint

ISBN 0 85696 292 9

©   J H Haynes and Company Limited 1977   ABCDE
                                                     FGHIJ

All rights reserved. No part of this book may be reproduced or transmitted in
any form or by any means, electronic or mechanical, including photocopying,
recording or by any information storage or retrieval system, without permission
in writing from the copyright holder.

Printed in England

HAYNES PUBLISHING GROUP
SPARKFORD YEOVIL SOMERSET ENGLAND
distributed in the USA by
HAYNES PUBLICATIONS INC
861 LAWRENCE DRIVE
NEWBURY PARK
CALIFORNIA 91320
USA

Acknowledgements

Few books are the work of one person and this one is no exception. Thanks are due to Alfa Romeo (GB) for their ever ready technical information and permission to reproduce some line illustrations. Many of their franchised garages have also unknowingly given helpful advice and helped to point out some of the more obscure differences between the Alfasud models which might otherwise have escaped mention.

Car mechanics magazine kindly supplied many of the photographs in the bodywork repair sequence of Chapter eleven.

Castrol Limited provided lubrication details.

Brian Horsfall and Les Brazier once again have helped in photographic preparation and Ted Frenchum aided the layout of the manual after Rod Grainger and John Rose had completed their usual excellent editing job.

About this manual

Its aims

The aim of this book is to help you get the best value from your car. It can do so in two ways. First it can help you decide what work must be done, even should you choose to get it done by a garage, the routine maintenance and the diagnosis and course of action when random faults occur. However, it is hoped that you will also use the second, and fuller, purpose by tackling the work yourself. This can give you the satisfaction of doing the job personally. On the simpler jobs it may even be quicker than booking the car into a garage and going there twice, to leave and collect it. Perhaps most important, much money can be saved by avoiding the costs a garage must charge to cover its labour costs and overheads.

To avoid labour costs a garage will often give a cheaper repair by fitting a reconditioned assembly. The home mechanic can be helped by this book to diagnose the fault and make a repair using only a minor spare part.

The book has drawings and descriptions to show the function of the various components so that their layout can be understood. Then the tasks are described and photographed in a step-by-step sequence so that even a novice can cope with complicated work.

The jobs are described assuming only normal tools are available, and not special tools. However, a reasonable outfit of tools will be a worthwhile investment. Many special workshop tools produced by the makers merely speed the work, and in these cases guidance is given as to how to do the job without them, the oft quoted example being the use of a large hose clip to compress the piston rings for insertion in the cylinder. However, on a very few occasions the special tool is essential to prevent damage to components, then its use is described. Though it might be possible to borrow the tool, such work may have to be entrusted to the official agent.

Using the manual

The book is divided into eleven Chapters. Each Chapter is divided into numbered Sections which are headed in **bold type** between horizontal lines. Each Section consists of serially numbered paragraphs.

There are two types of illustration: (1) Figures which are numbered according to Chapter and sequence of occurrence in that Chapter. (2) Photographs which have a reference number in their caption. All photographs apply to the Chapter in which they occur so that the reference figure pinpoints the pertinent Section and paragraph number.

Procedures, once described in the text, are not normally repeated. If it is necessary to refer to another Chapter the reference will be given in Chapter number and Section number thus: Chapter 1/16.

If it is considered necessary to refer to a particular paragraph in another Chapter the reference is usually given in this form: 1/5:5'. Cross-references given without use of the word 'Chapter' apply to Sections and/or paragraphs in the same Chapter (eg; 'see Section 8') means also 'in this Chapter'.

When the left or right side of the car is mentioned it is as if looking forward from the rear of the car.

Great effort has been made to ensure that this book is complete and up-to-date. However, it should be realised that manufacturers continually modify their cars, even in retrospect.

Whilst every care is taken to ensure that the information in this manual is correct no liability can be accepted by the authors or publishers for loss, damage or injury caused by any errors in, or omissions from, the information given.

Introduction to the Alfasud

Introduction

The Alfasud is built close to Naples in Southern Italy unlike all the other Alfa Romeo models which are made in Milan — hence Alfa Romeo Alfa*sud*. The Alfasud is not a typical Alfa Romeo on paper, many longstanding Alfa enthusiasts say it is not a 'real' one even on the road. In the author's opinion the Alfasud is as much a 'real' Alfa as any of them. If in doubt, drive one!

The Alfa Romeo company is partially government owned and because of this Alfasud is very much a product of government organized employment. There was need for mass employment opportunity in Southern Italy and this coupled with the lack of a small car in the Alfa Romeo range prompted the setting up of a factory outside Naples early in 1968. Within three years the factory was ready; soon after the first Alfasud rolled off the production line. Alfa Romeo had hired Rudolf Hruschka (a member of the original Porsche design team) to design the mechanics and Giugiaro of Italdesign the body. It is surprising therefore, to see a radical change from the familiar Alfa twin overhead-cam alloy engine and rear wheel drive?

The Alfasud was born in the shadow of the Citroen GS, many people feared for its success because of this. They need not have worried for the Alfasud is as much a complete car as is the GS but it behaves differently. It is an outstanding car on many counts perhaps its most praiseworthy feature is its steering. The Alfasud must be one of the five best cars in the world, no matter what the price, in terms of its steering.

It's an Alfa for the masses, a cheap, compact and economic car scoring on functionality and style, but its still an Alfa.

Modifications to the Alfasud range

Such is the complexity of modern car production in all its aspects, it is not possible to list all the modifications that may have been made to one range of cars. Component detail may change overnight without any announcement. This will happen because of either a change of supplier of a given component or simply because of design improvement. All major design modifications are mentioned in this book but some minor ones may not be included, however this in no way invalidates the book, for all changes which will alter repair or maintenance sequences are covered in full. What it does mean is that you should know precisely what you are buying in the way of spare parts and that you should be quite clear at the outset what you are doing before you tackle any task. It can, nevertheless, be stated that Alfa Romeo are not a company which indulges in multitudinous minor changes to their products almost for the sake of it. In over two years of production the cars in the Alfasud range there have been very few major changes.

Contents

Note: *Specifications, torque wrench settings and general descriptions are given in each Chapter immediately after the list of contents. Where applicable, fault diagnosis is given at the end of each appropriate Chapter.*

1973 4-door Alfasud Saloon, the project car used for this manual

1975 group of Alfasud TIs. The external differences are obvious

Buying spare parts
and vehicle identification numbers

Buying spare parts

Spare parts are available from many sources, for example: Alfa Romeo garages, other garages and accessory shops, and motor factors. Our advice regarding spare part sources is as follows:

Officially appointed Alfa Romeo garages - This is the best source of parts which are peculiar to your vehicle and are otherwise not generally available (eg complete cylinder heads, internal gearbox components, badges, interior trim etc). It is also the only place at which you should buy parts if your car is still under warranty - non - Alfa Romeo components may invalidate the warranty. To be sure of obtaining the correct parts it will always be necessary to give the storeman your car's engine and chassis number, and if possible, to take the 'old' part along for positive identification. Remember that many parts are available on a factory exchange scheme - any parts returned should always be clean! It obviously makes good sense to go straight to the specialists on your car for this type of part for they are best equipped to supply you.

Other garages and accessory shops - These are often very good places to buy materials and components needed for the maintenance of your car (eg oil filters, spark plugs, bulbs, fan belts, oils and greases, touch-up paint, filler paste etc). They also sell general accessories, usually have convenient opening hours, charge lower prices and can often be found not far from home.

Motor factors - Good factors will stock all of the more important components which wear out relatively quickly (eg clutch components, pistons, valves, exhaust system, brake cylinders/pipes/hoses/seals/shoes and pads etc). Motor factors will often provide new or reconditioned components on a part exchange basis - this can save a considerable

amount of money.

Gaskets - special note

With gasket sets - for both engine and gearbox - do not be alarmed if there seem to be many items included in the set you buy, which do not fit your vehicle. To save a lot of variety of kits they include in one enough to cover a variety of types over a period of time so you are certain to have some left over. However, it is a good idea to check the set before leaving the parts store. Some of the ones you may need could be omitted. Oil seals particularly are not all included - and this applies to some of the smaller ones.

Vehicle identification numbers

When buying spare parts it is necessary to properly identify your car. First give the car model and date (ie; Alfasud TI, June 1975). The *chassis number* is stamped on a plate affixed to the front side of the intermediate bulkhead. The *Identification plate* is fixed to the off-side inner wing - this gives the car model and type approval. The *engine number* is stamped into the engine block casting on the right bank of cylinders at the number 3 cylinder. (The gearbox is identified with the engine number). The *paint finish* plate is fixed to the underside of the boot lid. It is a foil plate. Commonsense will tell you which number you want and when. However, it is a good idea to record all these numbers from your car and have them ready whenever you are buying new parts.

Note the location illustration.

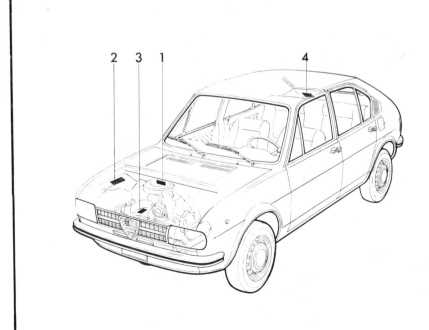

Location of engine and chassis numbers

1 *Chassis number*
2 *Car model and type approval plate*
3 *Engine number*
4 *Finish paint plate*

Tools and working facilities

Introduction

A selection of good tools is a fundamental requirement for anyone contemplating the maintenance and repair of a motor vehicle. For the owner who does not possess any, their purchase will prove a considerable expense, offsetting some of the savings made by doing-it-yourself. However, provided that the tools purchased are of good quality, they will last for many years and prove an extremely worthwhile investment.

To help the average owner to decide which tools are needed to carry out the various tasks detailed in this manual, we have compiled three lists of tools under the following headings: Maintenance and minor repair, Repair and overhaul, and Special. The newcomer to practical mechanics should start off with the 'Maintenance and minor repair' tool kit and confine himself to the simpler jobs around the vehicle. Then, as his confidence and experience grows, he can undertake more difficult tasks, buying extra tools as, and when, they are needed. In this way, a 'Maintenance and minor repair' tool kit can be built-up into a 'Repair and overhaul' tool kit over a considerable period of time without any major cash outlays. The experienced do-it-yourselfer will have a tool kit good enough for most repair and overhaul procedures and will add tools from the 'Special' category when he feels the expense is justified by the amount of use these tools will be put to.

It is obviously not possible to cover the subject of tools fully here. For those who wish to learn more about tools and their use there is a book entitled 'How to Choose and Use Car Tools' available from the publishers of this manual.

Maintenance and minor repair tool kit

The tools given in this list should be considered as a minimum requirement if routine maintenance, servicing and minor repair operations are to be undertaken. We recommend the purchase of combination spanners (ring one end, open-ended the other); although more expensive than open-ended ones, they do give the advantages of both types of spanner.

Combination spanners - 10, 11, 13, 14, 17 mm
Adjustable spanner - 9 inch
Engine sump/gearbox/rear axle drain plug key (where applicable)
Spark plug spanner (with rubber insert)
Spark plug gap adjustment tool
Set of feeler gauges
Brake adjuster spanner (where applicable)
Brake bleed nipple spanner
Screwdriver - 4 in. long x ¼ in. dia. (plain)
Screwdriver - 4 in. long x ¼ in. dia. (crosshead)
Combination pliers - 6 inch
Hacksaw, junior
Tyre pump
Tyre pressure gauge
Grease gun (where applicable)
Oil can
Fine emery cloth (1 sheet)
Wire brush (small)
Funnel (medium size)

Repair and overhaul tool kit

These tools are virtually essential for anyone undertaking any major repairs to a motor vehicle, and are additional to those given in the Basic list. Include in this list is a comprehensive set of sockets. Although these are expensive they will be found invaluable as they are so versatile-particularly if various drives are included in the set. We recommend the ½ square-drive type, as this can be used with most proprietary torque wrenches. If you cannot afford a socket set, even bought piecemeal, then inexpensive tubular box spanners are a useful alternative.

The tools in this list will occasionally need to supplemented by tools from the Special list.

Sockets (or box spanners) to cover range 6 to 27 mm
Reversible ratchet drive (for use with sockets)
Extension piece, 10 inch (for use with sockets)
Universal joint (for use with sockets)
Torque wrench (for use with sockets)
Mole wrench - 8 inch
Ball pein hammer
Soft-faced hammer, plastic or rubber
Screwdriver - 6 in. long x 5/16 in. dia. (plain)
Screwdriver - 2 in. long x 5/16 in. square (plain)
Screwdriver - 1½ in. long x ¼ in. dia. (crosshead)
Screwdriver - 3 in. long x 1/8 in. dia. (electricians)
Pliers - electricians side cutters
Pliers - needle nosed
Pliers - circlip (internal and external)
Cold chisel - ½ inch
Scriber (this can be made by grinding the end of a broken hacksaw blade)
Scraper (this can be made by flattening and sharpening one end of a piece of copper pipe)
Centre punch
Pin punch
Hacksaw
Valve grinding tool
Steel rule/straight edge
Allen keys
Selection of files
Wire brush (large)
Axle stands
Jack (strong scissor or hydraulic type)

Special tools

The tools in this list are those which are not used regularly, are expensive to buy, or which need to be used in accordance with their manufacturers instructions. Unless relatively difficult mechanical jobs are undertaken frequently, it will not be economic to buy many of these tools. Where this is the case, you could consider clubbing together with friends (or a motorists club) to make a joint purchase, or borrowing the tools against deposit from a local garage or tool hire specialist.

The following list contains only those tools and instruments freely available to the public, and not those special tools produced by the vehicle manufacturer specifically for its dealer network. You will find occasional reference to these manufacturers special tools in the text of this manual. Generally, an alternative method of doing the job without the vehicle manufacturers special tool is given. However, sometimes, there is no alternative to using them. Where this is the case and the relevant tool cannot be bought or borrowed you will have to entrust the work to a franchised garage.

Valve spring compressor
Piston ring compressor
Ball joint separator
Universal hub/bearing puller
Impact screwdriver
Micrometer and/or vernier gauge
Carburettor flow balancing device (where applicable)
Dial gauge
Stroboscopic timing light
Dwell angle meter/tachometer
Universal electrical multi-meter
Cylinder compression gauge
Lifting tackle
Trolley jack
Light with extension lead

Buying tools

For practically all tools, a tool factor is the best source since he will have a very comprehensive range compared with the average garage or accessory shop. Having said that, accessory shops often offer excellent quality tools at discount prices, so it pays to shop around.

Remember, you don't have to buy the most expensive items on the shelf, but it is always advisable to steer clear of the very cheap tools. There are plenty of good tools around, at reasonable prices, so ask the proprietor or manager of the shop for advice before making a purchase.

Care and maintenance of tools

Having purchased a reasonable tool kit, it is necessary to keep the tools in a clean and serviceable condition, After use, always wipe off any dirt, grease and metal particles using a clean, dry cloth, before putting the tools away. Never leave them lying around after they have been used. A simple tool rack on the garage or workshop wall, for items such as screwdrivers and pliers is a good idea. Store all normal spanners and sockets in a metal box. Any measuring instruments, gauges, meters, etc., must be carefully stored where they cannot be damaged or become rusty.

Take a little care when the tools are used. Hammer heads inevitably become marked and screwdrivers lose the keen edge on their blades from time-to-time. A little timely attention with emery cloth or a file will soon restore items like this to a good serviceable finish.

Working facilities

Not to be forgotten when discussing tools, is the workshop itself. If anything more than routine maintenance is to be carried out, some form of suitable working area becomes essential.

It is appreciated that many an owner mechanic is forced by circumstances to remove the engine or similar item, without the benefit of a garage or workshop. Having done this, any repairs should always be done under the cover of a roof.

Wherever possible, any dismantling should be done on a clean flat workbench or table at a suitable working height.

Any workbench needs a vice: one with a jaw opening of 4 in. (100 mm) is suitable for most jobs. As mentioned previously, some clean dry storage space is also required for tools, as well as the lubricants, cleaning fluids, touch-up paints and so on which soon become necessary.

Another item which may be required, and which has a much more general usage, is an electric drill with a chuck capacity of at least 5/16 in. (8 mm). This, together with a good range of twist drills, is virtually essential for fitting accessories such as wing mirrors and reversing lights.

Last, but not least, always keep a supply of old newspapers and clean, lint-free rags available, and try to keep any working area as clean as possible.

Spanner jaw gap comparison table

Jaw gap (in.)	Spanner size
0.250	1/4 in. AF
0.275	7 mm AF
0.312	5/16 in. AF
0.315	8 mm AF
0.340	11/32 in. AF/1/8 in. Whitworth
0.354	9 mm AF
0.375	3/8 in. AF
0.393	10 mm AF
0.433	11 mm AF
0.437	7/16 in. AF
0.445	3/16 in. Whitworth 1/4 in. BSF
0.472	12 mm AF
0.500	1/2 in. AF
0.512	13 mm AF
0.525	1/4 in. Whitworth/ 5/16 in. BSF
0.551	14 mm AF
0.562	9/16 in. AF
0.590	15 mm AF
0.600	5/16 in. Whitworth/ 3/8 in. BSF
0.625	5/8 in. AF
0.629	16 mm AF
0.669	17 mm AF
0.687	11/16 in. AF
0.708	18 mm AF
0.710	3/8 in. Whitworth/ 7/16 in. BSF
0.748	19 mm AF
0.750	3/4 in. AF
0.812	13/16 in. AF
0.820	7/16 in. Whitworth/ 1/2 in. BSF
0.866	22 mm AF
0.875	7/8 in. AF
0.920	1/2 in. Whitworth / 9/16 in. BSF
0.937	15/16 in. AF
0.944	24 mm AF
1.000	1 in. AF
1.010	9/16 in. Whitworth/ 5/8 in. BSF
1.023	26 mm AF
1.062	1 1/16 in. AF/27 mm AF
1.100	5/8 in. Whitworth/ 11/16 in. BSF
1.125	1 1/8 in. AF
1.181	30 mm AF
1.200	11/16 in. Whitworth /3/4 in. BSF
1.250	1 1/4 in. AF
1.259	32 mm AF
1.300	3/4 in. Whitworth/ 7/8 in. BSF
1.312	1 5/16 in. AF
1.390	13/16 in. Whitworth/ 15/16 in. BSF
1.417	36 mm AF
1.437	1 7/6 in. AF
1.480	7/8 in. Whitworth/ 1 in. BSF
1.500	1½ in. AF / 15/16 in. Whitworth
1.574	40 mm AF 15/16 in. Whitworth
1.614	41 mm AF
1.625	1 5/8 in. AF
1.670	1 in. Whitworth/ 1 1/8 in. BSF
1.687	1 11/16 in. AF
1.811	46 mm AF
1.812	1 13/16 in. AF
1.860	1 1/8 in. Whitworth/ 1 1/4 in. BSF
1.875	1 7/8 in. AF
1.968	50 mm AF
2.000	2 in. AF
2.050	1 1/4 in. Whitworth/ 1 3/8 in. BSF
2.165	55 mm AF
2.362	60 mm AF

Routine maintenance

Maintenance is essential for ensuring safety and desirable for the purpose of getting the best in terms of performance and economy from the car. Over the years the need for periodic lubrication - oiling, greasing and so on - has been drastically reduced if not totally eliminated. This has unfortunately tended to lead some owners to think that because no such action is required the items either no longer exist or will last for ever. This is a serious delusion. It follows therefore that the largest initial element of maintenance is visual examination. This may lead to repairs or renewals.

In the summary given here the 'essential for safety' items are shown in **Bold type**. These **must** be attended to at the regular frequencies shown in order to avoid the possibility of accidents and loss of life. Other neglect results in unreliability, increased running costs, more rapid wear and more rapid depreciation of the vehicle in general.

Starting procedure: Starting from cold the Alfasud needs careful warming up. Once the engine is running carefully coax it. Do not accelerate the engine until it is warm, since when the engine is cold the oil cannot reach all points requiring lubrication. A red light exhibited on the facia will not go out until the oil becomes sufficiently warm.

Every 250 miles (400 km) travelled or weekly - whichever comes first

Steering
Check the tyre pressures.
Examine tyres for wear or damage.
Is steering smooth and accurate?

Brakes
Check reservoir fluid level.
Is there any fall off in braking efficiency?
Try an emergency stop. Is adjustment necessary?

Lights, wipers and horns
Do all bulbs work at the front and rear?
Are the headlamp beams aligned properly?
Do the wipers and horns work?
Check windscreen washer fluid level.

Engine
Check the sump oil level and top-up if required
Check the radiator coolant level and top-up if required
Check the battery electrolyte level and top-up to the level of the plates with distilled water, as needed

---

3000 miles (4800 km) or 4 monthly, whichever comes first

Steering
Examine all steering linkage and bushes for wear or damage.
Check front wheel hub bearings and driveshafts.

Brakes
Examine disc pads front and rear to determine the amount of friction material left. Renew if necessary.
Examine all hydraulic pipes, cylinder and unions for signs of corrosion, dents or any other form of deterioration or leaks.

Suspension
Examine all nuts and bolts for security on all suspension components.

Tighten if necessary.
Examine all bushes for wear and play

Engine
Change oil
Check distributor points gap
Check spark plugs for wear
Check tension or alternator drivebelt
Check coolant in cooling system header tank.

Gearbox
Check oil level and top-up as necessary

Clutch
Check hydraulic pipe for deterioration or leaks

Bodyshell
Lubricate all locks and hinges, particularly the boot hinges
Check that all water drain holes are free

9,000 miles (13,600 km) or 12 monthly whichever comes first. All previous tasks plus:

Engine
Check camshaft drivebelt tension and adjust if necessary
Check cylinder heads for torque settings
Check valve clearances and adjust if necessary
Renew oil filter
Lubricate distributor
Clean air cleaner element
Check ignition timing and adjust if necessary
Clean fuel pump internally
Adjust engine idle speed and adjust accelerator linkage if necessary

Steering
Rotate road wheels and rebalance if necessary

Brakes and clutch
Check pedals free-movement and fluid leakage of hydraulic fluid

18,000 miles (27,200 km) or 2 yearly whichever comes first. All previous tasks plus:

Engine
Clean carburettor float chamber and jets
Fit new spark plugs
Check HT leads for deterioration
Renew air cleaner element
Flush cooling system and refill with antifreeze mixture of correct strength
Renew distributor contact points

Steering and suspension
Check wheel alignment
Check rear wheel bearing clearance and replace grease
Check shock absorber operation

Brakes
Change brake fluid by draining system (Note clutch too)

27,000 miles (40,800 km) or every three years whichever comes first. All previous tasks plus:

Transmission
Drain gearbox and refill with fresh oil

Engine
Change alternator drivebelt
Change camshaft drivebelt

54,000 miles (81,600 km) or every six years whichever comes first. All previous tasks plus:

Brakes and clutch
Drain hydraulic system, renew all cylinder seals and refill with fresh fluid. Bleed system

Additionally the following items should be attended to as time can be spared:

Cleaning
Examination of components requires that they be cleaned. The same applies to the body of the car, inside and out, in order that deterioration due to rust or unknown damage may be detected. Certain parts of the body frame, if rusted badly, can result in the vehicle being declared unsafe and it will not pass the annual test for roadworthiness.

Exhaust system
An exhaust system must be leakproof, and the noise level below a certain minimum. Excessive leaks may cause carbon monoxide fumes to enter the passenger compartment. Excessive noise constitutes a public nuisance. Both these faults may cause the vehicle to be kept off the road. Repair or replace defective sections when symptoms are apparent.

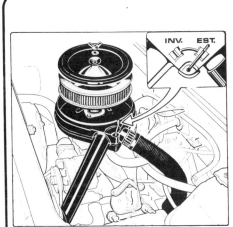

The air filter components. Inset
INV - winter setting,   EST - summer setting

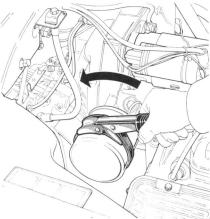

Oil filter removal - the arrow points in the removal direction

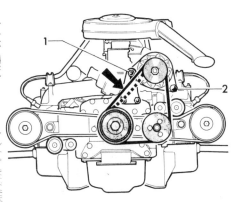

Alternator/water pump drive belt adjustment

1   Adjusting bolt   2   Pivot bolt

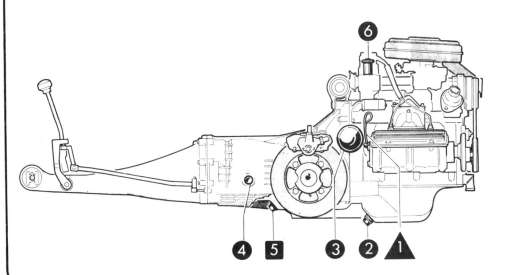

Lubrication schedule

1   Dipstick
2   Sump drain plug
3   Oil filter
4   Gearbox filler plug
5   Gearbox drain plug
6   Oil filler

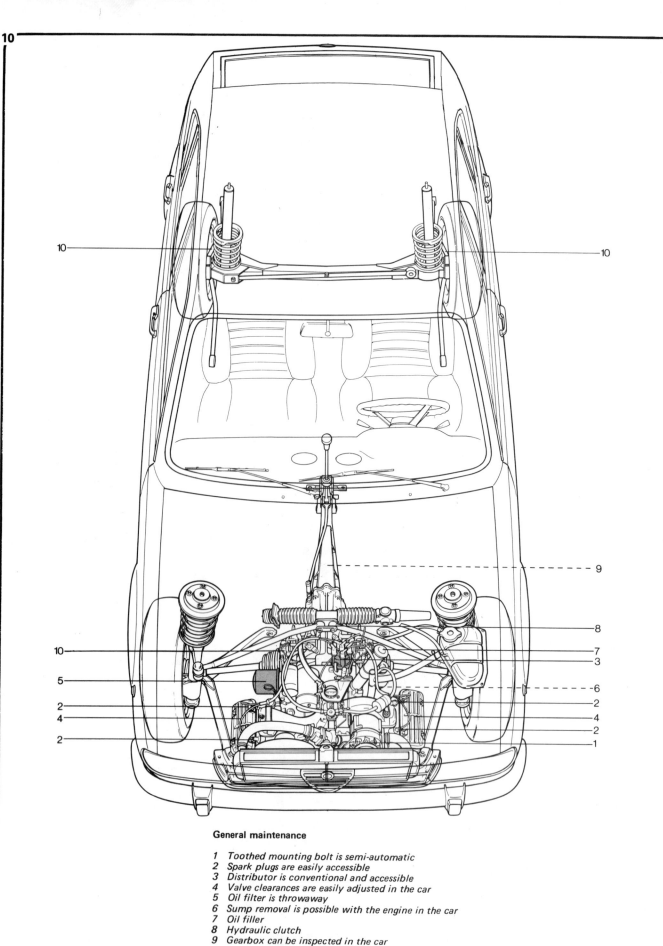

General maintenance

1 Toothed mounting bolt is semi-automatic
2 Spark plugs are easily accessible
3 Distributor is conventional and accessible
4 Valve clearances are easily adjusted in the car
5 Oil filter is throwaway
6 Sump removal is possible with the engine in the car
7 Oil filler
8 Hydraulic clutch
9 Gearbox can be inspected in the car
10 Front disc pads are not easy to change, but the rear ones are

General data

Refill capacities

	Metric	Imperial
Fuel tank	50 litres	11 gallons
Cooling system (inc. heater)	7.3 litres	1.6 gallons
Engine oil (sump and filter) *	4 litres	7 pints
Gearbox/differential	3.4 litres	5.9 pints

Figure given is when full or quantity for regular changing. The total amount of oil in the circuit is 4.6 litres. The 'danger level' quantity is 2.8 litres.

Overall dimensions and weights (all models)

	Metric	Imperial
Length (overall)	3890 mm	151.7 in.
Width (overall)	1590 mm	62 in.
Height (overall)	1370 mm	53.4 in.
Wheelbase	2455 mm	95.7 in.
Front track	1384 mm	53.9 in.
Rear track	1351 mm	52.6 in.
Body overhang from front axle centre	730 mm	28.4 in
Body overhang from rear axle centre	705 mm	27.4 in.
Turning circle	9400 mm	366.6 in.
Kerb weight (full fuel tank)	830 kg	1830 lb

Jacking and towing

Jacking points

The scissor-jack supplied with the vehicle is stored in a specially constructed jig in the boot. The wheelbrace-cum-jack handle is kept with the tool roll. The jack must only be used at the proper positions below the bodyshell. The jack has a special lug which sits under an opening/locating ring just behind the front wheels and just in front of the rear wheels

Towing points

When being towed secure the rope or cable through the eye of the special bracket attached to the front underside centre of the car. Do not tow from any other point or you may find your car changing shape! When towing another vehicle secure the rope or cable to the rigid back axle, on the off side. Make certain that the tow rope does not foul the hydraulic brake pipes and the linkage for the brake pressure limiter valve. This is not difficult to do properly but careful attachment is necessary.

Do not tow too heavy a vehicle. Towing tends to lift the front of any vehicle - the Alfasud can lose traction because of this.

Location of jacking point at the rear

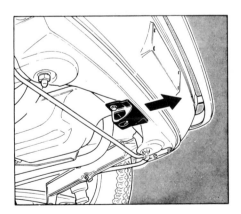

Only permissible towing hook

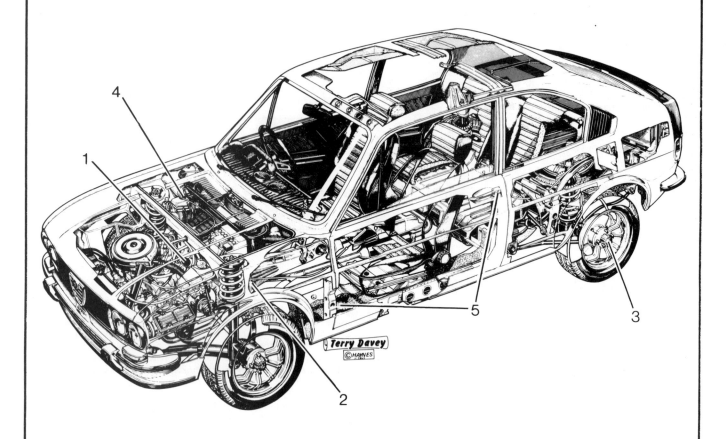

Recommended lubricants

Note: The following lubricants are recommended for use in temperate climates only. Different operating conditions require different lubricants. Consult the handbook supplied with the car.

Component	Castrol product
1 Engine	**Castrol GTX (20W/50)**
2 Gearbox/differential	**Castrol Hypoy (EP90)**
3 Wheel bearings	**Castrol LM grease**
4 Brake and clutch system	**Castrol Girling Universal Brake and Clutch fluid**
5 Hinges, locks and catches	**Castrol Everyman**

Chapter 1 Engine

Contents

Specifications

Engine - general

Type ... ... Horizontally opposed, flat 4-cylinder, water cooled, single overhead camshaft on each cylinder bank

	Alfasud	Alfasud TI
Code number	301.00	—
Bore		80mm (3.15 in)
Stroke		59mm (2.32 in)
Capacity		1186cc (72.4 cu in)
Compression ratio	8.8 : 1	90 : 1
Octane rating		99
Horsepower:		
SAE	73 at 6000 rpm	—
DIN	63 at 6000 rpm	68 at 6000 rpm
Torque:		
SAE	9.8 kgm at 3500 rpm	—
DIN	8.5 kgm at 3500 rpm	—
Idling speed		800 to 1000 rpm
Firing order		1 - 3 - 2 - 4
Oil capacity (both)		4 litres (17 Imp. pints) (sump and filter)

Essential differences between the Alfasud and Alfasud TI engines:

1   *Camshafts and valve timing*
2   *Cylinder heads*
3   *Valves*
4   *Carburettor*

Lubrication system

Type	Wet sump, pressure and splash
Filter	Full flow - replaceable cartridge
Capacity:	
With filter change	4 litres (7 Imp. pints)
Without filter change	3.6 litres (6.3 Imp. pints)
Oil required to fill from lower to upper marks on the dipstick	1.2 litres (2.1 Imp. pints)
Oil pump	Twin gear
Oil pump gear/body end-clearance	Nil
Oil pump gear/backlash	Nil
Oil pressure relief valve set at	4.5 kg/sq cm

Crankshaft and main bearings

No. of bearings, and type	3, thin wall shell
Journal diameters	59.944 - 59.957 mm
Undersize main bearing shells	0.25, 0.50, 0.75, 1 mm
Bearing clearance	0.028 - 0.063 mm
Crankshaft endfloat limits	0.05 - 0.24 mm
Journals, maximum ovality	0.02 mm

Crankcase

Main bearing bore diameter	63.663 - 63.673 mm
Thickness of seating for thrust washers (side-to-side)	23.68 - 23.73 mm
Maximum allowable misalignment of bearing	0.02 mm

Camshafts and bearings

Camshafts drive	2 gear driven toothed belts, external
Bearings	Direct in carrier
Journal diameters:	
Front	34.94 - 34.956 mm
Centre	46.445 - 46.456 mm
Rear	46.94 - 46.956 mm
Bearing housing diameter:	
Front	35.015 - 35.040 mm
Centre	46.515 - 46.54 mm
Rear	47.015 - 47.040 mm
Endfloat	0.1 - 0.3 mm
Width of camshaft register housing	5.45 - 5.5 mm
Thickness of rear cover gasket	0.21 - 0.33 mm
Width of camshaft register	5.5 - 5.55 mm
Diameter of tappet bucket housing	36 - 36.025 mm
Diameter of tappet housing	35.973 - 35.989 mm
Maximum total misalignment of camshaft bearings	0.02 mm
Truth of machined faces	0.03 mm

Connecting rods and bearings

Type	Forged steel
Big-end bearings	Thin wall shell
Small-end bush	Steel bush, lead bronze coated
Big-end journal diameter	49.987 - 50 mm
Big-end diameter	53.696 - 53.708 mm
Undersize big-end bearing shells	0.25, 0.50, 0.75, 1 mm
Clearance of big-end bearing to journal	0.026 - 0.063 mm
Gudgeon (wrist) pin/bush clearance	0.024 - 0.039 mm
Crankpin, maximum ovality	0.02 mm

Cylinders

Type	Machine into cylinder block with liners
Oversize (liner diameter)	0.2, 0.4, 0.6 mm
Maximum divergence from measurement	0.010 mm

Cylinder heads

Type	Aluminium alloy, one per pair of cylinders, cross flow. Alfasud and Alfasud TI use different heads

Pistons and rings

Type	Light alloy. Alfasud and Alfasud TI use the same pistons
Cylinder clearance limit	0.03 - 0.05 mm

Height of piston ring grooves:

Top compression	1.525 - 1.545 mm
Lower compression	1.775 - 1.795 mm
Oil control	4.015 - 4.035 mm

Piston ring thickness:

Top compression	1.478 - 1.490 mm
Lower compression	1.728 - 1.740 mm
Oil control	3.978 - 3.990 mm
Piston oversizes	0.2, 0.4, 0.6 mm
Gudgeon wrist pin	Steel tube
Clearance of gudgeon pin to piston	0.007 0.016 mm
Top compression ring gap	0.30 - 0.45 mm
Lower compression ring gap	0.30 - 0.45 mm
Oil control ring gap	0.25 - 0.40 mm
Gudgeon pin diameter	20.006 - 21.00 mm

Tappet cam followers

Type	Bucket type, encasing valve spring, bearing directly onto camshafts
Diameter of tappet bucket	35.973 - 35.989 mm

Valves, valve seats and timing

Inlet:

Valve head diameter	38 - 38.2 mm
Stem diameter	7.985 - 8 mm
Seat width	1.07 - 1.37 mm
Seat angle	90° - 90° 30' (included angle of seat faces)
Guide bore diameter	8.013 - 8.031 mm

Exhaust:

Valve head diameter	33 - 33.2 mm
Stem diameter	7.985 - 8 mm
Seat width	1.26 - 1.56 mm
Seat angle	90° - 90° 30' (included angle of seat faces)
Guide bore diameter	8.030 - 8.048 mm
Maximum rock in guide (both)	0.9 mm

Valve springs:

Height of free spring	46 mm
External spring: spring length and load with valve closed	33.75 mm/22.95 - 24.35 Kg
Internal spring: spring length and load with valve closed	31.75 mm/11.35 - 12.15 Kg

Valve (tappet) clearance (oil removed from camshaft chest) (cold)

Inlet	0.35 - 0.40 mm (0.014/0.016 in)
Exhaust	0.45 - 0.50 mm (0.018/0.020 in)

Valve timing

	Alfasud	Alfasud TI
Inlet opens btdc	6°	12°
Inlet closes abdc	54°	48°
Exhaust opens bbdc	54°	45°
Exhaust closes atdc	6°	7°

Torque wrench settings

	kg f m	lb f ft
Main bearing cap bolts	6.7 - 7.4	48.5 - 53.5
Side brace bolts	4.1 - 5.0	29.5 - 36.0
Connecting rod bolts	4.4 - 4.9	31.8 - 35.4
Flywheel bolts	9.6 - 10.7	69.4 - 77.3
Crankshaft nut	12.0 - 14.7	86.7 - 106.4
Drive pulley to camshaft	6.4 - 7.1	46.2 - 51.3
Cylinder head bolts	8.3 - 8.9	60.0 - 64.3
Camshaft housing/cylinder head bolts	1.9 - 2.4	13.7 - 17.3

Oil pump set screws:

	kg f m	lb f ft
Large	1.9 - 2.4	13.7 - 17.3
Small	0.8 - 1.0	5.7 - 7.2
Fuel pump nuts	1.9 - 2.4	13.7 - 17.3
Inlet manifold	1.9 - 2.4	13.7 - 17.3

1 General description

The Alfasud engine is not particularly conventional. As a flat four, single overhead camshaft, water cooled engine it is unique at the present time. The specifications explain the basic workings of the engine adequately, this paragraph will explain its significance to the home mechanic. Do not be put off the Alfasud engine by its 'paper' description, nor by what it looks like sitting in the car. It is a relatively simple unit to remove and equally so to dismantle. No special tools are strictly necessary but it is a **must** to use a wide selection of good quality tools. Many spanner (metric) sizes are used; it would be unwise to tackle the job without a full metric socket set, open and ring spanner set, screw drivers, hammers, punches etc. Have some easing fluid available as the majority of the engine components are assembled at the factory with gasket cement and thread locking fluid. Have engine and grease cleaner available, too, as a clean engine is much easier to work on in this case, than a dirty one. Lots of lint free rag and wooden blocks to support the components will help. Follow the instructions very carefully, one sequence out could cost extra time and money. At times it is necessary to have someone else help you; you will be told when this is so.

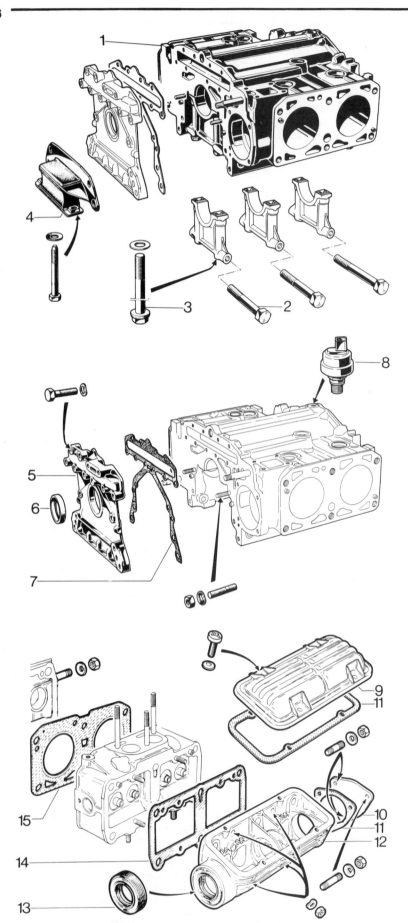

1 Cylinder block
2 Main bearing cross-bolts
3 Main bearing cap bolts
4 Front engine mounting

5 Front cover
6 Oil seal
7 Gasket
8 Pressure sensor

9 Rocker cover
10 End cover
11 Gasket
12 Cam housing
13 Oil seal
14 Gasket
15 Head gasket

Fig. 1.1. Basic, static engine components

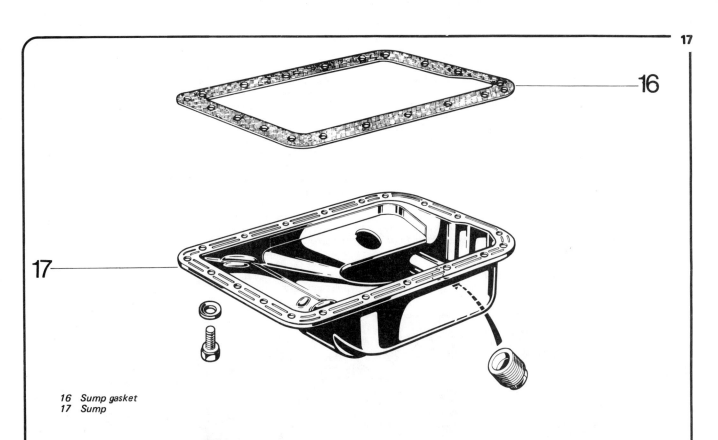

16 Sump gasket
17 Sump

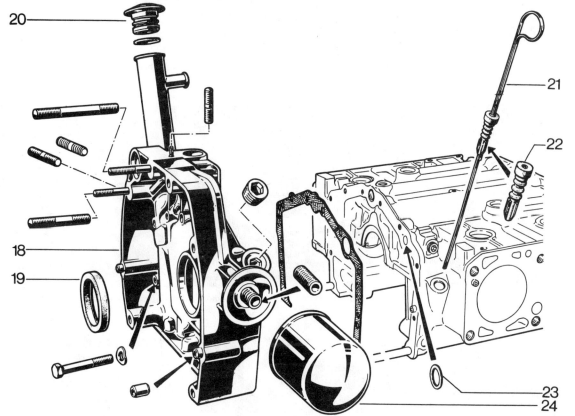

18 Crankcase rear cover
19 Oil seal
20 Oil filler
21 Dipstick
22 Dipstick stop
23 'O' ring
24 Oil filter

2   Major operations which may be carried out with the engine in the car

Little major work can be carried out upon the engine with it still in the car. As it is relatively easy to take the engine and gearbox out of the car you may find that nothing more than routine servicing can be easily carried out with the engine in the car. Here is a list of those tasks which can be carried out with some indication as to whether or not it would be better to remove the engine:

1   *Replacement of timing toothed belts (easy)*
2   *Replacement of inlet manifold, carburettor, distributor, exhaust, alternator and alternator drive belt, radiator and spark plugs (easy)*
3   *Water pump (possible but very difficult due to interference fit of pump)*
4   *Sump (easy)*
5   *Big-end bearings (difficult and from below)*
6   *Oil pump (easy)*

3   Major operations which entail engine removal

It is necessary to remove the engine and gearbox from the car to carry out the replacement of the following components:

1   *Clutch and gearbox*
2   *Crankshaft, flywheel, main bearings, pistons and connecting rods, cylinder heads, valves and camshafts, and oil seals*

4   Method of engine removal

The engine and gearbox must be removed together complete and must always be done from below. This may mean either lowering the engine/gearbox from a hoist under the bodyshell, having jacked up the bodyshell to sufficient height, or to wheel the engine and gearbox from under the car on a trolley jack and physically lift the bodyshell over it. Whatever happens ideal conditions are necessary: flat floor, elbow room, hoist and tall stacks.

4.8a This is the all important radiator top support

4.8b Some parts are left in the photograph to help location

4.9 This return spring is very tight

4.10 The starter motor cables

4.15 Once the air cleaner is off a lot of engine is clear

4.17 Note the cover over the carburettor - the choke cable

4.22 It's a curious system, but it works

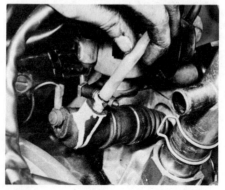
4.23 The slave cylinder is located very sensibly

4.27 The engine oil sump plug. Clean it first

4.28 Pull off both leads from the reverse light switch

4.29 Releasing agent is essential

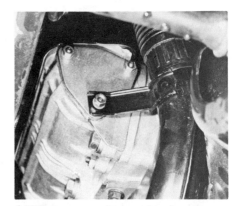

4.30 The cam cover is cleaned to show the location of the bracket

4.31 Note the two rubber doughnuts for exhaust fixing

4.32 Clean up the location first

4.33 Check all the tin ware fixing points

4.34 This shows well the allen screw location

4.36 Engine mounting to crossmember

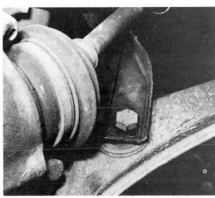

4.37a Bodyshell bolts for the front crossmember

4.37b Do not remove these bolts

4.37c The crossmember and anti-roll bar complete

4.38 One of the bolts is clearly visible

4.39 This is the major centre mounting

4.40 The handbrake cable is visible to the rear of the engine mounting

4.41a We use a hoist - the engine is on a piece of wood

4.41b The car needs to be raised as high as this

5   Engine removal

1   Place the car in a convenient spot where it is possible to gain access underneath it for its full length and where it is possible to leave it jacked up and supported on stands. A hoist can be used or instead a trolley jack to lift the bodyshell or lower the engine, and room to use them.

2   Run the engine until it is at its normal working temperature. Switch off and chock the rear wheels on both sides of the car. Open the bonnet and disconnect the battery earth lead.

3   Remove the front grille. It is fixed by one screw on each side and four on the bottom edge. Pull off the central badge (it is a push-on fit) and remove the last screw which is mounted behind it.

4   The four bonnet hinge bolts are now exposed. Have someone hold the bonnet and rémove the four bolts. Squeeze the bonnet support, unclip it and remove the bonnet to a safe place.

5   It is not necessary but it will give greater working space if you now drain the cooling system and then remove the radiator. Jack up the front of the car and support it. Obtain two receptacles which will hold about a gallon each and place them under the coolant drain plugs, one under the centre of each cylinder block. Undo the plugs and allow the radiator and the cylinder blocks to drain, once you have removed the expansion chamber filler cap. Remove the receptacles and lower the car.

6   Remove the bottom and top hoses to the radiator by pinching the two hose clips on each hose, one at each end, and carefully levering off the tight hoses. Remove the expansion chamber hose at the radiator by unscrewing the hose clip and slipping it off.

7   Pull off the electrical connections to the thermostatically controlled fan switch and one of these to the fan. The other wire to the fan is an earth wire and should be disconnected at earth which is one of the headlamp support studs.

8   Undo the one radiator support which is in the centre of its top chamber. This is a one stud with a nut fixing, on rubber. Undo the nut and carefully pull the radiator back at the top towards the bulkhead, and lift out.

9   Disconnect the accelerator control linkage from the lever on the carburettor. You will need to unhook the return spring and a special connecting ring, a sort of circlip.

10 Disconnect the engine and transmission earth cable which is connected to an end cover nut adjacent to the starter motor. Disconnect the two starter motor cables. Pull off the water temperature warning light wire from the sender unit on the right hand bank of cylinders. All these wires are in the same harness. Tie them all back out of the way.

11 Pull off the terminals from the alternator and then release the cables from the retaining clip on the engine lifting hook which is on the outer end of the inlet manifold fixing. Tie back.

12 Pull off the high tension and low tension cables from the distributor and tie back.

13 Pull off the cable from the sender unit for the engine oil pressure warning light.

14 Pull off the carburettor air cleaner warm air intake pipe from its lower fixing and unclip the hose clip at its top end on the air cleaner. Remove.

15 Unscrew the wing nut on the top of the air cleaner, remove cover and the element inside. Now remove the air cleaner body and gasket from the carburettor. This is fixed by two nuts and studs on the Alfasud and four on the Alfasud TI. Pull off the breather pipes which come with it.

16 Release the support bracket for the accelerator cable from the top of the carburettor which is now exposed. It fits over the top of the inlet.

17 Disconnect the flexible cable and the outer cable of the choke at the clamp and screw. Two small spanners will be necessary here.

18 For ease of movement remove the plug caps and leads together with the distributor cap. Then remove the rotor arm.

19 Pull off the brake servo pipe to the inlet manifold and tie back, on those models so fitted.

20 Unclip the hose clips and remove as many of the heater hoses as possible. Remove them from the front side of the inner bulkhead only; do not remove them at the heater itself. A screwdriver, carefully used to lever off the hoses, always helps. Some of them are clipped to the engine oil filler pipe, disconnect here too. Do not forget the pipe to the expansion chamber also.

21 Disconnect the petrol feed pipe to the fuel pump and tie back.

22 Remove the cap to the brake fluid master cylinder reservoir and place a piece of thin polythene over the opening and replace the cap. This prevents brake fluid leakage for the next operation. Disconnect the front brake flexible pipes from the rigid pipes which come direct from the master cylinder at the special unions, one on each side of the inner bulkhead, on the front side. Two spanners will be necessary. Seal off the pipes with suitable plugs.

23 To remove the clutch slave cylinder from the engine block locate it close to the engine oil filler pipe. On the far side there is a large circlip which holds the body of the slave cylinder in place. Release this circlip and the slave cylinder will come back through its fixing and can be placed out of harm's way on the other side of the inner bulkhead. There is no need to disconnect the piping.

24 Inside the car pull off the gearlever knob. Then pull out the 'bag' at the foot of the gearlever and the rubber gaiter below that. They are nothing more than simply clipped in.

25 Inside the car pull off the handbrake lever gaiter and release the handbrake. Undo the nut on the handbrake lever pivot pin, remove the pivot pin so that the lever is loose. Now remove the circlip on the handbrake cable ferrule which locates the cable to the lever. Juggle the cable inner about to enable the ferrule to release itself from the cable and be pushed through. It has a step on it and this has to be pushed through the lever at an angle.

26 Everything that needs to be done from above the engine has been completed. Now jack up the car as high as you can at the front in the place that you can let it rest whilst the engine is out. Support the front of the car. Remove the front wheels.

27 Drain the engine and gearbox oils. A large container will be necessary for both oils. Both the drain plugs are fitted with sealing washers and appear in the centre of their respective sumps. Replace the plugs when the oil has drained.

28 From below the gearbox at the rear, disconnect the reverse light switch cable by pulling it off. Then disconnect the speedometer drive cable from the side of the gearbox by unclipping the special retaining spring.

29 Go to the left-hand rear road wheel and just in front of it spray the exhaust connection (the exhaust splits here into two parts) with a releasing agent. The joint is bound to be rusted together and its breaking will be helped if you use releasing fluid now.

30 Now go to the front of the car to the right-hand exhaust below the engine. There is a tin moulding which is bolted to a bracket on the exhaust and to the end of the camshaft cover. This is the carburettor air cleaner warm air intake. Remove the two bolts and release the intake.

31 Go back to the exhaust system, split and release the exhaust clamp completely. Tap the connection with a copper-headed hammer and try to make the joint move in some way. Eventually you will have to split them. Use a large screwdriver or punch to try to tap back the tail pipe off the front part of the system. Undo the two sets of rubber 'O' ring exhaust supports and remove the tail pipe and rear silencer.

32 Undo and remove the eight nuts which support the four pipes of the exhaust manifolds at the cylinder heads. Then remove the two rubber 'O' ring exhaust system supports at the other end of the front part of the total system. The system should now drop away. Obviously it will help to have another person under the car to hold the front or the back as it is released.

33 Now remove the two front disc dust covers. These are individually fixed with four bolts. Two appear from below and bolt into a special bracket on the underside of the gearbox sump and the other two are on the top top side of the cover located into the side of the gearbox.

34 With the appropriate allen key undo and release the allen screws which bolts the two front drive shafts to the disc/hub flanges. These Allen screws will be tight as they are 'Loctited' into position. It may be necessary to use a piece of tubing on the Allen key plus some releasing agent. Watch the rubber bellows as you do this for they are expensive to replace. Never 'bodge' the proper tool. Release the half shafts and tie them back, preferably upwards with string or wire to the inner bulkhead.

35 From above support the engine and gearbox with a sling and a hoist. There are two lifting eyes, one on each end of the inlet manifold. Use these plus a third point when it becomes visible through the top of the gearbox. For the moment support the engine on the two eyes. Another method is to support the engine from below with a trolley jack with the lifting head protected with a piece of wood. This method is not so good but it will work if no hoist is available.

36 The front crossmember should come out with the anti-roll bar attached. Undo the bolt which locates the rear end of the suspension arm/crossmember to the transverse suspension arm at the strut, close to the inner side of the front hub. Do this on each side. Slacken and remove the two bolts from below that fix the front engine mounting to the crossmember. These are located just in front of the anti-roll bar, in the centre.

37 At each end of the front crossmember are two bolts which locate it to the bodyshell. With these four removed the front crossmember, engine support (front) and both trailing suspension links with the anti-roll bar still fixed, should come away. The engine and gearbox should be supported, of course, by the sling or trolley jack together with the rear centre mounting and the rear gearbox mounting.

38 Remove the two support bolts for the rear gearbox mounting located at the end of the tail shaft.

39 From above with the tail shaft of the gearbox supported by another person under the car (no strength is needed, just a steadying hand) slacken and remove the centre engine mounting bolt located under the centre of the inner bulkhead. The engine and gearbox are now loose.

40 If you are using a hoist allow the engine/gearbox to be lowered to the ground. Now disconnect the handbrake cable from both the front brake calipers. A pair of grips and a stout screwdriver are necessary to do this with some force. The return spring on the cable is very stiff. Once done, tie the handbrake cable back. Now relocate the hoist so that it is mounted at three points, the third being through the support on the gearbox from whence the handbrake cable came. Raise the engine and gearbox unit just off the ground and pull it forward and out from under the car. At some point you will again have to remove the hoist to clear the front of the car. Take the engine and gearbox to the point where you intend to work. Three strong men could lift the total unit complete.

41 If you are using a trolley jack, lower the engine and gearbox unit and remove the handbrake cable as described in the previous paragraph. At the jack's lowest point pull the whole unit forward until you are ready to clear the underside of the car. It is necessary to lift the car over the engine and gearbox. One person will have to pull the engine and two will have to lift the bodyshell. This is a minimum number of persons.

6 Engine removal from gearbox

1 Place the engine and gearbox (preferably) on a strong working surface still with the sling just supporting the total unit. If not place the pair on the ground.

2 Remove the nuts, bolts and washers which support the starter motor to the bell housing. Remove the starter motor.

3 Remove from the underside of both units the flywheel protection cover. This is retained by a number of bolts and washers to the rear engine cover and by one at the bottom to the gearbox casing.

4 Remove all the remaining nuts and washers from the studs around the bell housing. Both engine and gearbox may now be split by lifting the gearbox from the engine. Take care with the gearbox shaft which locates through the centre of the clutch. Do not allow any pressure on it - pull off straight.

Dismantling

7 Engine dismantling - general

1 Owners who have dismantled engines will know the need for a strong work bench and many tools and pieces of equipment, which make their life much easier when going through the process of dismantling an engine. For those who are doing a dismantling job for the first time, there are a few 'musts' in the way of preparation which, if not acquired, will only cause frustration and long delays to the job in the long run. It is essential to have sufficient space in which to work. Dismantling and reassembly is not going to be completed all in one go and it is therefore absolutely essential that you have sufficient area to leave things as they are when necessary. A strong work bench is also necessary together with a good engineer's vice. If you have no alternative other than to work at ground level, make sure that the floor is at least level and covered with a suitable wooden or wood composition material on which to work. If dirt and grit are allowed to get into any of the component parts all work which you carry out may be completely wasted. Before actually placing the engine wherever it is that you may be carrying out the dismantling, make sure that the exterior is now completely and thoroughly cleaned.

2 Once dismantling begins it is advisable to clean the parts as they are removed. A small bath of paraffin is about the best thing to use for this, but do not let parts which have oilways in them become immersed in paraffin otherwise there may be a residue which could cause harmful effects later on. If paraffin does get into oilways every effort should be made to blow it out. For this it may be necessary to carry the particular part to a garage fitted with a high pressure air hose. Short oilways such as there are in the crankshaft can be cleared

easily with pipe cleaners.

3   Always obtain a complete set of gaskets when the engine is being dismantled - no gaskets on an engine are re-usable and any attempt to do so is quite unjustified in view of the relatively small cost involved. Before throwing any gaskets away, however, make sure that you have the replacement to hand. If, for example, a particular gasket cannot be obtained it may be necessary to make one, and the pattern of the old one is useful in such cases.

4   Generally speaking, it is best to start dismantling the engine from the top downwards. In any case, make sure it is firmly supported at all times so that it does not topple over whilst you are undoing the very tight nuts and bolts which will be encountered. Always replace nuts and bolts into their locations once the particular part has been removed, if possible. Otherwise keep them in convenient tins or pots in their groups, so that when the time comes to reassemble there is the minimum of confusion.

8   Distributor - removal

1   The distributor cap, plug leads and caps should have been removed already. So should the rotor arm. Pull off the vacuum advance pipe at the carburettor and leave it attached to the distributor.

2   There is no need to record the position in which the distributor is fixed to enable quick and accurate ignition timing upon replacement as static timing marks are provided on a dowelled flywheel and there is a cut on the rim of the distributor body where the caps fit to align the rotor arm. Also there are adequate instructions for ignition timing in Chapter 4. The distributor is therefore quickly removed.

3   Slacken the nut fixing the distributor to the adjusting plate on the rear crankcase cover. Remove the nut and pull the distributor away.

9   Oil filter - removal

1   Withdraw the dipstick.

2   Hold a rag under the oil seal to catch the oil which will flow out when you release the oil filter. Now use a strap or chain wrench around the oil filter body and release, unscrew and discard it. An alternate method if a proper wrench is not available is to unscrew the filter body using a hammer and screwdriver to drive it in an anticlockwise direction.

3   Always use a new filter on a rebuilt engine.

10   Alternator - removal

1   First slacken the bolts which adjust the alternator drive belt using the alternator body as a fulcrum. Loosen and remove the alternator drive belt. You must of course slacken two bolts to do this, one is on the adjuster plate and the other is the alternator pivot bolt.

2   Slacken and remove the two bolts which attach the adjuster plate to the front crankcase cover. Now remove the alternator pivot bolt and remove the alternator still attached to the alternator adjuster plate.

11   Carburettor - removal

1   The carburettor is easily removed from the inlet manifold. The Alfasud carburettor is attached by two studs and nuts whilst the Alfasud TI is attached by four studs and nuts. First, however, slacken the hose clip to the fuel line on the carburettor and pull off the fuel line. Do the same at the fuel pump and remove the pipe.

2   Now carefully slacken the carburettor fixing nuts, remove and then lift off the carburettor, followed by the spacer and gasket.

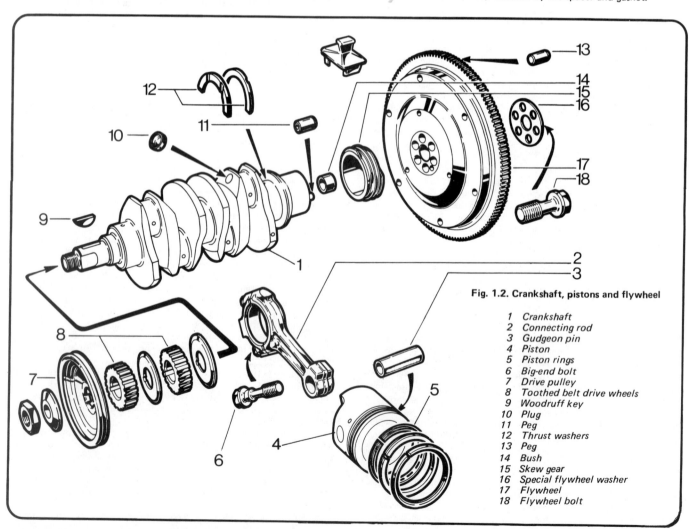

Fig. 1.2. Crankshaft, pistons and flywheel

1   Crankshaft
2   Connecting rod
3   Gudgeon pin
4   Piston
5   Piston rings
6   Big-end bolt
7   Drive pulley
8   Toothed belt drive wheels
9   Woodruff key
10 Plug
11 Peg
12 Thrust washers
13 Peg
14 Bush
15 Skew gear
16 Special flywheel washer
17 Flywheel
18 Flywheel bolt

12 Inlet manifold and thermostat housing - removal

1   The inlet manifold is held at each end, on each bank of cylinders, by three studs and nuts. See paragraph 3 before attempting to remove. To remove, unscrew gradually the six nuts, three at each end, remove, and then carefully lift the whole manifold off. Of course, the two engine lifting hooks come away with the manifold nuts. To undo some of the nuts it may be necessary to first pull off the HT lead clips held by the lifting hooks.
2   The thermostat housing is a little more complicated as it should include the water inlet adapter.
3   The thermostat housing is attached to the inlet manifold by two studs and nuts. It is easiest to remove the thermostat housing once the inlet manifold has been removed from the engine. This is quite possible if you first slacken and then pull off the coolant hose which connects the thermostat housing to the water inlet adapter.
4   To remove the thermostat housing from the inlet manifold remove the two nuts from the fixing studs and pull off.
5   To remove the water inlet adapter from the crankcase, slacken and remove the four fixing nuts from the studs and lift off. The connecting hose should still be located to the water inlet adapter.

13 Fuel pump - removal

1   The fuel pump is fixed to the crankcase adjacent to the flywheel close to the engine oil filler tube. It is fixed by two studs and nuts.
2   Slacken and remove the two nuts on the fixing studs, remove the pump, gasket, spacer and operating rod which come away loose.

14 Camshaft drive belts - removal

1   There is no need to record the position of the belts on the camshaft or crankshaft drive wheels. Simple repositioning is available.
2   With the engine sitting on the bench remove the belt on the left first. You should be facing the front of the engine. Slacken the belt tensioner which is located in the centre of the lower run of the belt. Only slacken the bolt holding the tensioner first, release the tension and then carefully thread the belt over. If necessary it is possible to remove the belt tensioner completely; this will disturb the tensioner spring. Simply slacken further and remove the locating bolt and pull

off the tensioner and body.
3   The right hand belt is removed in the same way as the left. The other tensioner is located just above the water pump.

15 Cylinder heads and camshafts - removal

1   The camshaft housing with the camshaft installed can be removed from the cylinder head with the head still attached to the crankcase. For a complete stripdown it is easier to remove the cylinder head with the camshaft housing still attached and then remove the camshaft housing from the head afterwards.
2   Using a Phillips screwdriver slacken and remove the camshaft housing cover and gasket. Held inside the housing is a quantity of oil if you have a suitable syringe suck up this oil to avoid an undue mess; if not leave the oil there and pour it away after the head is removed.
3   Slacken the six large cylinder head bolts - three are outside the housing and three are inside. Slacken these diagonally, remove and then pull off the cylinder head and camshaft housing intact (watch the oil if still in the housing). If the head will not shift tap it gently with a copper-headed hammer to loosen.
4   Repeat for the other cylinder head and camshaft housing.
5   To remove the camshaft housing from the cylinder head pour off the oil if not already sucked out. Slacken and remove the three nuts on the camshaft end cover, and then remove the cover and gasket.
6   The camshaft housing is attached to the cylinder head by four nuts on studs, between the cylinder head bolts. Slacken the four nuts diagonally, remove and pull off the camshaft housing. Together with the tappet buckets, record which valve they are removed from and put them in a safe place.
7   Place the camshaft drive pulley in the jaws of a 'soft' mouthed vice and tighten the vice enough to grip the pulley. Slacken the centre fixing nut. Remove the whole thing from the vice, remove the fixing nut, pull off the pulley and washer. Now remove the camshaft very carefully through the rear cover end. Pull it through straight to protect the camshaft lobes.
8   Repeat the whole operation for the other cylinder head and camshaft housing and record the fit of the various parts so that they can be replaced in the same place.
9   Valve and spring removal is described in Section 31.

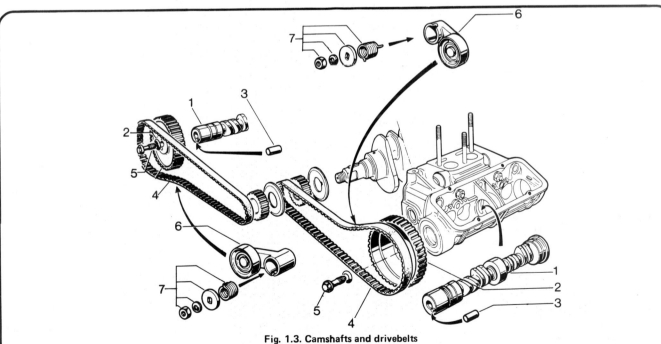

Fig. 1.3. Camshafts and drivebelts

| 1 Camshaft | 3 Peg | 5 Bolt | 7 Adjuster wheel springs |
| 2 Drive wheel | 4 Belt | 6 Adjuster wheel | |

16 Water pump and pulley - removal

1   The water pump is unusual on the Alfasud in that it is an integral interference fit in the crankcase rather than a face fit as is normal. It is not easy to remove.
2   Carefully 'hold' the water pump pulley and slacken the three fixing bolts. Remove the bolts and tap off the pulley.
3   Slacken the four fixing bolts of the water pump. Spray the whole unit, particularly the point at which the rim of the pump fits the crankcase, with releasing fluid. Leave for a minute and then carefully tap one of the ribs of the pump with a piece of wood using a copper-headed hammer in an anti-clockwise direction. With luck you will break the seal - carefully now tap out the water pump in a 'to' and 'fro' motion.

17 Crankshaft pulley and drives - removal

1   Hold the flywheel by jamming (carefully) a screwdriver in the starter ring gear and then slacken the crankshaft pulley securing nut. Some force may be necessary. Remove the nut, the washer, the alternator drive pulley, and then the two camshaft drive pulleys and spacers. Note their strict order.
2   Remove the screwdriver from the starter ring gear.

18 Sump - removal

1   Turn the engine over so that the sump is fully exposed.
2   Slacken all the bolts which fix the sump, remove them with their washers and then lift off the sump.

19 Oil pump - removal

1   The oil pump is fixed direct to the rear crankcase cover and is exposed by removing the sump. It is fixed by three bolts to the cover, those nearest the flywheel. (The other two bolts on the opposite side of the oil pump fix the pump to the pump support. These two can be slackened and removed once the whole unit is removed).
2   Slacken the three pump-to-cover bolts and then remove. Remove the pump which pulls straight up.

20 Crankcase front cover - removal

1   Still attached to the front crankcase cover is the front engine mounting. To remove this slacken and remove the four mounting bolts, and then pull off the mounting.
2   The front cover is located by eight bolts and two studs and nuts. Slacken all these and then remove. The front cover will be stuck to the crankcase with gasket cement. Using releasing fluid on the joints, wait a minute and then very, very carefully tap the cover using a piece of wood and a copper-headed hammer. Do not lever and do not be rough. Take your time and work progressively and slowly.
3   When released, pull off straight to save the oil seal if possible.

21 Big-end bearings and piston - removal

1   Rotate the flywheel to gain access to the big-end caps and bolts. Each big-end cap and connecting rod are stamped with their number.
2   Slacken each big-end bearing cap bolt, two per connecting rod, remove a pair, then the cap with bearing installed and push the piston and rod through the cylinder bore. Be careful not to scratch the cylinder with the end of the connecting rod. Rotate the crankshaft and proceed with the next piston.
3   Store the piston, connecting rod and big-end bearing cap with bolts replaced, in oil if you wish to retain and refit the bearings. This should stop corrosion to the bearing which may occur from exposure to the air if not so covered.
4   Removing piston from connecting rod is discussed in Section 27.

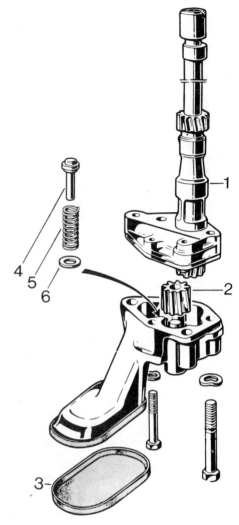

Fig. 1.4. Oil pump

1	Top body and spindle	4	Valve
2	Gear	5	Spring
3	Gauze filter	6	Washer

22 Flywheel - removal

1   Remove the clutch (see Chapter 5).
2   Hold the flywheel with a screwdriver jammed into the starter ring gear as you did in Section 17.
3   Slacken the six flywheel bolts, remove with their drilled washer and then pull off the flywheel. It is dowelled in one place.

23 Crankcase rear cover - removal

1   The rear crankcase cover is removed in the same way as the front, see Section 20, except that there are eight fixing bolts only.

24 Main bearings and crankshaft - removal

1   The three main bearings are capped and braced with transverse bolts.
2   Unscrew the transverse locking bolts from the main bearing caps, then the bolts and washers fixing the main bearing caps to their supports.
3   Remove the caps and keep the bearing halves in order of removal so that they can be refitted in their original position if reused.
4   Lift the crankshaft from the crankcase.
5   Retain the main bearing halves and the thrust washer halves and mark their exact position to aid replacement if necessary.

Inspection and renovation

25 Cylinder compression test

1 A great deal can be told about an engine's condition by a cylinder compression test. It may not give a specific answer but it will confirm that action should be taken with the engine's internals. Fortunately a compression test is an easy thing to undertake on an Alfasud engine.
2 Buy or borrow a cylinder compression tester. Run the engine until it has reached its normal working temperature. Take out one spark plug, start the engine on 'three cylinders' and press in the cylinder compression tester into the plug hole. Record the compression given on the dial of the tester. Remove and replace the spark plug and cap.
3 Now repeat the operation of compression testing on the three other cylinders. What is important is that the compression should be similar on each cylinder within a few pounds per square inch. Now check with the Specifications as to what the normal compression should be. Provided all cylinders are much the same and that they are all within 15% of the norm, there is little to worry about - at least, with regard to the pistons, piston rings, cylinders and valve gear.
4 Obviously, the test will help diagnose and pinpoint trouble in a particular engine to a particular cylinder.

26 Crankcase/cylinder block

1 Make sure both sides of the crankcase are spotlessly clean and dry.
2 Examine each side. Look for cracks, burrs, loose studs and any sign of rotating parts fouling the crankcase. Do not be afraid of asking an 'experienced engine man', particularly if he has knowledge of the Alfasud. If you are not close to an Alfa Romeo agency, a Volkswagen agency should be able to confirm any thoughts you may have about the condition of your crankcases, for the Beetle engine is very close in this respect.

27 Liners, pistons, piston rings and connecting rods

1 A new cylinder is perfectly round and the walls parallel throughout its length. The action of the piston tends to wear the walls at right angles to the gudgeon pin due to side thrust. This wear takes place principally on that section of the cylinder swept by the piston rings.
2 It is possible to get an indication of bore wear by removing the cylinder heads. With the piston down in the bore first signs of wear can be seen and felt just below the top of the bore where the top piston ring reaches and there will be a noticeable lip. If there is no lip it is fairly reasonable to expect that bore wear is not severe and any lack of compression or excessive oil consumption is due to worn or broken piston rings or pistons.
3 If it is possible to obtain a bore measuring micrometer measure the bore in the thrust plane below the lip and again at the bottom of the cylinder in the same plane. If the difference is more than 0.0762 mm then a rebore is necessary. Similarly, a difference of 0.0762 mm or more across the bore diameter is a sign of ovality calling for a new liner or rebore.
4 Any bore which is significantly scratched or scored will need replacement of the liner or reboring. This symptom usually indicates that the piston or rings are damaged also in that cylinder. In the event of only one cylinder being in need of reboring it will still be necessary for all four liners to be replaced or to be bored and fitted with new oversize pistons and rings.
5 Your Alfa Romeo agent or local motor engineering specialist will be able to rebore and obtain the necessary matched pistons. If the crankshaft is undergoing regrinding also it is a good idea to let the same firm renovate and reassemble the crankshaft and pistons to the block. A reputable firm normally gives a guarantee for such work. In cases where engines have been rebored already to their maximum, new cylinder liners are available which may be fitted. In such cases the same reboring processes have to be followed and the services of a specialist engineering firm are required.
6 Worn pistons and rings can usually be diagnosed when the symptoms of excessive oil consumption and low compression occur

and are sometimes, though not always, associated with worn cylinder bores. Compression testers that fit into the spark plug holes are available and these can indicate where low compression is occuring. Wear usually accelerates the more it is left so when the symptoms occur, early action can possibly save the expense of a rebore.
7 Another symptom of piston wear is piston slap - a knocking noise from the crankcase not to be confused with big-end bearing failure. It can be heard clearly at low engine speed when there is no load (idling for example) and is much less audible when the engine speed increases. Piston wear usually occurs in the skirt or lower end of the piston and is indicated by vertical streaks in the worn area which is always on the thrust side. It can also be seen where the skirt thickness differs.
8 Piston ring wear can be checked by first removing the rings from the pistons. Then place the rings in the cylinder bores from the top, pushing them down about 44mm with the head of a piston (from which the rings have been removed) so that they rest square in the cylinder. Then measure the gap at the ends of the ring with a feeler gauge. If it exceeds 0.45mm for the two top compression rings, and 0.40mm for the oil control ring then they need renewal.
9 The groove in which the rings locate in the piston can also become enlarged in use. The clearance between ring and piston, in the groove, should not exceed 0.035-0.067mm for the top two compression rings and 0.025-0.057mm for the lower oil control ring.
10 However, it is rare that a piston is only worn in the ring grooves and the need to replace them for this fault alone is hardly ever encountered. Wherever pistons are renewed the weight of the four piston/connecting rod assemblies should be kept within the limit variation of 13 g to maintain engine balance.
11 Any wear or distortion found in the gudgeon pin, small end or connecting rod will mean fitting a complete piston/connecting rod assembly.
12 Connecting rods are not subject to wear but in extreme circumstances such as engine seizure they could be distorted. Such conditions may be visually apparent but where doubt exists they should be changed. The bearing caps should also be examined for indications of filing down which may have been attempted in the mistaken idea that bearing slackness could be remedied in this way. If there are such signs then the connecting rods should be replaced.
13 It is not possible to remove a piston from its connecting rod without special and sophisticated tools. If you anticipate the need to replace the connecting rod, gudgeon pin or piston then you must take the complete rod/piston assembly to a specialist engine builder or to an Alfa Romeo agency. They should be able to remove the piston from the connecting rod.
14 In the same way that you cannot remove a piston from a connecting rod, so you cannot fit one either. Get your specialist to do both jobs for you.
15 Do not attempt to disregard this - if you try to remove the piston without the proper equipment, you will destroy it.

28 Crankshaft, big-end and main bearings

1 Look at the three main bearing journals and the four crankpins and if there are any scratches or score marks then the shaft will need regrinding. Such conditions will nearly always be accompanied by similar deterioration in the matching bearing shells.
2 Each bearing journal should also be round and can be checked with a micrometer or caliper gauge around the periphery at several points. If there is more than 0.0254 mm of ovality regrinding is necessary.
3 An Alfa Romeo agent or motor engineering specialist will be able to decide to what extent regrinding is necessary and also supply the special undersize shell bearings to match whatever may need grinding off.
4 Before taking the crankshaft for regrinding check also the cylinder bores and pistons as it may be advantageous to have the whole engine done together.
5 With careful servicing and regular oil and filter changes bearings will last for a very long time but they can still fail for unforeseen reasons. With big-end bearings the indications are regular rhythmic knocking from the crankcase, the frequency depending on engine speed. It is particularly noticeable when the engine is under load. This symptom is accompanied by a fall in oil pressure although this is not normally noticeable unless an oil pressure gauge is fitted. Main bearing failure is usually indicated by serious vibration, particularly

at higher engine revolutions, accompanied by a more significant drop in oil pressure and a 'rumbling' noise.

6   Bearing shells in good condition have bearing surfaces with a smooth, even, matt silver/grey colour all over. Worn bearings will show patches of a different colour where the bearing metal has worn away and exposed the underlay. Damaged bearings will be pitted or scored. It is **always** well worthwhile fitting new shells as their cost is relatively low. If the crankshaft is in good condition it is merely a question of obtaining another set of standard size. A reground crank-shaft will need new bearing shells as a matter of course.

29 Flywheel (and starter ring gear)

1   There are two areas in which the flywheel may have been worn or damaged. Firstly, is on the driving face where the clutch friction plate bears against it. Should the clutch plate have been permitted to wear down beyond the level of the rivets, it is possible that the flywheel has been scored. If this scoring is severe it may be necessary to have it refaced or even renewed.

2   The other part to examine is the teeth of the starter ring gear around the periphery of the flywheel. If several of the teeth are broken or missing, or the front edges of all teeth are obviously very badly chewed up, then it would be advisable to fit a new ring gear.

3   The old ring gear can be removed by cutting a slot with a hacksaw down between two of the teeth as far as possible, without cutting into the flywheel itself. Once the cut is made a chisel will split the ring gear which can then be drawn off. To fit a new ring gear requires it to be heated first to a temperature of 435°F, no more. This is best done in a bath of oil or an oven, but not, preferably, with a naked flame. It is much more difficult to spread and heat evenly and control it to the required temperature with a naked flame. Once the ring gear has attained the correct temperature it can be placed onto the flywheel making sure that it beds down properly onto the register. It should then be allowed to cool down naturally. If by mischance, the ring gear is overheated, it should not be used. The temper will have been lost, therefore softening it, and it will wear out in a very short space of time.

4   Although it is not actually fitted into the flywheel itself, there is a bush in the centre of the crankshaft flange onto which the flywheel fits. Although this bush is more correctly associated with the gearbox or clutch, it is mentioned here as well as it would be a pity to ignore it whilst carrying out work on the flywheel. If it shows signs of wear it should be renewed. If suitable extractors are not available to get it out another method is to fill the recess with grease and then drive in a piece of close fitting steel bar. This should force the bush out. A new bush may be pressed in.

30 Oil pump

1   Only work on the oil pump with it removed from the block.

2   With the pump clear pull apart the cover face and filter to the main body.

3   Take care with the valve boss, the valve and the pressure relief spring which will come away when the cover face is removed.

4   Take out the driven gear and then the drive gear and the shaft.

5   Clean all the parts with petrol or paraffin and check the condition of the splines on the driveshaft. They should be unchewed and straight.

6   Check the condition of the valve and its seating. There should be no irregularity or ridges in either. The valve should be replaced anyway if you have reached this stage.

7   Check the spring. If possible replace it anyway at this stage. Obtain the correct replacement without fail.

8   Check the clearance between the pump gears and their body. If over 0.008 in (0.20 mm) replace the gears. Also check the cover joint face for marks and irregularities. Replace if scored.

9   It may be found that if two or more parts need replacing that it is more economic and quicker to replace the whole pump. There is no exchange scheme.

31 Cylinder heads and valves, plus decarbonisation

1   Alfasud cylinder heads are expensive to replace. Handle them with care for they are of aluminium alloy - whilst efficient, reliable and well

made they will suffer if dropped and they can become distorted. With a straight edge check the surface for 'flatness' - if in doubt have them checked by your agent. This is especially important if you have suffered from a blown head gasket.

2   In fact, apart from the facility to check the cylinder heads, little can be done to Alfasud cylinder heads by the man at home, except for valve grinding and spring replacement.

3   The valves can be removed from the cylinder head by the following method. Compress each spring in turn with a valve spring compressor until the two halves of the collets can be removed. Release the compressor and remove the spring and spring retainer.

4   If, when the valve spring compressor is screwed down, the valve spring retaining cap refuses to free to expose the split collet, do not continue to screw down on the compressor as there is a likelihood of damaging it.

5   Gently tap the top of the tool directly over the cap with a light hammer. This will free the cap. To avoid the compressor jumping off the valve spring retaining cap when it is tapped, hold the compressor firmly in position with one hand.

6   Slide the rubber oil control seal off the top of each valve stem and then drop out each valve through the cylinder head.

7   It is essential that the valves are kept in their correct sequence unless they are so badly worn that they are to be renewed.

8   Provided there are no obvious signs of serious pitting the valve should be ground with its seat. This may be done by placing a smear of carborundum paste on the edge of the valve and using a suction type valve holder, grinding the valve in situ. This is done with a semi-rotary action, twirling the handle of the valve holder between the hands and lifting it occasionally to re-distribute the paste. Use a coarse paste to start with. As soon as a matt grey unbroken line appears on both the valve and seat the valve is 'ground in'. All traces of carbon should also be cleaned from the head and neck of the valve stem. A wire brush mounted in a power drill is a quick and effective way of doing this.

9   Valve guides seldom require replacement. As the valves work in a horizontal plane the problem of oil running down worn guides is not nearly so serious. The rock at the end of the stem is 0.013-0.046 mm for a new valve and guide, and a wear limit of 0.900 mm is permitted.

10 Inside diameters vary somewhat but the 'rock' test will decide whether replacement is required.

If new guides are required this is a job for the Alfa Romeo agent. The old guides must be drilled out partially before removal and the new ones reamed to size after installation.

11 If the valves cannot be ground in satisfactorily by hand using the traditional method of a rubber sucker and paste, then, again, the agent must be consulted. Exhaust valves may only be ground in, not refaced on a machine, inlets may be refaced but the owner is unlikely to possess a machine, so the agent must again be sought.

12 Cylinder head inserts may be installed where valve seats are damaged but this is a factory job. Check the head for cracks between seats, and check the threads of the plug sockets.

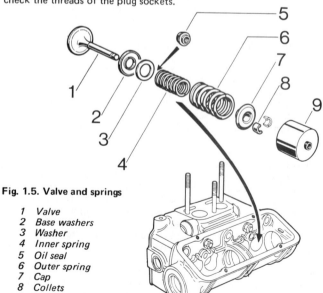

Fig. 1.5. Valve and springs

1   Valve
2   Base washers
3   Washer
4   Inner spring
5   Oil seal
6   Outer spring
7   Cap
8   Collets
9   Tappet bucket

Decarbonisation

13 Modern engines, together with modern fuels and lubricants have virtually nullified the need for the engine to have a 'decoke' which was common enough only a few years ago. Carbon deposits are formed mostly on the modern engine only when it has to do a great deal of slow speed, stop/start running, for example, in busy traffic conditions. If carbon deposit symptoms are apparent, such as pinking or pre-ignition and running on after the engine has been switched off, then a good high speed run on a motorway or straight stretch of road is usually sufficient to clear these deposits out. It is beneficial to any motor car to give it a good high speed run from time to time.

14 There will always be some carbon deposits, of course, so if the occasion demands the removal of the cylinder heads for some reason or another, it is a good idea to remove the carbon deposits when the opportunity presents itself. Carbon deposits in the combustion chambers of the cylinder head (TI only) can be dealt with as described. The other carbon deposits which have to be dealt with are those on the crowns of the pistons. This work can easily be carried out with the engine in the car, but great care must be taken to ensure that no particles of dislodged carbon fall either into the cylinder bores and down past the piston rings or into the water jacket orifices in the cylinder block.

15 Bring the first piston to be cleaned to the top of its stroke and then using a sheet of strong paper and some self-adhesive tape, mask off the other three cylinders and surrounding block to prevent any particles falling into the open orifice in the block. To prevent small particles of dislodged carbon from finding their way down the side of the piston which is actually being decarbonised press grease into the gap between the piston and the cylinder wall. Carbon deposits should then be scraped away carefully with a flat blade from the top of the crown of the piston and the surrounding top edge of the cylinder. Great care must be taken to ensure that the scraper does not gouge away into the soft aluminium surface of the piston crown.

16 A wire brush, either operated by hand or a power drill, should not be used if decarbonising is being done with the engine still in the car. It is virtually impossible to prevent carbon particles being distributed over a large area and the time saved by this method is very little.

17 After each piston has been attended to clean out the grease and carbon particles from the gap where it has been pressed in. As the engine is revolved to bring the next piston to the top of its stroke for attention, check the bore of the cylinder which has just been decarbonised and make sure that no traces of carbon or grease are adhering to the inside of the bore.

32 Camshafts, tappets, camshaft pulleys and belts

1 The camshafts run in housings without removable bushes. If there is any damage or wear replacement is the only answer. Fortunately there is no indication that wear is prevalent in this area.

2 Carefully inspect the working surfaces of the camshafts, and the camshaft journals - there should be no sign of scratches, binding, overheating or uneven wear. If necessary, replace the components. Check the housings too, in the same way.

3 Examine the surfaces of the tappets in the housing, the housing itself and the lobe seats for binding, scratching, overheating and uneven wear. Again, if necessary, replacement is the only answer.

4 The camshaft pulleys should be 100% reliable provided the teeth are not broken, kept clean and undented. If in doubt, replace.

5 'Never use steel brushes, metal tools or similar for cleaning' say Alfa Romeo, as this will damage the teeth and wear out pulley belts quickly.

6 The toothed belts should last 40,000 miles without any trouble, maybe a lot longer. Alfa Romeo recommend that they are auto-matically replaced after 30,000 miles for absolute safety. Essentially you have nothing to do to them except inspect them for cracks, deterioration and excessive wear. Provided no other contingency has occured which could effect them (like being immersed in oil) there should be no problem. Do not clean them - they will not break under normal usage. If in doubt, replace them both.

Reassembly

33 Engine - reassembly general

1 Everything has been checked and rectified and it is all laid out neatly ready for reassembly. Start with a clean bench top, an oil can of light oil, all the tools clean, plenty of clean non-fluffy rags, and clean hands and overalls.

2 Gaskets, 'O' rings and seals should be replaced by new ones and the set should be laid out conveniently on a clean flat surface.

3 Finally - take your time. The engine is a well made piece of machinery which goes together in a most satisfactory way, but each job must be completed properly and checked before going on to the next one.

34 Crankcase preparation

1 As the crankcase is the largest single component of the engine and because it holds together the other components, it is important that you start reassembly with this component in the best of condition - its significance is that you should intend to complete the engine in a similar frame of mind. The crankcase must be spotless. You should be able to apply the time old phrase, 'clean enough to eat your lunch from'.

2 Check several things. Are all gasket surfaces clean and smooth? Have you removed the old gasket cement? Are the drillings clean all the way through? Are all the threads clean and good? Check everything and then check it again. Did you want to paint the outside of the crankcase with engine paint? If so, do it now and wait until dry before assembly, do not leave it until the engine is assembled.

3 Now place the crankcase on the bench ready to replace the main bearing shells, ie with the bottom facing upwards.

35 Crankshaft and main bearings reassembly

1 If removed (very unlikely) replace the distributor and oil pump gear drive wheel to the end of the crankshaft. You will need to heat the gear to 150ºC to re-install it. The gear should be positioned on the crank-shaft in such a way that the start of a tooth is at an angle of between 22º and 26º to the centreline of the dowel. This refitment procedure is so for all engines including those which were not so fitted originally (see Fig. 1.6).

2 Fit the shell bearings into the main bearing webs of the crankcase in the usual way. Use only your fingers to do it. Oil them liberally with fresh oil, once you have cleaned them of their protective film (before fitting).

3 Now very carefully lower the crankshaft onto the main bearing shells.

4 Fit the thrust half rings, with the oilways facing the crankshaft webs, either side of the main bearing journal adjacent to the flywheel end of the crankshaft. Remember from whence they came. Make sure they are clean before fitting, and well oiled.

5 Fit the other half of the main bearing shells to the main bearing caps in the conventional manner. It is impossible to fit them incorrectly. Oil them.

6 Install the main bearing caps. Note the number stamped on their backs. They should obviously be fitted in order - No 1 is the timing end, No 2 in the middle and No 3 at the flywheel end. Fit all three before installing any main bearing cap bolts. If all looks good and fits well, as it should, proceed by fitting the main bearing cap bolts. Alfa Romeo describe these bolts as 'lubetorque screws' - fit them in the normal way and then tighten them to the specified torque wrench setting. Now fit the 'side brace' bolts - these hold the main bearing caps through the sides of the crankcase. Again, tighten these in a diagonal pattern to the specified torque wrench setting. The strength of the crankcase design structure relies on the proper installation of the main bearing caps in this way. Now check that the crankshaft rotates smoothly when turned by hand - it may be stiff but it should turn smoothly.

7 Now check crankshaft end float by inserting a 0.25mm feeler blade

between one side of a thrust washer half and the adjacent crankshaft web. If you can insert the feeler blade and there is still a little movement then end float is too much. If the crankshaft has just been reground, you have not fitted the correct oversize thrust washers. If it has not been reground then you should disassemble the crankcase completely and have the rear main journal shoulders ground so that oversize thrust washers can be fitted.

8   If you feel that end float is outside the limits mentioned seek the advice of the company who have worked on your engine or your bearing supplier, or of course go to your Alfa Romeo agent.

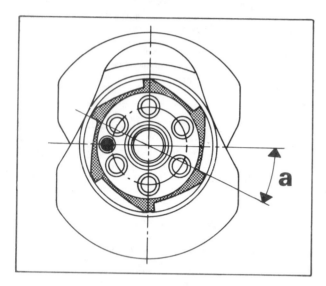

Fig. 1.6. Position the gear so that the start of a tooth is at an angle 'a' - 22/26° to the centre line of the dowel

36 Pistons and connecting rods - reassembly and replacement

1   If you have found it necessary to replace pistons and are therefore faced with the task of refitting the pistons to the connecting rods you should now read Section 27. You cannot do-it-yourself but must seek professional help.

2   Fitting the connecting rods, therefore big-end bearings, must be undertaken with the pistons already fitted. They must obviously have their piston rings fitted.

3   Before fitting new piston rings to the old pistons, make sure the ring grooves in the piston are completely clean and free of carbon deposits. A piece of old, broken piston ring is a useful tool for doing this, but make sure that the sharp edge is not permitted to gouge out any pieces of metal. Check also that the specified gap between the edge of the new piston ring and the groove is correct.

4   All rings must be fitted from the top of the piston. To get the new rings into position involves spreading them sufficiently to clear the diameter of the piston itself and then moving them down over the existing grooves into their appropriate positions. Care must be taken to avoid straining them to a point where they could break. A piece of thin shim steel or an old feeler gauge blade is a very useful means of guiding the ends of the rings over the grooves to prevent them inadvertently dropping in, rather than passing over each groove.

5   Before fitting the rings to the piston it is important to check that the end gap matches the cylinder bore into which they will eventually be fitted. Push the rings down the bores using the piston until they are about 44mm below the top surface of the top of the bore. Then measure the gap. If the gap is too large you have either got the wrong piston rings or the cylinder bores are worn more than you had anticipated. If the gap is too small then it will be necessary to remove a piece of material from the end of the ring. The gap may be increased to the correct specification by clamping the end of the ring in a vice so that a very small portion of the end projects above the top of the vice. Then use a fine file to take off the material in very small quantities at a time. Do not clamp the ring so that the end being filed projects too far above the vice jaws or it may easily be snapped off while the filing is being done.

6   When every ring has been checked and the gaps made correct the rings should be assembled to the piston to prevent them being mixed up with other rings which will be fitted to other bores. Fit the bottom scraper ring first placing it over the top of the piston and spreading the ends. Move it down the piston a little at a time, taking care to prevent it from snagging in the grooves over which it will pass. The next ring to be fitted is the lower compression ring and this only goes on one way up. The top edge of the ring will be marked 'top' and this, of course, means that the ring is the top one on the piston. The top compression ring, which is the last one to go on, then can be fitted either way up on the piston. When all the rings are in position in their grooves, try and arrange the gaps to be equally spaced around the piston. Place the gap of the oil control ring over an undrilled portion of the groove. Obviously, if the gaps of all the rings are in a straight line there will be a much greater tendency for compression loss at that point.

7   Now fit the big-end bearing shells to the connecting rod and the end cap.

8   Oil the shells and the cylinder bores, the crankpins and the piston rings.

9   Install the piston/connecting rod assembly through the relevant cylinder bore. You will need to turn the crankshaft so that the appropriate journal is ready to mate up with the connecting rod. It is impossible to fit the connecting rod incorrectly to the journal. Fit one bank of cylinders first, then the other. You must use a piston ring compressor to enable easy fitment of the piston and its rings into a bore. The photograph shows how this is done. As soon as one connecting rod is fitted to its journal fit the big-end cap and insert the big-end bolts, tighten them finger tight and then go onto the next connecting rod.

10 When all four connecting rods are installed and bolted up finger tight you are ready to tighten them all down to the specified torque wrench setting, once you have obtained a 0.15mm feeler blade. As you torque down each big-end bolt, you must place the feeler blade between the big-end cap and one of the webs of the crankshaft either side of it. This will ensure that all is correctly aligned while you are tightening that particular connecting rod.

11 Check now that it is possible to turn the crankshaft, pistons and connecting rods - this will be difficult but should be possible.

37 Rear crankcase cover - replacement

1   If you have gone to the trouble to recondition the engine or have found it necessary to dismantle it, you should always fit new oil seals. It is like an insurance policy.

2   Prise out the old oil seal with a screwdriver. Be careful not to damage the housing surface.

3   Grease the inside and outside of the new seal and tap it gently into the housing. Note the arrow of direction on the new seal. This ensures that you fit the seal the right way round. The lips of the seal should face inwards, towards the centre of the engine.

4   Replace the 'O' ring on the main oilway of the end cover.

5   Carefully place the end cover onto the crankcase. It is best to place the crankcase on its end. You should use a new gasket and gasket cement on both surfaces. There are six bolts which should be fitted now to hold the cover on before the flywheel is fitted. These are obviously in the centre of the cover. Tighten them progressively.

38 Flywheel - replacement

1   Place the flywheel onto the crankshaft. It can only fit in one position because the crankshaft end has an eccentric dowel. Fit the six bolts. Again, if you can, you are wise to fit new bolts.

2   To tighten the bolts to the specified torque wrench setting you are going to need to hold the crankshaft. The best way is to use the shaft of a hammer inside the crankcase, wedged safely under one of the crankshaft webs. Two people will help here, one to tighten, the other to hold the hammer and crankcase.

35.2 Cleanliness is essential

35.3 Three main bearings are used because the crank is short

35.4 Although the crank is installed the thrust washers are well visible

35.5 Push the shell around this way

35.6a Note the number on the cap

35.6b Note the serrated mating face

35.6c Torque these bolts first, then the six brace bolts not shown here

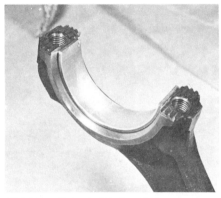
36.8 Now oil the shell before fitting

36.9 Use a proper piston ring compressor

36.10a Fit the right cap to the right rod

36.10b Fit all four, then torque them. Note alignment instruction

37.3a This is the right way round

37.3b Note the arrow direction. Read the text

37.4 Always use a new 'O' ring. Never skimp

37.5a Stick the gasket to the block

37.5b Lower it carefully and straight

38.1 One bolt is installed. Torque all six when they are finger tight

39.1 This is the right way round

39.2 New gasket, cement and cleanliness

40.1 Ease the pump body carefully

40.2 We fitted the pulley later, but here it is

39 Front crankcase cover - replacement

1 Install a new oil seal in the front crankcase cover, just as you have done in the rear crankcase cover described in Section 37. Remember you are going to need the front end mounting as well for this uses the same through-bolts for its mounting.
2 Use a new gasket and coat each surface with a smear of gasket cement. Oil the oil seal and install the cover.
3 Finger tighten all the bolts, including those for the engine mounting. Then tighten them all diagonally. Again check that it is possible to turn the crankshaft.

40 Water pump and pulley - replacement

1 Whilst it will have proven difficult to remove the water pump, it is easy to replace it. Always replace it without the pulley fitted. Use a new gasket and smear gasket cement to each surface.
2 Fit the water pump and start the four set screws and washers. Then tighten progressively.
3 Now you can fit the water pump pulley. Push on the pulley and then start the three set screws and washers. Again tighten progressively.

41 Cylinder heads and camshafts - reassembly and replacement

1 Before fitting either the cylinder heads or camshafts it is necessary to assemble the various integral components. But even before this it is suitable to fit the crankshaft belt pulley and the two belt tensioners.
2 Fit to the crankshaft the inner belt guide (a large smooth shim), the left hand or inner camshaft belt drive pulley, the spacer and then the right hand or outer camshaft belt drive pulley. Now press on the crankshaft to alternator/water pump pulley. Hold the crankshaft with

the shaft of a hammer as previously described when fitting the flywheel and tighten the nut and washer. Tighten this to the specified torque wrench setting.

3 Refitting the two belt tensioners is tricky because of the strength of the tensioner springs. It is not possible to fit them in their wrong locations. Do not tighten them down but simply finger tighten them so that they hold together. The assembly order is tensioner pulley body, the spring, the washers and the lock nut. See the photograph for positions.

4 Assembly of the camshafts into their housings is an exact reversal of their disassembly. See Section 15. Care, oiled bushes, a new oil seal and new gaskets and gasket cement are essential. You should now have two camshafts and housings ready to fit with the tappet buckets installed. Fit the drive pulley to each camshaft. The pulley is a dowelled fit. Press on the pulley and start the bolt and washer. Tighten to the specified torque wrench setting, carefully holding the camshaft so that it does not twist.

5 Now reassemble the valves and springs into the cylinder heads. The procedure is an exact reverse sequence to their disassembly given in Section 31.

6 You should now fit the camshaft housings to the cylinder heads before installing each complete component to the crankcase. It is much easier to do it in this fashion than to assemble the single components once the heads are attached to the crankcase.

7 Using a new gasket, with gasket cement each side, fit the relevant camshaft housing to its cylinder head. Of course, make sure the tappet buckets are installed in their correct place. Install only the four fixing nuts and washers onto the locating studs and then progressively tighten these nuts. Once you have fitted the heads to the crankcase you will have to double check the tightness here.

8 Refit the left bank cylinder head first. Rotate the crankshaft until the semi-circular mark on the flywheel is opposite the pointer on the rear cover: the piston in No 1 bore should now be at Top Dead Centre. Check through the bore that this is so.

9 Place the new head gasket onto the crankcase - it is marked for its top side.

10 Rotate the camshaft in the appropriate camshaft housing - the one you are about to fit - so that the mark on the rear flange of the camshaft aligns with the mark on the rear camshaft flange support.

11 Now place that cylinder head onto the crankcase. Check that the open valves of that head do not foul a piston in the crankcase as you fit and start the cylinder head bolts on that side. If possible use new cylinder head bolts. Tighten them now progressively in the sequence shown in Fig. 1.7. Finally check the tightness of the camshaft housing nuts as previously described. Tighten the cylinder head bolts to the specified torque wrench setting.

12 Leave the position of the crankshaft as it is, align the camshaft in the second housing and fit the second cylinder head using the same method just described.

13 There should now be a near completed engine of some weight and width. Continue to support it carefully on wooden blocks.

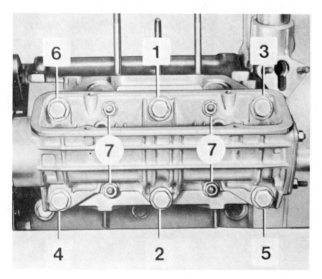

Fig. 1.7. The cylinder head torque tightening sequence

42 Camshaft belts and valve timing

1 Check again that No 1 piston is at TDC.

2 Make sure that the camshaft marks on the left hand bank are aligned as just described in Section 41.

3 Fit the inner camshaft belt over the various pulleys having slackened the tensioner. Actually fit it into the appropriate grooves in the following fashion. Ensure that the driving side, ie, **not** the side affected by the belt tensioner is **taut**. Now allow the belt tensioner to tension the belt, and lock its fixing nut. That camshaft is now 'timed'. (One further check should be made - see Fig. 1.10, S should be not less than 9mm. If it is, the engine mounting flange should be modified until it is. This is an unlikely occurrence).

4 Repeat the procedure for the right hand bank camshaft but remember to keep No 1 piston at Top Dead Centre (TDC). Both valves on No 1 cylinder should be closed.

5 Rotate the crankshaft and check all is well. It is a simple procedure provided care is taken.

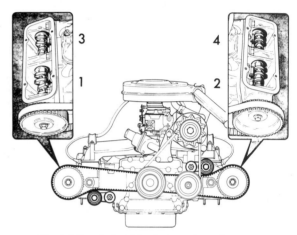

Fig. 1.8 Camshaft driving belt tension adjustment

1 and 3 cylinders belt is adjusted when that camshaft has none of its lobes touching the respective valves. 2 and 4 cylinders belt is adjusted using the same procedure for that bank

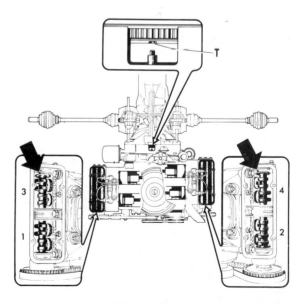

Fig. 1.9. Valve timing

Valve timing is correct when No 1 piston is on compression (TDC, both valves closed) and the timing mark T aligns with the reference pointer, also when the timing marks cut on the camshaft journals are in line with those on the journal bearings.

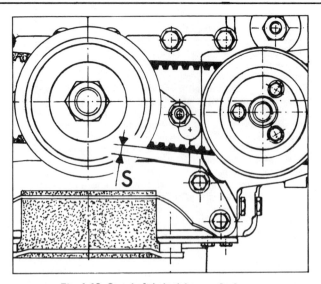

Fig. 1.10. Camshaft belt tightness, S - 9 mm

43 Tappet clearance adjustment

1   For an overhead camshaft design the Alfasud engine is brilliant in
its simplicity of tappet clearance adjustment. You require two sets of
feeler blades, an Allen key of the appropriate size and a solid punch - a
pin punch of the appropriate size. The feeler blades are used to check
the measurement, the Allen key is used to adjust the clearance and the
punch is used to lock the tappet buckets so that they do not rotate.
2   Our two photographs show exactly what has to be done. You must,
of course, obtain a set of metric Allen keys, find the one that fits and
then cut it to size. Look at the photograph again. The feeler blades,
not shown in the photograph for clarity's sake, should be inserted in
turn under each cam lobe, two per valve. Hence the need for two
sets of feeler blades at once.

3   Rotate the crankshaft to bring both valves of any one cylinder to
the fully closed position. Insert the Allen key in the cross-drilling in the
camshaft. Gently rotate the camshaft to bring the key in line with the
adjustment Allen screw on the tappet bucket.
4   Lock the pin punch between that tappet and the adjacent tappet
to prevent them from rotating whilst adjustment takes place.
5   Place the two feeler blades under the lobes and adjust the clearance
with the Allen key. Inlet valves take 0.35-0.40 mm, whilst the exhaust
0.45-0.50mm. The engine should, of course, be cold.
6   Remove all the tools and attempt the next valve. Do not leave
anything still in the tappet/camshaft housing once you have finished.
7   Using new camshaft housing cover gaskets and gasket cement on
both surfaces, install the covers. Before you do this pour in enough
clean engine oil into the housing to just cover the camshaft until its
level is about half way. (We did not do this until later - but you should).

44 Oil pump - replacement

1   Turn the engine over, and support it on blocks of wood so that you
do not damage the inlet manifold studs.
2   With No 1 piston still at TDC fit the oil pump in the following
manner - no gasket is used. Oil the pump spindle.
3   Rotate the pump spindle in such a way so that when the drive gear
on the pump spindle is eased into mesh with the drive gear on the
crankshaft, the slot in the drive coupling is at an angle 'B' (see
Fig. 1.13) of 45°. Note the offset - you are obviously looking at the
offset through the distributor location, effectively from the top of
the engine.
4   Tighten the two sizes of fixing set screws to different torques as
specified in the Specifications.

45 Sump - replacement

1   Once the oil pump is fitted you should fit the sump.
2   Use a new gasket and smear gasket cement on both surfaces.
3   Refit and start all the screws and washers. Then tighten all
progressively until the sump is located firmly and unstressed.

41.2a Note the order of fitment, and the key
and ...

41.2b ... then fit the pulley, washer and nut

41.3a The tensioner wheel and spring

41.3b Tension the wheel, now tighten the nut

41.3c This shows proper location (the water
pump pulley is off)

41.4a A new oil seal is fitted

41.4b Carefully insert the camshafts to their mountings

41.4c Note the location of the buckets

41.4d Now the end cover and gasket

41.4e Put the pulley on before the housing is fixed to the cylinder

41.5a Put the right valve into the right valve guide

41.5b Note the oil seal on the valve stem on the right

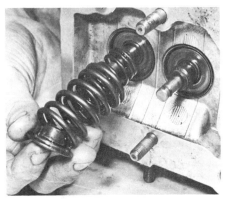
41.5c Spring seat, both springs and the valve cap

41.5d Place the collets carefully when the spring is compressed

41.6 This illustrates how the housing fits the cylinder head

41.8 Lower the cylinder heads this way

41.10 Note the two marks on the camshaft and its housing

42.3 The inner camshaft belt first ...

42.4 ... then the outer, as shown here

43.3 We made up a special Allen key for tappet adjustment

43.4 We used a steel punch to stop the buckets rotating

43.7 Pour oil into the housings before fitting the cover

44.3 Check the position of the spindle constantly

45.2 The sump gasket is cemented

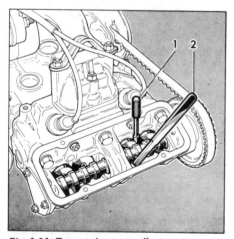

Fig. 1.11. Tappet clearance adjustment

1 Special tappet locking tool
2 Special tappet adjusting tool - an Allen key

Fig. 1.12. Tappet clearance
- in cross-section
G = intake   0.35 - 0.40 mm
G = exhaust   0.45 - 0.50 mm

Fig. 1.13. 'B' - 45⁰ if the angle given in Figure 1.6 is 22/26⁰ when the oil pump spindle is meshed with the gear on the crankshaft

46 Distributor - replacement

1 Make sure No 1 piston is still at TDC.
2 Rotate the distributor shaft so as to align the rotor arm with the reference mark on the distributor body.
3 Insert the distributor into the rear cover housing and engage the driving coupling's dog and the offset slot.
4 Obviously you should check the oil ring on the outer distributor shaft is in good condition before fitting the distributor.
5 Install the distributor clamp bolt on the housing and tighten. For the time being tighten this clampbracket to the distributor body. You should be somewhere near the correct ignition timing when you come to start the engine. See Chapter 4 for final ignition timing.

47 Fuel pump - replacement

1 Replacement of the fuel pump is no real problem. If the engine is one which has covered considerable mileage, say over 60,000 then you should automatically consult your Alfa Romeo agency and purchase a new fuel pump actuating rod. See Chapter 3.
2 Place a new gasket over the locating studs.
3 Place the actuating rod through the opening onto the cam. Then fit over the fuel pump having oiled the actuating rod along its whole length. Start the attaching nuts and tighten them to the specified torque.

48 Alternator and drive belt - replacement and tension

1   Fit the alternator belt tension adjusting mounting flange to the crankcase. You will find that this fits and is located onto the two bolt holes just above the crankshaft pulley on the front cover.
2   Now fix the alternator onto the adjusting bracket and the crankcase on the opposite side. Tighten each bolt finger tight only.
3   Fit over the drive belt onto the crankshaft, water pump and alternator pulleys. Tension the belt by moving the alternator until the belt tension amounts to a sag of 15mm at the centre point of the run between the crankshaft pulley and the alternator pulley. Tighten first the tension bolt on the tension bracket. Then tighten the pivot bolt on the opposite side of the alternator.

49 Ancillary sender units, oil filter and other parts

1   Replace the dipstick into its housing.

2   Replace the water temperature sender unit. This is the unusual unit which is fitted at right angles to the rear of the left hand cylinder head adjacent to the engine number plate. This unit is in two parts but is obviously fitted. Do not overtighten - make sure the washer is fitted.
3   The other sender unit is for oil pressure. On the Alfasud this is fitted to the centre at the front, on the top of the crankcase. On the Alfasud TI it is fitted to the rear crankcase cover close to the oil filter. In each case you must fit the washer and not overtighten.
4   Fit a new oil filter. Grease the internal sealing ring with some light grease and screw in hard by hand.
5   You should now fit the coolant take off casting. This fits on the top of the crankcase near the centre. Use a new gasket and smear both sides with gasket cement.
6   Check with the photograph and bolt on the component with its small hose already installed. Tighten the flange progressively.
7   Install the correct spark plugs into the cylinder heads. Check the specification, it is critical on this engine.
8   Do not install the distributor cap yet.

46.3 Note the 'O' ring on the spindle

47.3 Actuating rod and gasket ready for the pump

48.1 Mounting the bracket on the front cover

48.2 The pivot bolt is the lower one, well shown here

48.3 The proper location of all the components

49.2 Note the exact position of this sender unit

49.3 Do not overtighten and use the appropriate washer

49.4 Hand tighten the filter only. Grease the seal

49.6a Fit this way with the bolts installed as shown

49.6b Always keep the hose fitted

49.6c Putting the hose onto the thremostat housing is not easy (once the thermostat is installed)

50.1 Do not use any cement here

50.2 This photo illustrates how the manifold is lowered. Some components would not normally be on it

50.3 These lifting pieces are an essential fitment

51.4a Pipe on the fuel pump ...

51.4b ... then push onto the carburettor

50 Inlet manifold - replacement

1   Place new gaskets to each of the cylinder heads, over the studs.
2   Fit the manifold down onto the gaskets. Push the small hose on the coolant take off flange out of the way and then persuade it onto its fitting on the manifold. Install the proper hose clip.
3   Add the lifting bridge pieces to the top of the inlet manifold over each cylinder head. Now install and start all the nuts onto the fixing studs. Tighten progressively to the specified torque wrench setting.

51 Carburettor replacement

1   Use a new carburettor gasket.
2   Place the carburettor onto the studs and then start the fixing nuts.
3   Tighten these progressively.
4   Install the fuel pump to carburettor pipe and use hose clips.
5   Install the distributor cap and the plug leads, clipping the plug leads onto their guides on the inlet manifold, around the carburettor.

Engine replacement in the car

52 Engine attachment to the gearbox

1   Install the clutch (see Chapter 5).
2   Attach the gearbox to the engine in the conventional manner. You will need the help of a second person. Proceed in an exact reverse sequence to its removal as given in Section 6. Watch the gearbox primary shaft - do not hang the gearbox on this!

53 Engine replacement in the car

Generally speaking, the replacement of the engine is a reversal of the removal procedure but the following points should be borne in mind.
1   The engine and gearbox have been removed together, they should be reassembled and replaced together. This takes care of the possible difficulties one may encounter fitting the gearbox input shaft into the clutch.
2   When raising the engine into the car make sure first that it is suspended at the correct attitude. It is difficult and possibly dangerous to have to alter the angle of tilt whilst it is suspended.
3   Always raise the engine very slowly and watch it all round all the way. It is easy to wrench out wire and pipes due to being in too much of a hurry and not noticing these things when they flip back in the way - as they always seem to do.
4   If the engine will not go where it should, look and find out why. Do not try and force anything.
5   Always fit a new oil filter, air cleaner element, spark plugs and contact points, and fill with fresh oil and coolant.

6 Replace all the suspension and steering parts as well as the driveshafts before attempting to start the engine. Always lower the car to the ground and use the following check list, as well as reading the relevant parts in the rest of this book concerning those components which you have had to touch to remove the engine but which are not actually engine components, before attempting to start the car.

7 Once the engine has started and all is well you must have the car retracked at the front wheels before undertaking any regular use.

8 The following check list should ensure that the engine starts safely and with little or no delay and that the car is ready to move:

a) *Fuel pipes to fuel pump and carburettor connected and tight.*
b) *Coolant hoses to radiator and heater connected and tight.*
c) *Coolant drain plugs shut and tight.*
d) *Cooling system filled and bled.*
e) *Sump drain plug screwed and tight.*
f) *Oil filter cartridge tight.*
g) *Oil in sump and dipstick replaced.*
h) *Oil in transmission unit and plug tight.*
i) *LT wires connected to the distributor.*
j) *Spark plugs clean and tight.*
k) *Valve rocker clearance set.*
l) *HT leads all connected and secure.*
m) *Distributor rotor arm fitted.*
n) *Choke and accelerator cable fitted and working through their total range.*
o) *Earthing cable from engine block to battery and battery*

to earth secure.
p) *Starter motor cable to battery connected and secure.*
q) *Generator leads connected.*
r) *Oil pressure warning, coolant temperature sender unit and electric fan cables connected.*
s) *Battery charged and secure in position.*
t) *All loose tools removed from the engine compartment.*
u) *Clutch slave cylinder refitted, and bled if necessary.*
v) *Gear change linkage replaced.*
w) *Driveshafts refitted to transmission unit and greased, and speedometer cable replaced. See Chapter 7.*
x) *Handbrake cables, linkage and engine mountings secure.*
y) *Brakes bled.*

Leave the bonnet off and the lights unconnected for the initial start but replace before venturing on to the road!

54 Starting engine and running-in

1 As soon as the engine starts, run it steadily at a fast tick-over for several minutes and look all round for signs of leaks and loose or unclipped pipes and wires. Watch the instrument and warning lights and stop the engine at the first indications of anything nasty!

2 Check with Chapters 2 (Cooling), 3 (Carburation) and 4 (Ignition) for final tuning.

3 Running in is a matter of taste. Simply do not abuse the engine while stiff and new. Do not run it harshly and do not labour it.

55 Fault diagnosis - engine

Note: *When investigating starting and uneven running faults do not be tempted into snap diagnosis. Start from the beginning of the check procedure and follow it through. It will take less time in the long run. Poor performance from an engine in terms of power and economy is not normally diagnosed quickly. In any event the ignition and fuel systems must be checked first before assuming any further investigation needs to be made.*

Symptom	Reason/s	Remedy
Engine will not turn over when starter switch is operated	Flat battery Bad battery connections Bad connections at solenoid switch and/or starter motor	Check that battery is fully charged and that all connections are clean and tight.
	Starter motor jammed	Rock car back and forth with a gear engaged. If ineffective remove starter.
	Defective solenoid	Remove starter and check solenoid.
	Starter motor defective	Remove starter and overhaul.
Engine turns over normally but fails to fire and run	No spark at plugs	Check ignition system according to procedures given in Chapter 4.
	No fuel reaching engine	Check fuel system according to procedures given in Chapter 3.
	Too much fuel reaching the engine (flooding)	Slowly depress accelerator pedal to floor and keep it there while operating starter motor until engine fires. Check fuel system if necessary as described in Chapter 3.
Engine starts but runs unevenly and misfires	Ignition and/or fuel system faults	Check the ignition and fuel systems as though the engine had failed to start.
	Incorrect valve clearances	Check and reset clearances.
	Burnt out valves	Remove cylinder heads and examine and overhaul as necessary.
Lack of power	Ignition and/or fuel system faults	Check the ignition and fuel systems for correct ignition timing and carburettor settings.
	Incorrect valve clearances	Check and reset the clearances.
	Burnt out valves	Remove cylinder heads and examine and overhaul as necessary.
	Worn out pistons or cylinder bores	Remove cylinder heads and examine pistons

Excessive oil consumption	Oil leaks from crankshaft oil seal, cam cover gasket, oil pump, or oil filter	Identify source of leak and repair as appropriate.
	Worn piston rings or cylinder bores resulting in oil being burnt by engine (Smoky exhaust is an indication)	Fit new rings or rebore cylinders and fit new pistons, depending on degree of wear.
	Worn valve guides	Remove cylinder heads and recondition valve stem bores and valves as necessary.
Excessive mechanical noise from engine	Wrong valve clearances	Adjust valve clearances.
	Worn crankshaft bearings	Inspect and overhaul where necessary.
	Worn cylinders (piston slap)	
Unusual vibration	Misfiring on one or more cylinders	Check ignition system.
	Loose mounting bolts	Check tightness of bolts and condition of flexible mountings.
Engine backfires or overruns	Faulty fuel circuit	Check fuel system.

Chapter 2 Cooling and heating systems

Contents

Specifications

Cooling system
Type .. ..   Thermo-syphon with pump assistance

Radiator
Type ... ...   Corrugated fin
Filler cap relief pressure ... ...   13 lb/sq. in (0.9 Kg/sq. cm)

Thermostat
Type ... ...   Bimetal spring

Coolant capacity (with heater) ... .   12.9 Imp pints (7.31 litres)

Fan
Type ... ...   Electric thermostatically controlled
Cut in temperature ... .   190 - 196°F (88 - 92°C)
Cut out temperature ... ...   180 - 172°F (82 - 78°C)
Warning light extinguishes (from cold) at ... ...   110 - 120°F (43 - 49°C)
Warning light comes on to indicate overheating at ... ...   220 - 228°F (104 - 108°C)

Antifreeze
Quantity required to protect engine to minus 4°F (20°C) ... ...   4.6 Imp pints (2.6 litres)

1 General description

The engine cooling liquid is circulated round the system on the thermosyphon principle, assisted by a belt-driven impeller type pump.

The system is pressurised and sealed so that boiling will only occur at abnormally high temperatures and so that there is no loss of coolant. As the coolant heats up it expands and flows into the expansion chamber, which is fitted with a blow-off valve should the pressure, and therefore the temperature, get too great. No coolant should ever be lost as air pressure and not water pressure is vented because the expansion chamber is never more than about 1/3 filled with coolant. As the coolant becomes cool it will flow back into the radiator under the vacuum principle.

The circuit also incorporates a thermostatically controlled valve which restricts the amount of water passing through the radiator until the correct engine operating temperature is reached. This assists rapid warming up and keeps the engine at a constant running temperature regardless of ambient conditions.

The principle of operation is as follows. The water heated by the engine rises out of the cylinder heads towards the thermostat which, if cold, is closed. It then diverts straight to the pump and thence back to the engine via the heater (if open).

When the engine warms up a proportion of the warm water will pass via the thermostat valve to the top of the radiator down through which it will pass and cool. The pump will then draw the cold water from the bottom of the radiator and pass it back to the engine (the pump has two inlets). If the engine temperature should rise excessively the thermostat valve will close off the by-pass outlet, thus directing all water through the radiator.

It is important that the system is always sealed properly and that it is filled with the correct coolant which ideally is 50% antifreeze (glycol) and 50% distilled water. To maintain correct antifreeze properties and to safeguard against internal damage to the aluminium cylinder heads this mixture should be adhered to at all times. Because of the sealed system this mixture is safe during the whole year in any climate.

The Alfasud utilises a thermostatically controlled electric fan for cooling the radiator. The thermostatically controlled switch is in the lower half of the radiator.

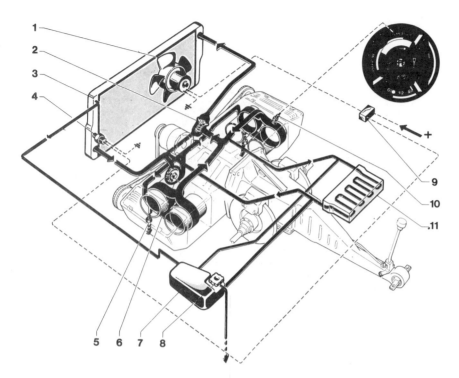

Fig. 2.1. The cooling system circuit

1   Electric fan
2   Thermostatic valve
3   Radiator
4   Electric fan thermostat
    switch
5   Drain plug (one for each bank
    of cylinders)
6   Pump
7   Header tank
8   Cap with calibrated valve
9   Electric fan relay
10 Thermostat switch for coolant
    temperature warning light
11 Heater

2 Cooling system - draining

1   The Alfasud is unconventional in terms of coolant draining. There is no radiator drain plug nor is there one in the crankcase. The coolant is drained through two plugs, one under each cylinder head.
2   To drain fully, find three receptacles of a reasonable size and place one under the bottom hose of the radiator and one under each of the cylinder heads. If it means placing the front of the car on ramps or jacking it up, this will help. Remove the cap from the cooling system expansion chamber.
3   Undo the two drain plugs, one roughly in the centre of each cylinder head, on the underside.
4   When coolant has stopped pouring from each plug, remove the bottom radiator hose. This will allow for a thorough draining and enable proper flushing of the radiator alone.
5   The heater valve should, of course, be open all the time during the operation.

3 Cooling system - flushing

1   Every so often it is a good practice to flush out the system to remove any loose sediment, and scale which may have accumulated. The time to do this is when the coolant is being drained. With the sealed system, however, the need for topping-up should be very infrequent so that the deposits of lime and so on, from regular addition of new water, are negligible. The need for flushing, therefore, is usually only caused by some other factor - such as a leak which allows air to enter the system and cause oxidisation or the use of an antifreeze of a type which may cause corrosion.
2   To check the need for flushing remove the bottom hose and if the liquid coming out is obviously very dirty, although it can be a deep colour, and full of solid particles, let it run out. If it clears as more runs out and the outflow is in no way restricted then there is no great problem. If, however, constant poking with a piece of wire is needed and the liquid continues very dirty then obviously a flush is needed.
3   To flush out, simply leave the engine drain plugs open and after removing the radiator cap, run a hose through the system for about 15 minutes (ordinary water is quite safe). If the plug openings show signs of blockage keep poking them out. If the blocking is persistent remove

the tap completely so that a larger orifice may permit the obstruction to clear itself. In some bad cases a reverse flush may help and this is easily done by removing the radiator and running the hose into the bottom tank so that it flows out of the filler neck.
4   If the radiator flow is restricted by something other than loose sediment then no amount of flushing will shift it and it is then that a proprietary chemical, suitable for aluminium heads, is needed Use this according to the directions and make sure that the residue is fully out afterwards. If leaks develop after using a chemical cleaner, a proprietary radiator sealer may cure them but the signs are that the radiator has suffered considerable chemical corrosion and that the metal is obviously getting very thin in places.

4 Cooling system - filling

1   Make sure the cylinder head drain plugs are in and fixed properly. Make sure all hoses are attached and secured with hose clips properly. Open the heater valve. Turn to 'on'.
2   Fill the expansion chamber with the appropriate coolant until coolant reaches the bottom edge of the filler orifice. Leave the cap off.
3   Start the engine and warm it up until you are sure the thermostat is open. This will cause the level of the coolant in the expansion chamber orifice to 'vibrate' greatly; it does, however, mean that the air trapped in the total system is being bled out. Let the engine run a little longer, then stop it and allow it to cool down.
4   Top-up again until coolant level is above the pointer inside the expansion chamber and visible through the orifice. Replace the filler cap, run the engine again and check for correct function and leaks.

5 Antifreeze mixture

1   In climatic conditions where the ambient temperature is likely to drop below freezing point the use of antifreeze is essential. If the coolant is permitted to freeze in the car serious damage can result.
2   A good proprietary brand should be used and may be left in the cooling system for at least a year. All antifreeze solutions contain corrosion inhibitors which will keep the system in good condition whatever the climatic conditions.
3   The quantity of antifreeze which should be used for various levels of protection is given in the table below, expressed as a percentage of

the cooling system capacity.

Antifreeze volume	Protection to	Spec. gravity
10%	-8°C (17°F)	1.017
15%	-13°C (7°F)	1.024
20%	-19°C (-3°F)	1.032

4   Always be guided by the antifreeze manufacturers instructions, however, as variations in strength do occur between products of different makes.

6   Radiator and expansion chamber - removal, inspection, cleaning and refitting

1   The radiator is easily removed. Drain it by taking off the expansion chamber cap and removing the bottom radiator hose. Catch the coolant in a suitable receptacle. Remove the top hose, and overflow pipe to the expansion chamber.
2   Disconnect the thermostatic switch on the radiator by pulling off the electrical connectors.
3   Disconnect the cooling fan electrical connections at the joint.
4   Undo the centre top nut on the central mounting stud. This is the only radiator mounting. Pull the radiator towards the engine by about an inch at the top. This should help to free the rubber mountings and the washers. Now carefully lift the radiator and cooling fan complete up and out. Retrieve bottom radiator seats.
5   The cooling fan is easily removed from the radiator shell by undoing the four fan frame mounting screws. The thermostatic switch is equally simply removed by gently unscrewing it and retaining the soft washer beneath it.
6   Radiator repair is best left to a specialist but minor leaks may be tackled with a proprietary compound.
7   The radiator matrix may be cleared of flies by brushing with a soft brush or by hosing.
8   Flush the radiator as described in Section 3 according to its degree of contamination. Examine and renew any hoses or clips which have deteriorated.
9   Replacement is an opposite procedure. Refill the cooling system and bleed.
10 The expansion chamber on header tank is attached to the inner ring by three self-tapping screws. It is, therefore, easily removed.

Check it regularly for leaks.
11 If there is any doubt that the expansion chamber filler pressure cap is not functioning properly it should be replaced without hesitation.

7   Thermostat - removal, testing and refitting

1   The thermostat is located on the left side of the engine and is easily located by looking at the radiator top hose and following it back to the engine. There is the thermostat.
2   To remove the thermostat disconnect the radiator top hose on the engine. Undo the two nuts on the thermostat housing, remove and pull off the housing top. Inside is the thermostat which can be easily picked out. Expect to have a certain amount of coolant flow out unless the cooling system has been drained.
3   Do not treat the thermostat badly. It is quite delicate and needs careful handling to encourage long life.
4   To test whether the thermostat functions as it should, suspend it in a pan of water with a piece of string. Then, with a thermometer in the water (not touching the pan) note at what temperature it starts to open. This should be 81 - 85°C. Check that the thermostat closes once again (after cooling naturally). Should it fail on any of these checks it must be renewed. Note that the operation of the thermostat is not instantaneous so allow sufficient time when testing it. Should the thermostat have stuck open it would have been apparent when the housing cover was removed.
5   Replacement of the thermostat is a reversal of the removal procedure. Ensure that the mating faces of the two flanges are clean and use a new gasket. It is a sensible insurance to use a sealing compound also such as 'Hermetite'. If the housing is very deeply corroded it should be renewed.
6   Always top-up the cooling system and bleed if necessary.

8   Water pump - description

The water pump is of conventional impeller type, driven by a drivebelt. The impeller chamber is built into, and forms part of, the timing cover. The water pump detachable body is of die-cast aluminium in which runs the shaft. The shaft is fitted with bearings which are a shrink fit in the body and in the event of leakage or failure of the water pump, then it must be renewed as an assembly on an exchange basis.

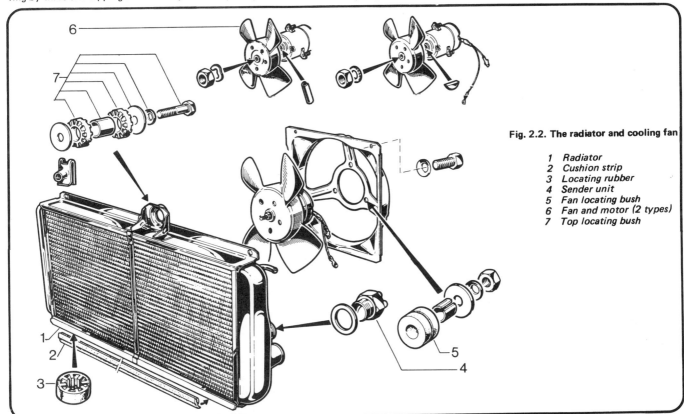

Fig. 2.2. The radiator and cooling fan

1   Radiator
2   Cushion strip
3   Locating rubber
4   Sender unit
5   Fan locating bush
6   Fan and motor (2 types)
7   Top locating bush

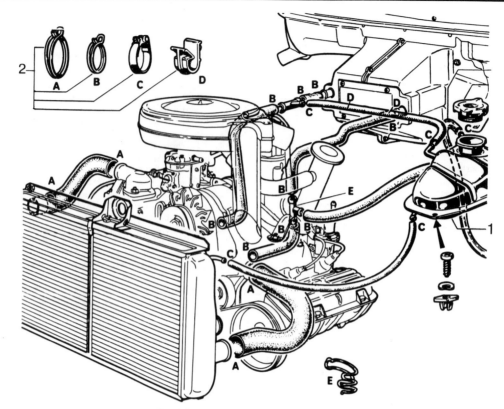

Fig. 2.3. Hoses and expansion chamber

1   Expansion chamber   2   4 types of hose clips with their application

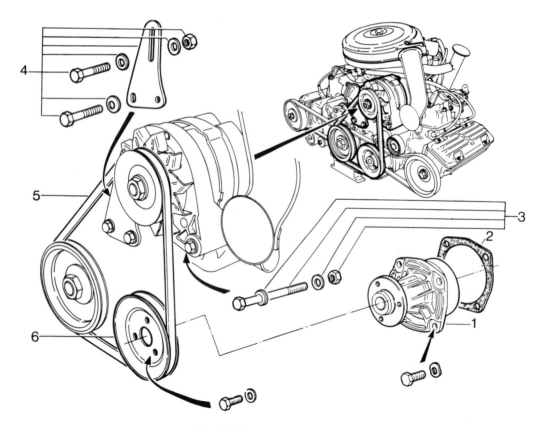

Fig. 2.4. Water pump and drive belt

| 1 Water pump | 3 Pivot bolt | 4 Adjusting quadrant | 5 Drive belt |
| 2 Water pump gasket | | | 6 Drive pulley |

6.10 Expansion chamber and pressure release cap

11.4 Just above the oil filter is a heater hose

9 Water pump - removal and replacement

See Section 16 of Chapter 1. This describes how the water pump is removed and replaced with the engine out of the car. If this operation is undertaken with the engine in the car remove only the radiator, the alternator and drivebelt and the water pump pulley. It is possible to work on the water pump, with care, without touching the camshaft belt on that side.

10 Water temperature - fault finding

1   Correct operation of the water temperature gauge is very important as the engine can otherwise overheat without it being observed.
2   The gauge is an electrically operated instrument comprising a transmitter unit screwed into the top of the cylinder head and transmitting through a spade type connector and cable to a light mounted on the facia instrument panel. The light only operates when the ignition is switched on.
3   Where the water temperature gauge reads intermittently, or not at all, then first check the security of the connecting cable between the transmitter unit and the light.
4   Disconnect the spade connector from the transmitter unit, switch on the ignition when the light should be on. Now earth the cable to the engine block when the light should be out. This test proves the light to be functional and the fault must therefore lie in the cable or transmitter unit. Renew as appropriate.

11 Heater - removal, investigation and replacement

1   Unlike most cars of this type, the heater unit and heater blower are readily accessible, and all from underneath the bonnet. In fact the heater blower and matrix are an integral unit. Neither should be worked upon without removing the whole thing from the car.
2   Open the bonnet and remove the large piece of black plastic channel which crosses the car in the inner bulkhead. It is secured in six places and has two vent pipes connected to it at each end. Undo and remove the two end fixing screws which are visible beneath the vent pipes at each end. Then undo and remove the four crosshead screws which fix it to the top of the heater unit. Lift up the ducting channel and pull off each of the vent pipes. You can now see the heater unit, in the centre.
3   To remove the complete unit pull off but record the electrical connections to it. Now disconnect the heater control cables at the fixing points on the heater unit. The heater unit is located by four studs and nuts on its base. Undo and remove the nuts and pull up the heater to just loosen it. (It sits on a rubber base gasket).

4   Undo the hose clips and pull off the heater/coolant hoses on the inner end, right next to the heater unit. The heater unit should now be free to be lifted upwards and out. Record all the gaskets and their positions.
5   It is now possible to split the heater unit by undoing and removing all the through setscrews and nuts. Once this has been done it is possible to pull the two halves or cases apart to reveal the heater matrix and blower motor and fan.
6   The heater matrix is either in good order or finished; it cannot be repaired. If damaged in any way, replace it.
7   Similarly the heater blower motor cannot be repaired. If not functioning, replace it.
8   Reassembly is an exact reverse procedure of dismantling.
9   The control cables will have to be adjusted to make sure they work through their full potential of travel. They should not be kinked or abused in any way otherwise trouble will occur.
10 The heater control inside the car is easily removed, from inside the car. Unclip the slide cover. Disconnect the cables from the heater unit as just described and then loosen and remove the two vertical fixing screws which hold the lever plate to the dashboard. The lever plate with the cables still attached should now pull away.
11 Replacement is a reverse procedure of removal.
Special Note: By British standards the heater is very weak on these cars. The car is built in Southern Italy where the temperature is usually fairly warm. The engine runs fairly cool and the heater matrix is a small one. There is little one can do!

12 Hoses - general

1   All hoses deteriorate over a period of time. They crack, split or sometimes soften. Check often on the condition of the hoses, particularly on any sharp bends over particularly hot parts of the engine, or under the hose clips. Never patch, always replace unhealthy hoses.
2   Hose clips used on the Alfasud are invariably pressure clips rather than worm-drive clips. If they weaken replace with good quality clips of the proper size.

13 Cooling fan - general

1   The cooling fan is attached to the radiator by a special locating frame which is removed as described in Section 6. The fan blades are removed from the motor by releasing the end nut. The motor itself is mounted to the locating frame by three rubber mounts secured by three nuts, ferrules and washers. All are obviously removed.
2   It is not a good idea to tamper with the fan motor. If it is faulty take it to an auto-electrician but expect it to be exchanged, rather than repaired.

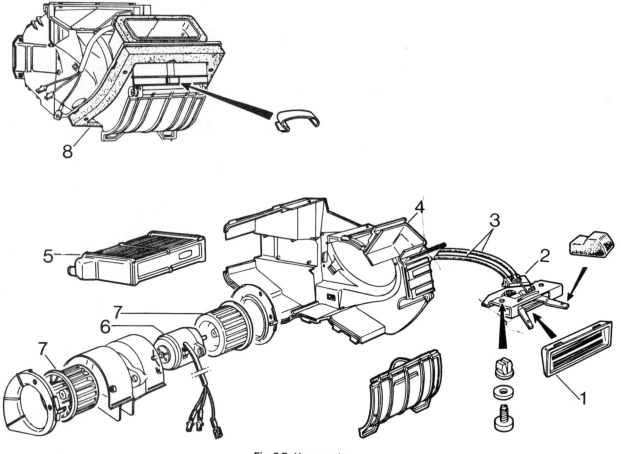

Fig. 2.5. Heater unit

| 1 Heater control bezel | 3 Control cables | 5 Matrix | 7 Fans |
| 2 Heater control | 4 Heater casing half | 6 Motor | 8 Heater complete |

14 Fault diagnosis - cooling and heating systems

Symptom	Reason/s	Remedy
Loss of coolant but no overheating provided	Expansion chamber empty Small leaks in system	Half fill expansion chamber. Examine all hoses and connections for signs of cracks and leaks when engine is both cold and hot, stationary and running. If no signs, use proprietary sealer in coolant to stop any invisible leaks.
Overheating and loss of coolant only when overheated	Faulty thermostat Fan belt slipping/electric fan fault Engine out of tune due to ignition and/or fuel system settings being incorrect Blockage or restriction in circulation of cooling water Radiator cooling fins clogged up Blown cylinder head gasket or cracked cylinder head Sheared water pump impeller shaft Cracked cylinder body New engine still tight	Check and renew if faulty. Check and adjust. Check ignition and fuel systems and adjust as required. Check that no hoses have collapsed. Drain, flush out and refill cooling system. Use chemical flushing compound if necessary. Remove radiator and clean exterior as needed. Remove cylinder head for examination. Remove pump and check. Remove engine and examine and repair (if possible). Adjust engine speeds to suit until run in.
Engine runs too cool and heater inefficient	Thermostat missing or stuck open	Remove housing cover and inspect.

Chapter 3 Carburation; fuel and exhaust systems

Contents

Specifications

Fuel tank capacity ... ... 11 Imp. gallons (50 litres)

Fuel pump

Type ... ... Diaphragm, mechanically operated by a cam on the distributor manufactured by either Fispa or Savara.

Delivery pressure ... ... 2.56 - 4.27 psi (18 - 30 kg/sq cm) at 5000rpm Fispa pump or 6000rpm for Savara.

Air cleaner ... ... Pancake type with dry paper element

Carburettor

	Alfasud	Alfasud TI
Type	Solex C32 DISA21 single choke downdraught	Weber 32 DIR 41 twin choke downdraught
Main jet	127.5	125/135
Main air metering jet	150	170/120
Idling jet	65	50/50
Idling air metering jet	80	—
Choke jet	55	—
Accelerator pump jet	45	45
Venturi	24mm	—
Idling speed	800/1000rpm	800/1000rpm

Torque wrench settings	lb f ft	kg f m
Inlet manifold to cylinder head	14	2
Fuel pump to rear cover	14	2
Carburettor to inlet manifold	14	2
Air cleaner to carburettor	7	1

1 General description

The fuel system of the Alfasud range is entirely conventional, although it could be said that the inlet manifolds are extremely long, to allow the carburettor to sit in the centre of the engine between the two banks of cylinders.

The Alfasud uses a single choke downdraught Solex carburettor, while the Alfasud TI uses a twin choke downdraught Weber. Both models use a mechanical fuel pump and a water heated inlet manifold, and a replaceable paper filter element for the air cleaner.

A large fuel tank is mounted underneath the car at the rear. An unusual four-into-two-into-one exhaust system is used with two silencers.

2 Air filter element - removal and renewal

1 To remove the air filter element undo the large wing nut on the top of the air cleaner, lift the cover and sealing ring. The element can now be picked out. It is a replaceable element and once 'dirty' must be thrown away.

2 To remove the cleaner case release the 'Winter' flexible pipe top hose clip and pull off the pipe. Pull off the one (Alfasud) and two (Alfasud TI) breather pipes on the underside of the case. Undo the two (Alfasud) and four (Alfasud TI) fixing nuts in the base of the cleaner, remove and then remove the cleaner case. Note the two gaskets on the top of the carburettor.

3 Replacement of the case is an exactly opposite operation. Obviously

the new air cleaner element is put back into the case before the top is secured. Check the sealing ring and make sure there is no dust etc left in the case.

4   There are two inlet pipes into the air cleaner case. Pushing the operating lever to the rear of the car opens the 'Summer' inlet pipe, ie cold air from the radiator grill, while pushing it to the front of the car opens the 'Winter' pipe (the flexible pipe), ie warm air taken from the special housing on the exhaust manifold.

5   Always fit an air cleaner and always use the appropriate inlet pipe. Damage can occur if this is not strictly adhered to.

3 Carburettor - description and principle

The Alfasud uses a single choke downdraught Solex C32 DISA 21 mounted on a long inlet tract which is water heated. A manual choke is fitted to enable easy starting. The carburettor is fitted with a pump jet. The Alfasud TI is equipped with a twin choke downdraught Weber 32 DIR 41. It too, has a manual choke and a pump jet, and sits on a water heated manifold.

In each carburettor fuel is pumped through a filter into a float chamber. It is then fed into the venturi(s). The manual choke operates a butterfly in the venturi and shuts off the flow of the majority of the air. When the accelerator is pressed firmly fuel is pumped directly into the venturi and the butterfly is 'opened'; as soon as the 'initial' motion is completed fuel is fed into the venturi through the main jet. On the Alfasud TI this principle operates in the same way except it goes further, in that as the butterfly 'opens' in one venturi it progressively opens a butterfly in the second venturi, thereby enabling even more fuel to enter the inlet tracts.

4 Carburettor - removal and replacement

See Sections 11 and 51, of Chapter 1.

5 Carburettor - setting and adjustment

1   It must be emphasised that if the engine is running smoothly and performance and fuel consumption are satisfactory there are no adjustments that will materially improve any of these conditions beyond the manufacturers' specifications. If the engine is not performing as it should, be sure to check the ignition system before assuming that the carburettor is the cause of the trouble.

2   Assuming all components are clean and in good condition there are only two adjustments that can be made - these being the fuel level in the float chamber and the slow running speed.

3   To check the fuel level the carburettor must be fitted to the engine. The car should be standing on a level surface. Run the engine and then switch it off and remove the fuel line from the carburettor.

4   Remove the air cleaner assembly and then take out the five screws securing the upper half of the carburettor to the lower. Put a finger over the fuel inlet pipe (to prevent the little fuel in the top cover coming out when the top is lifted) and take off the top cover and gasket.

5   The level of the fuel - with the float in position - should be 12 - 14 mm below the top edge of the float chamber. This can be measured by using a depth gauge or by placing a straight edge across the top of the float chamber and measuring down with a suitable rule. Do not measure too near the edge as capillary action up the side of the chamber could cause a false reading. If the level is incorrect it may be altered by fitting a washer of a different thickness under the needle valve which is screwed into the top cover. Washers are available in a range of thicknesses from ½ to 1 mm. (It can be seen that the fuel level measurement has to be taken fairly accurately to be of any use in deciding whether alteration is necessary). If the level in the chamber needs raising, a thinner washer should be fitted, and vice versa. If you are tempted to try and alter the level by bending the bracket on the float - forget it. It cannot be done accurately enough to be of any use and more often than not the result of such attempts is either breakage or distortion. In the latter case the net result is a sticking float which

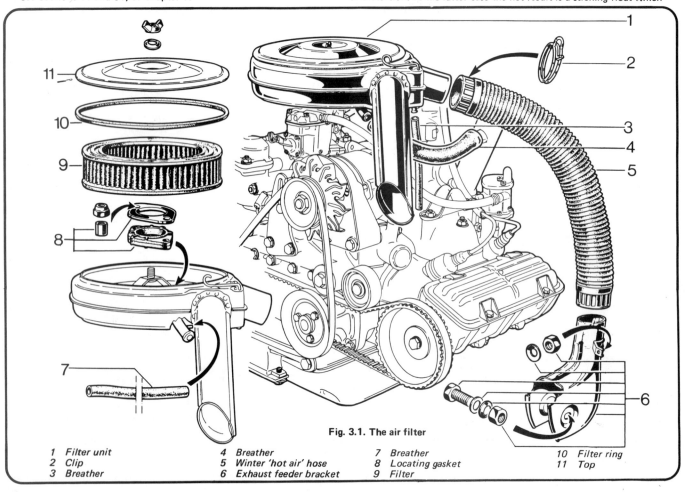

Fig. 3.1. The air filter

1	Filter unit	4	Breather	7	Breather	10	Filter ring
2	Clip	5	Winter 'hot air' hose	8	Locating gasket	11	Top
3	Breather	6	Exhaust feeder bracket	9	Filter		

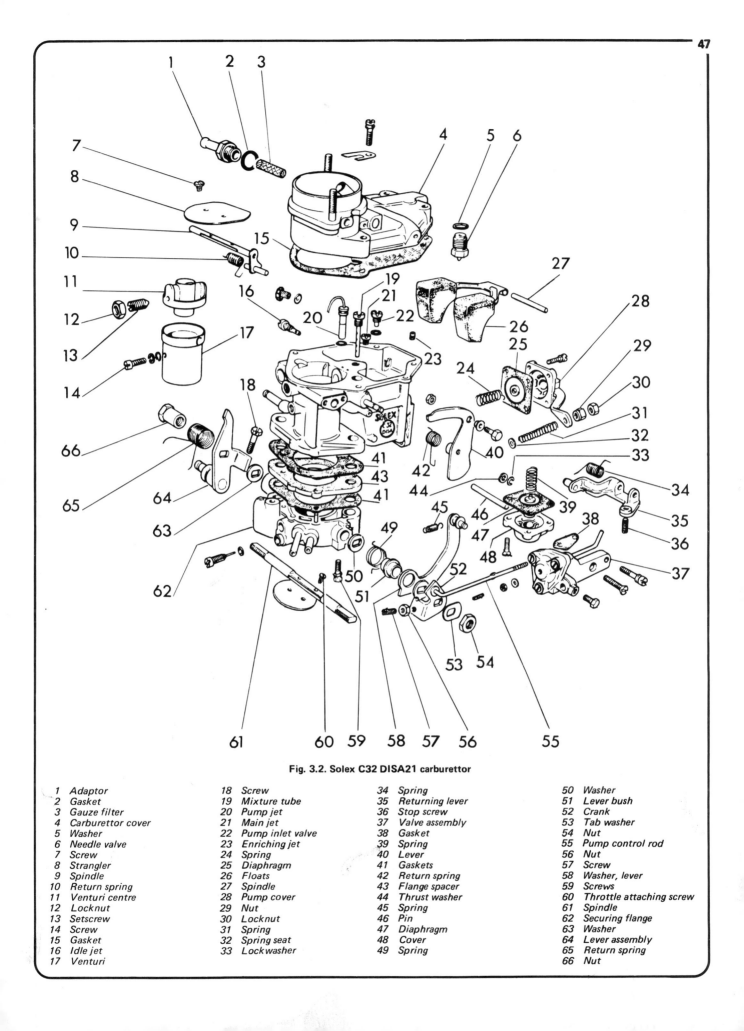

Fig. 3.2. Solex C32 DISA21 carburettor

1	Adaptor	18	Screw	34	Spring	50	Washer
2	Gasket	19	Mixture tube	35	Returning lever	51	Lever bush
3	Gauze filter	20	Pump jet	36	Stop screw	52	Crank
4	Carburettor cover	21	Main jet	37	Valve assembly	53	Tab washer
5	Washer	22	Pump inlet valve	38	Gasket	54	Nut
6	Needle valve	23	Enriching jet	39	Spring	55	Pump control rod
7	Screw	24	Spring	40	Lever	56	Nut
8	Strangler	25	Diaphragm	41	Gaskets	57	Screw
9	Spindle	26	Floats	42	Return spring	58	Washer, lever
10	Return spring	27	Spindle	43	Flange spacer	59	Screws
11	Venturi centre	28	Pump cover	44	Thrust washer	60	Throttle attaching screw
12	Locknut	29	Nut	45	Spring	61	Spindle
13	Setscrew	30	Locknut	46	Pin	62	Securing flange
14	Screw	31	Spring	47	Diaphragm	63	Washer
15	Gasket	32	Spring seat	48	Cover	64	Lever assembly
16	Idle jet	33	Lockwasher	49	Spring	65	Return spring
17	Venturi					66	Nut

2.2a How the 'cold'/'hot' air switch lever works

2.2b The base fixing studs use Nyloc nuts

gives you more problems than you had to start with.

6   Whilst the cover is removed it would be as well to check the condition of the needle valve as described in the previous section.

7   Reassemble the top cover with the gasket the correct way round, reconnect and clip the fuel line and replace the air cleaner. If wished the level may be checked again once any adjustment has been made but it should not be necessary provided the needle valve is in good order and the measurements were accurately taken.

8   Slow running adjustment is only carried out when the engine is warm and the strangler flap fully open.

9   With the engine adjusted on the throttle stop screw to a speed of 700 - 800 rpm (fast tickover) turn the volume control screw clockwise until the speed decreases. Then turn it back until even running occurs. Then continue to turn it another ¼ revolution. Note that if this adjustment is carried out before the engine is warm (and the automatic choke fully open) the throttle stop screw may still be resting on one of the steps of the cam attached to the strangler flap spindle. These steps are intended only to keep up the engine speed during the warm up period by restricting the throttle from closing fully even when the accelerator pedal may be released completely. When the volume control screw has been set the throttle stop screw may be re-adjusted to give a suitable idling speed. Do not try to set the idling speed too low - particularly if the engine is not in the first flush of youth. You will waste hours trying to achieve the impossible.

10   The setting of the accelerator cable into the throttle operating arm is important if full throttle opening is to be possible and also if excessive strain is to be avoided. Obviously one wants to have the throttle flap fully open when the accelerator pedal is fully depressed. At the same time one does not want to have the throttle fully open and up to the stop before the pedal has been fully depressed, otherwise the pedal pressure will stretch the cable and put considerable strain on the bracket and spindle. With the accelerator cable end in position but unclamped, move the throttle lever round to the fully open position, up to the stop. Then let it come back so that there is a gap of 1 mm between the stop and the lever. At the same time someone else should depress the accelerator pedal right to the floor. In this position the cable end may be tightened into position. Check the accelerator pedal movement to see that the gap is maintained when the pedal is pressed to the floor.

11   Remember the throttle pedal stop screw on the floor inside the car. This should be adjusted for foot comfort only.

12   The Weber 32 DIR fitted to the Alfasud TI is a twin progressive choke downdraught carburettor which has the same operating principle as the Solex varieties. It is basically two single choke carburettors in one body, one choke of which is open at tick-over whilst the other only begins to open at heavier throttle loadings, activated by the first choke as it itself is nearing a fully open state. This facility allows for comparative economy at low speeds (operating on one choke) and extra performance when needed (both chokes operating). It has a manual operated cold starting strangler (choke) by the cable from a lever near the gear lever on the floor of the car. This carburettor also has a water heated manifold but does not use a similar method to the Solex, in that heat from the coolant does not operate the choke

automatically.

13   This carburettor is an expensive component, relative to the price of a Solex and is better made. Consequently it is advised that under no circumstances should the carburettor be dismantled further than the removal of the float chamber/choke flaps cover, and this only to clean the float chamber and to check the level of the float. If you are certain that the carburettor is at fault, and not simply an adjustment or ignition fault, then the carburettor must be removed from the car and taken to a good experienced Alfa Romeo agency or a Weber agency. **Do not** attempt any home renovation - it will only make matters worse.

14   Removal of this carburettor is undertaken in exactly the same way as for the Solex except that you should remove the choke cable by undoing the locknut on the inner cable and then the clamp nut of the outer cable. Pull both through then. The carburettor is bolted down with four nuts instead of two.

15   The top cover of the carburettor is located by five screws. These should all be undone and then the cover lifted off. Make sure a new paper gasket is available. The float level and jet removal (only if absolutely necessary) should be undertaken in the same way as for the Solex. Make sure you understand what you are doing first. Read that section thoroughly.

16   Carburettor adjustment is undertaken in exactly the same way as for the Solex using the appropriate adjusting screws.

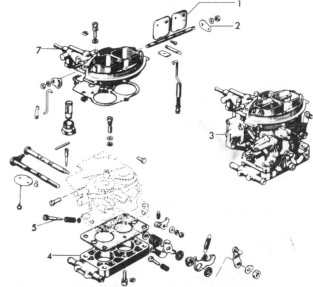

Fig. 3.3. Weber 32 DIR 41 Components (there will be some difference in exact specification on the Alfasud TI)

1 Top butterflies	3 Complete carburettor	5 Fuel screw
2 Spindle lever	showing diaphragm	6 Lower butterflies
	4 Carburettor base	7 Carburettor cover

Fig. 3.4. The solex carburettor idle adjusting screw 'A'

6 Carburettor - dismantling, inspection and reassembly

Alfasud

1 The carburettor should not be dismantled without reason. Such reasons would be for cleaning or renewal of the float and needle valve assembly and, in rare circumstances, the jets. Partial dismantling would also be necessary for checking and setting the float chamber fuel level.
2 The first stage of dismantling should be to remove the screws holding the top to the base. Separate the two halves carefully and remove the paper gasket, taking care to keep it from being damaged. It can be re-used.
3 To clean out the float chamber, invert the carburettor body; the float complete with pivot pin will fall out. If it needs a little help to get it out do not under any circumstances strain it in such a way that the pin or bracket are bent. When the float is removed the bowl may be flushed out and sediment removed with a small brush.
4 The needle valve is screwed into the top cover and when taking it out note the washer mounted underneath it. The simplest way to check this for leaks is to try blowing through it. It should not be possible to do so when the plunger is lightly pushed in. If in doubt, then renew the assembly, as a leaking valve will result in an over-rich mixture with consequent loss of performance and increased fuel consumption.
5 The accelerator pump diaphragm may be examined when the four cover securing screws, cover and spring have been removed. Be careful not to damage the diaphragm. Renew it if there are signs of holes or cracks which may reduce its efficiency.
6 The main jet is situated behind a hexagonal headed plug in the base of the float chamber. This can, of course, be removed without taking the carburettor off the car. Remove the plug and then unscrew the jet from behind it with a screwdriver. The pilot jet is fixed similarly in the body but alongside the accelerator pump housing, except that it is on the opposite side. When cleaning these jets do not use anything other than air pressure. Any poking with wire could damage the fine tolerance bores and upset the fuel mixtures.
7 The air correction jet and emulsion tube is mounted vertically in the body of the carburettor by the side of the choke tube. This too may be unscrewed for cleaning. Blow through the passageway in the carburettor also, when it is removed.
8 Before reassembly check that the float is undamaged and unpunctured. It can be checked by immersion in hot water.
9 The accelerator pump inspection tube may be inadvertently moved so check that the outlet points down in such a way that the jet of fuel cannot impinge on any part of the carburettor or open throttle on its way down to the inlet manifold.
10 If the throttle flap spindle should be very loose in its bearings in the main body of the carburettor then air may leak past and affect the air to fuel ratio of the mixture. In such cases the easiest remedy is a new carburettor. An alternative is to drill and fit bushes to suit but this needs some expertise and time.
11 Reassembly is a reversal of the dismantling procedure but the following points should be watched carefully. Do not forget the washer when replacing the needle valve. Make sure that the gasket between body and cover is correctly positioned. When refitting the accelerator pump cover, the screws should be tightened with the diaphragm centre pushed in. This means holding the operating lever out whilst the screws are tightened. Do not bend or distort the float arm when replacing it into the float chamber.
12 For the air and fuel screw see the next Section. Never dismantle further than described here.

Alfasud TI

13 See Section 5, paragraph 12 onwards. Follow the instructions given here.

7 Choke cable - general

The choke cable should not need touching unless it snaps or develops a permanent kink in it; it is of stiff steel wire. It is basically a conventional system, although it does have an electrical switch at its top end which will ignite a warning light on the instrument panel whilst it remains 'on'. The cable's removal and replacement, once the two electrical connections have been pulled off from underneath the steering column, is conventional and straightforward. Disconnect the cable at the carburettor and pull the choke knob right out - this removes the inner cable. It is now possible to unclip the outer cable from inside the car and remove it. It is necessary to purchase a complete cable; inners and outers and switches are not available separately.

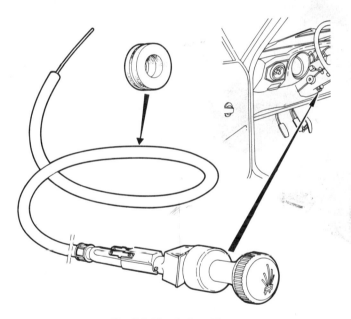

Fig. 3.5. The choke cable

8 Throttle cable - general

1 The throttle cable is easily replaced. Both the inner and outer cables are available separately as are all the other components.
2 Whilst the Alfasud and the Alfasud TI do not share exactly the same cable or fixing components, the removal and refitting technique is similar. If the cable snaps or simply will not travel properly, the inner cable at least should be replaced.
3 At the carburettor end there is a threaded ferrule connection. The throttle return spring should be disconnected and the ferrule unscrewed. Pull the outer cable through the various rubber grommets and stop washers.
4 On the inner bulkhead there is an outer cable stop which is attached to the bulkhead by one screw. Remove this and push the inner cable into the car.
5 Inside the car disconnect the inner cable from the throttle pedal up under the parcel shelf. Pull out the pedal end plug and disconnect

the cable. Pull the inner away and then push the whole thing back into the bonnet area and lift the whole cable away.

6   Replacement is a straightforward reverse procedure. It helps to oil the inner cable lightly. Make sure it does not have any kinks in it, and make sure it operates the carburettor through its full potential movement.

7   To achieve proper adjustment tape the throttle pedal cable connection end to the bulkhead so that it is fully released. Then adjust the cable slack at the carburettor so that there is 1 mm 'slack' between the bottom elongation of the cable plate and the throttle spindle lever pin. You do this with the adjuster on the outer cable. Now remove the tape and operate the pedal. Ignore the throttle pedal stop screw; it is used to inhibit maximum 'to the floor' throttle to be achieved. It is a stop, nothing more.

9   Fuel pump - removal and replacement

See Sections 13 and 47, of Chapter 1.

10 Fuel pump - dismantling, inspection and reassembly

1   Alfasud fuel pumps cannot be repaired. They can be dismantled, cleaned and reassembled but spare parts are not available. There is little point in doing anything more than removing the cover and cleaning the filter.

2   The pump top cover is fixed by two screws. Remove both these and lift the cover. Inside is a gauze filter. Carefully remove this and clean any sediment away from the gauze and from the body of the pump. Obviously this can be done with the engine in the car.

3   Carefully replace all the parts. Methylated spirits is a suitable cleaner.

4   However, before discarding a fuel pump, just check that the pump is at fault rather than any other component. Remove the pump and check the operation of the actuating arm. These actuating arms come in different lengths, although it is unlikely that yours will be too short. If you are concerned about it you will have to try to borrow the Alfa Romeo special tool for measuring actuating arm protrusion out of the crankcase. The arm should, in theory, protrude between 0.8/1.11 mm out from the fuel pump gasket placed on the mounting studs. Nevertheless it is most likely that your pump *is* at fault.

11 Fuel tank - general

1   The fuel tank is located across the car between the back seat and

the boot floor, below the floor. Its removal is simple, if a little messy. The quality of the tank is good and unlikely to need replacement unless it is holed or some foreign body finds its way into it and starts to destroy the inner surface to allow rusting to take place.

2   To remove the tank jack the rear of the car as high as possible and support it. Both wheels should be off the ground. Remove the rear roadwheels. (Try to have the tank as empty as possible).

3   Clean as much of the tank as you can now. Release the filler hose clip at the tank and pull off the hose. Start the two fixing bolts which fix the support straps around the tank, to the bodyshell underside.

4   Pull off the overflow pipe close to the filler hose. Remove the tank strap bolts and slowly lower the tank away. Before pulling well away, disconnect the sender unit electrical connections at the sender unit and pull off the fuel outlet pipe from that unit. The tank should now be free to lift out and away.

5   Replacement is a reverse process.

6   The fuel filler neck complete can be removed and replaced without the tank. Once the bottom filler hose and overflow pipe is disconnected from the tank end, the complete filler pipe can be removed by undoing the filler neck fixing plate from inside the little filler flap on the rear of the bodywork. It should then drop down.

7   Obviously the bodywork should be cleaned before replacement. Check all the hoses and their clips.

12 Fuel gauge - sender unit

1   The fuel gauge sender unit is mounted on the top of the tank where the fuel outlet pipe connection is also made, sucking up the petrol through a filter on the end of a tube. If the fuel gauge appears faulty first check the wiring connections at the base of the instrument panel. See Chapter 9. Then go on to the sender unit which is a variable resistance giving different readings with both a full and empty tank by the operation of a metal float. If the fault lies here and you are sure that the sender unit was properly connected, you will have to replace the whole unit. It is not possible to replace parts of it.

2   To remove the sender unit, you will have to remove the fuel tank. See Section 13. Having presumably pulled off the fuel and electrical contents, to remove, undo the fixing screws, break the seal and lift out carefully turning the body of the unit to release the float and filter tube. When replacing always use a new gasket and do not overtighten. Make sure that the two connections are clean and tight.

3   These are reliable instruments and are usually non-functioning because of some mechanical defect rather than electrical, ie; the float arm is bent, or the float has been perforated.

13 Inlet manifold - general

1   The Alfasud and Alfasud TI inlet manifolds (different components, but similar from a maintenance point of view), are beautiful pieces of alloy casting. Many other components are fitted to it, apart from the carburettor. It is water heated, internally, having the thermostat housing attached directly to it, beneath the carburettor.

2   Its removal and replacement, and the removal of the various components are described in Chapter 1, in full. Here all that needs to be stated is that care should be taken with it. Wherever any component is fixed to it, or it is attached to the crankcase, new gaskets should be used. Follow fixing instructions carefully, particularly with regard to torque loadings. Always keep it clean.

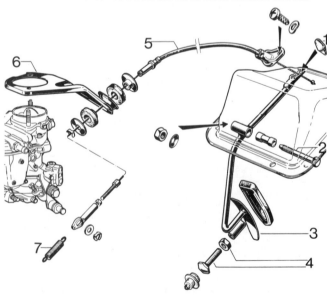

Fig. 3.6. The throttle pedal and cable

1 Top pedal stop	*5 Cable*
2 Pivot	*6 Carburettor bracing*
3 Pedal	*7 Return spring*
4 Bottom stop	

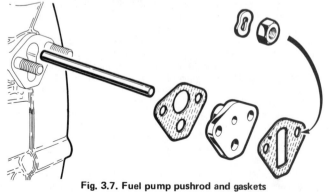

Fig. 3.7. Fuel pump pushrod and gaskets

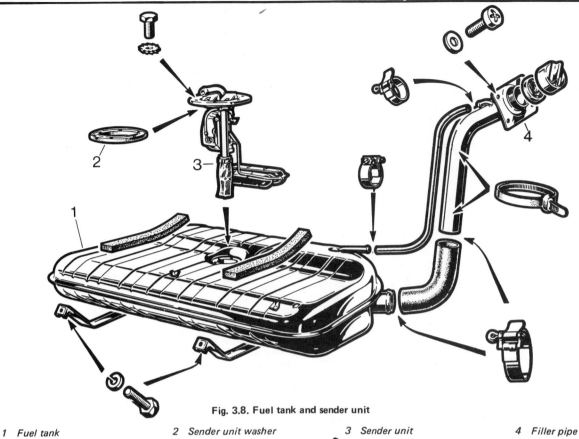

Fig. 3.8. Fuel tank and sender unit

1 Fuel tank	2 Sender unit washer	3 Sender unit	4 Filler pipe

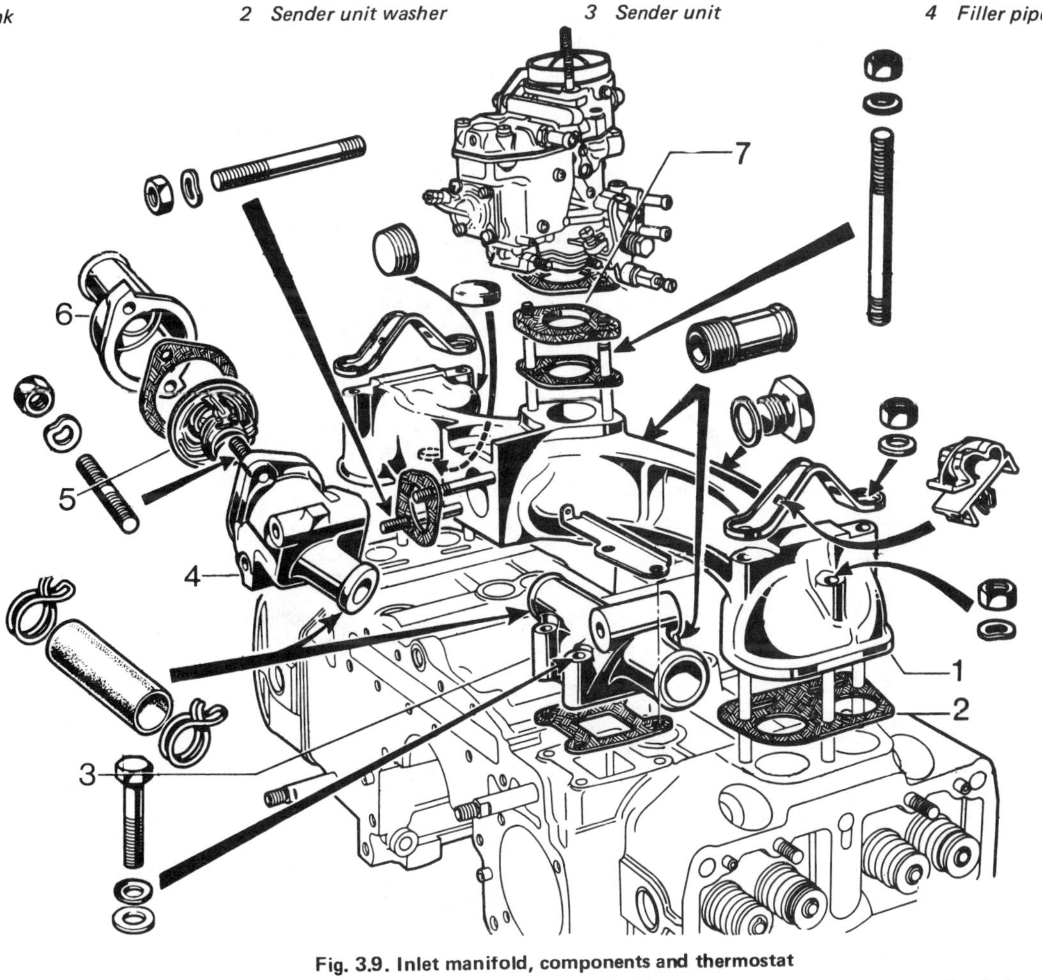

Fig. 3.9. Inlet manifold, components and thermostat

1 Inlet manifold	3 Cooling by-pass	5 Thermostat	7 Carburettor gasket
2 Gasket	4 Thermostat body	6 Thermostat top	

11.3a One of the two bolts ...

11.3b ... and the clips on the other end of the fixing straps

14 Exhaust system - general

1   The exhaust manifolding and exhaust system complete, comes only in two pieces. This is unusual. The individual exhaust manifolding comes from each cylinder to join, four into two into one, under the centre of the car, following the centre to the first silencer and then to branching at right angles, in front of the fuel tank. It then turns another right angle, again to the rear, just in front of the offside rear wheel and stops. That is the first part. The second part is simply a piece of pipe with a silencer in the middle and a tailpipe which curves gently to the rear of the car. A complete new exhaust system is expensive. Take care with it!

2   When any one section of the exhaust system needs renewal it often follows that the whole lot is best replaced.

3   It is most important when fitting exhaust systems that the twists and contours are carefully followed and that each connecting joint overlaps the correct distance. Any stresses or strain imparted, in order to force the system to fit the hanger rubbers, will result in early fractures and failures.

4   When fitting a new part of a complete system it is well worth removing **all** the system from the car and cleaning up all the joints so that they fit together easily. The time spent struggling with obstinate joints whilst flat on your back under the car is eliminated and the likelihood of distorting or even breaking a section is greatly reduced. Do not waste a lot of time trying to undo rusted and corroded clamps and bolts. Cut them off. New ones will be required anyway if they are that bad.

5   Two persons are better than one when working on this system.

6   Do not modify the system, by, for example, leaving off the tailpipe. Economy and performance will suffer.

7   Exhaust system removal and replacement is described in Chapter 1. See Section 4.

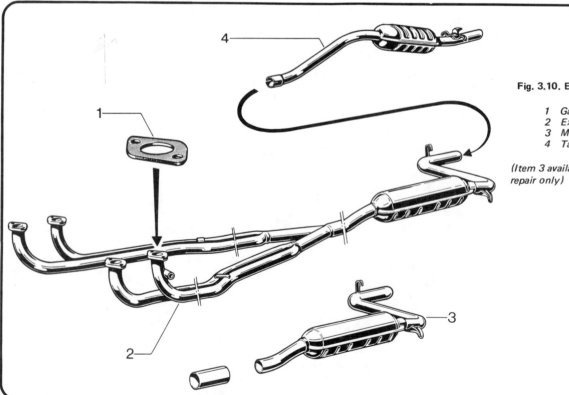

Fig. 3.10. Exhaust system

1 Gasket
2 Exhaust manifold
3 Middle silencer
4 Tail pipe

(Item 3 available separately as a repair only)

15 Fault diagnosis - fuel system and carburation

Symptom	Reason/s	Remedy
Excessive fuel consumption	Air cleaner choked and dirty giving rich mixture	Remove, clean and replace air cleaner.
	Fuel leaking from carburettor, fuel pump, or fuel lines	Check for and eliminate all fuel leaks. Tighten fuel line union.
	Float chamber flooding	Check and adjust float level.
	Generally worn carburettor	Remove, overhaul and replace.
	Distributor condenser faulty	Remove, and fit new unit.
	Balance weights or vacuum advance mechanism in distributor faulty	Remove and overhaul distributor.
	Carburettor incorrectly adjusted, mixture too rich	Tune and adjust carburettor.
	Idling speed too high	Adjust idling speed.
	Contact breaker gap incorrect	Check and reset gap.
	Valve clearances incorrect	Check clearances and adjust as necessary.
	Tyres under-inflated	Check tyre pressures and inflate if necessary.
	Wrong spark plugs fitted	Remove and replace with correct units.
	Brakes dragging	Check and adjust brakes.
Insufficient fuel delivery or weak mixture	Fuel tank air vent restricted	Clean out air vent.
	Partially clogged filter in pump	Remove and clean filter.
	Dirt lodged in float chamber needle housing	Remove and clean out float chamber and needle valve assembly.
	Incorrectly seating valves in fuel pump	Remove, dismantle, and clean out fuel pump.
	Fuel pump diaphragm leaking or damaged	Remove and overhaul fuel pump.
	Gasket in fuel pump damaged	Remove and overhaul fuel pump.
	Fuel pump valves sticking due to petrol gumming	Remove and thoroughly clean fuel pump.
	Too little fuel in fuel tank (prevalent when climbing steep hills)	Refill fuel tank.
	Union joints on pipe connections loose	Tighten joints and check for air leaks.
	Split in fuel pipe on suction side of fuel pump	Examine, locate and repair.
	Inlet manifold to block or inlet manifold to carburettor gasket leaking	Test by pouring oil along joints - bubbles indicate leak. Renew gasket as appropriate.
Difficult cold starting	Clogged jets	Clear.
	Loose main jet plug	Tighten.
	Choke flap not closing	Check mechanism.
	Weak mixture	Adjust slow-running.
Difficult starting when engine hot	Incorrect float level	Adjust or renew defective float.
	Flooded carburettor	Check needle valve.
Erratic idling	Clogged idling jet	Clear.
	Incorrect float level	Check level, also tightness of needle valve.
	Incorrectly set slow-running	Adjust.
	Leak in vacuum connection to distributor	Rectify.
'Pinking'	Use of fuel with too low an octane rating	Fill tank with correct grade.
	Incorrect carburettor jets (mixture too weak)	Compare with Specifications.
	Carbon deposits in combustion chamber	Decarbonise.
	Displaced or deformed cylinder head gasket causing pre-ignition particularly on overrun	Remove head and renew gasket.
	Incorrect type spark plugs	Renew.
Misfiring or lack of power	Water in fuel	Drain tank.
	Clogged fuel line	Clear.
	Faulty fuel pump	Overhaul.
	Clogged filters or air cleaner	Clean or renew.
	Carburettor icing	Move air cleaner intake to winter position.
	Incorrect slow-running	Adjust.

Chapter 4 Ignition system

Contents

Specifications

Spark plugs
Type	Golden Lodge 2HL*
Maximum renewal period	16,000 km (10,000 miles)

Firing order
Firing order	1 - 3 - 2 - 4 (RH front - RH rear - LH front - LH rear)

Coil
Coil	12 volt

Distributor
Type	Bosch JFU 4
Dwell angle at 500 rpm	60° - 64°
Opening of contacts (statically)	0.45 mm
Pressure of contacts	500 - 650 gr
Capacity of condenser	0.2 mF
Type	Ducellier 4435/A
Dwell angle at 500 rpm	54° - 60°
Opening of contacts (statically)	0.35 - 0.40 mm
Pressure of contacts	400 - 500 gr
Capacity of condenser	0.2 mF

Static ignition timing
Static ignition timing	$8^o \pm 1^o$

Location of timing mark
Location of timing mark	Flywheel '1' = static timing: 'III' - maximum advance

Contact breaker gap
Contact breaker gap	0.35 - 0.45 mm (0.014 - 0.018 in)

Only this type of plug is to be used in the Alfasud engine. It has a special 4-prong electrode which is not adjustable for gap. Any other type could ruin the engine.

Torque wrench setting
	lb f ft	Kg f m
Spark plugs	21	3

1 General description

In order that the engine can run correctly it is necessary for an electrical spark to ignite the fuel/air mixture in the combustion chamber at exactly the right moment in relation to engine speed and load. The ignition system is based on feeding low tension (LT) voltage from the battery to the coil where it is converted to high tension (HT) voltage. The high tension voltage is powerful enough to jump the spark plug gap in the cylinders many times a second under high compression pressures, providing that the system is in good condition and that all adjustments are correct.

The ignition system is divided into two circuits. The low tension circuit and the high tension circuit.

The low tension (sometimes known as the primary) circuit consists of the battery, the lead to the control box, to the ignition switch from the ignition switch to the low tension or primary coil windings (terminal SW), and from the low tension coil windings (coil terminal CB) to the contact breaker points and condenser on the distributor.

The high tension circuit consists of the high tension or secondary coil windings, the heavy ignition lead from the centre of the coil to the centre of the distributor cap, the rotor arm, and the spark plug leads and spark plugs.

The system functions in the following manner, Low tension voltage is changed by the coil into high tension voltage by the opening and closing of the contact breaker points in the low tension circuit. High tension voltage is then fed via the carbon brush in the centre of the distributor cap to the rotor arm of the distributor cap, and each time it comes in line with one of the four metal segments in the cap, which are connected to the spark plug leads, the opening and closing of the contact breaker points causes the high tension voltage to build up, jump the gap from the rotor arm to the appropriate metal segment and so, via the spark plug lead, to the spark plug; where it finally jumps the spark plug gap before going to earth.

The ignition is advanced and retarded automatically, to ensure the spark occurs at just the right instant for the particular load at the prevailing engine speed.

The ignition advance is controlled both mechanically and by a vacuum operated system. The mechanical governor mechanism comprises two weights, which move out from the distributor shaft as the engine speed rises due to centrifugal force. As they move outwards they rotate the cam relative to the distributor shaft, and so advance the spark. The weights are held in position by two light springs and it is the tension of the springs which is largely responsible for correct spark advancement.

The vacuum control consists of a diaphragm, one side of which is connected via a small bore tube to the carburettor, and the other side to the contact breaker plate. Depression in the inlet manifold and carburettor, which varies with engine speed and throttle opening, causes the diaphragm to move, so moving the contact breaker plate, and advancing or retarding the spark.

2 Routine maintenance

Spark plugs

Remove the plugs and thoroughly clean away all traces of carbon. Examine the porcelain insulation round the central electrodes inside the plug and if damaged discard the plug. Do not use a set of plugs for more than 15000 km (9000 miles). It is false economy.

At the same time check the plug caps. Always use the straight tubular ones normally fitted. Good replacements can come from an Alfa Romeo agent. Read the Section on spark plugs, Section 9.

Distributor

Every 15000 km (9000 miles) remove the cap and rotor arm and put one or two drops of engine oil into the centre of the cam recess. Smear the surfaces of the cam itself with petroleum jelly. Do not over lubricate as any excess could get onto the contact point surfaces and cause ignition difficulties.

Every 15000 km (9000 miles) examine the contact point surfaces. If there is a build-up of deposits on one face and a pit in the other it will be impossible to set the gap correctly, and they should be refaced or renewed. Set the gap when the contact surfaces are in order.

Check the proper functioning of the vacuum advance mechanism.

General

Examine all leads and terminals for signs of broken or cracked insulation. Also check all terminal connections for slackness or signs of fracturing of some strands of wire. Partly broken wire should be renewed.

The HT leads are particularly important as any insulation faults will cause the high voltage to 'jump' to the nearest earth and this will prevent a spark at the plug. Check that no HT leads are loose or in a position where the insulation could wear due to rubbing against part of the engine.

3 Distributor - contact points - adjustment

1 To adjust the contact breaker points to the correct gap, first pull off the two clips securing the distributor cap to the distributor body, and lift away the cap. Clean the cap inside and out with a dry cloth. It is unlikely that the four segments will be badly burned or scored, but if they are the cap will have to be renewed.
2 Inspect the carbon brush located in the top of the cap. See that it is unbroken and stands proud of the plastic surface.
3 Gently prise the contact breaker points open to examine the condition of their faces. If they are rough, pitted or dirty, it will be necessary to remove them for resurfacing, or for replacement points to be fitted.

4 Presuming the points are satisfactory, or that they have been cleaned and replaced, measure the gap between the points by turning the engine over until the heel of the breaker arm is on the highest point of the cam.
5 A 0.40 mm (0.016 in) feeler gauge should now just fit between the points.
6 If the gap varies from this amount slacken the contact plate securing screw.
7 Adjust the contact gap by inserting a screwdriver in the notched hole, in the breaker plate. Turn clockwise to increase and anticlockwise to decrease the gap. When the gap is correct tighten the securing screw and check the gap again.
8 Making sure the rotor is in position replace the distributor cap and clip the spring blade cap retainers into position.
9 A more precise method of setting the contact breaker gap to conform with the requirements of individual engines can be obtained with the use of a dwell angle tester. Any variation in the points gap (and in turn the dwell angle) will affect the timing. The correct dwell angle is 60° to 64° at 500 rpm.

4 Distributor - contact points - removal and replacement

1 Slip back the spring clips which secure the distributor cap in position. Remove the distributor cap and lay it to one side, only removing one or two of the HT leads from the plugs if necessary to provide greater movement of the cap.
2 Pull the rotor from the distributor shaft.
3 Disconnect the lead which runs from the moveable spring type contact breaker arm to the LT connecting clip.
4 A retaining clip and washers must be removed from the top of the contact breaker pivot post.
5 Press the spring arm of the moveable contact breaker from its support and withdraw the contact breaker arm.
6 Unscrew and remove the fixed contact breaker arm from the distributor baseplate.
7 Inspect the faces of the contact points. If they are only lightly burned or pitted then they may be ground square on an oilstone or by rubbing a carborundum strip between them. Where the points are found to be severely burned or pitted, then they must be renewed and at the same time the cause of the erosion of the points established. This is most likely to be due to poor earth connections from the battery negative lead to body earth or the engine strap. Remove the connecting bolts at these points, scrape the surfaces free from rust and corrosion, and tighten the bolts using a star type lock washer. Other screws to check for security are: the baseplate to distributor body securing screws, the condenser securing screw and the distributor body to lockplate bolt. Looseness in any of these could contribute to a poor earth connection. Check the condenser (Section 5).
8 Refitting is a reversal of removal but some distributors include shims at the spring contact arm anchorage to ensure correct alignment of the contact point faces. Apply a trace of engine oil to the breaker pivot post and to the felt pad at the top of the distributor shaft. Smear the high points of the cam with petroleum jelly.
9 Reset the contact breaker gap as described in Section 3.

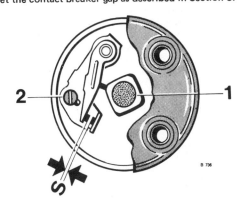

Fig. 4.1. Contact points adjustment

1 *Breaker cam*   2 *Adjuster screw*
S = *gap 0.35 - 0.45 mm*

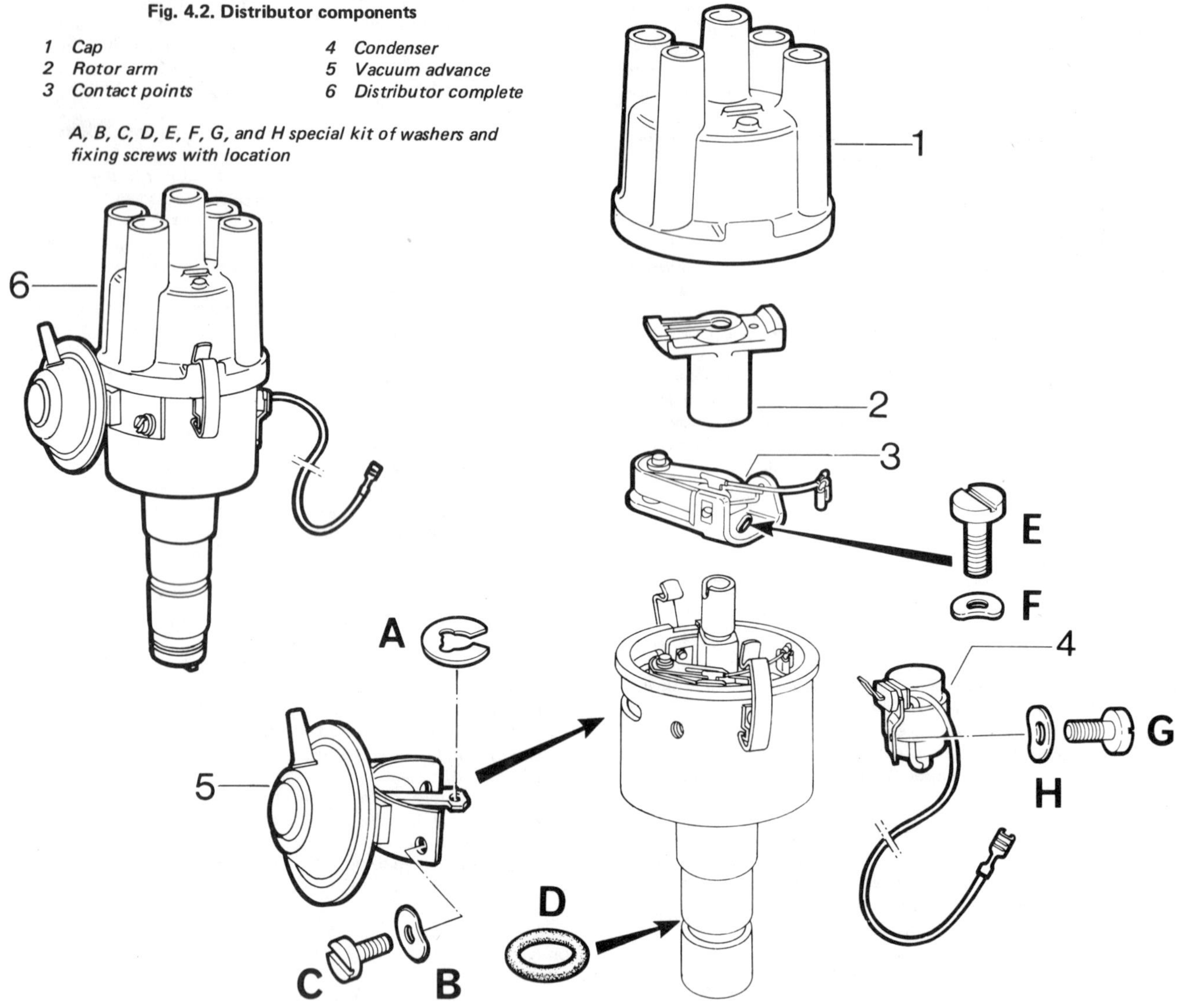

Fig. 4.2. Distributor components

1	Cap	4	Condenser
2	Rotor arm	5	Vacuum advance
3	Contact points	6	Distributor complete

A, B, C, D, E, F, G, and H special kit of washers and fixing screws with location

5 Distributor - condenser - testing, removal and replacement

1 The condenser ensures that with the contact breaker points open, the sparking between them is not excessive, to cause severe pitting. The condenser is fitted in parallel and its failure will automatically cause failure of the ignition system as the points will be prevented from interrupting the low tension circuit.

2 Testing for an unserviceable condenser may be effected by switching on the ignition and separating the contact points by hand. If this action is accompanied by a blue flash then condenser failure is indicated. Difficult starting, missing of the engine after several miles running or badly pitted points are other indications of a faulty condenser.

3 The surest test is by substitution of a new unit.

4 Removal and refitting of the externally mounted condenser is by means of a single securing screw.

6 Distributor - removal and replacement

See Chapter 1, Sections 8 and 46.

7 Distributor - dismantling, inspection and reassembly

1 Remove the rotor.

2 Disconnect the LT lead from the terminal clip within the distributor.

3 Remove the condenser and its lead.

4 Remove the circlip from the top of the vacuum unit control rod pivot post.

5 Unscrew and remove the two screws which secure the vacuum unit to the distributor body and withdraw the unit.

6 Unscrew and remove the two screws which serve to hold the distributor cap retaining clips and also the fixed baseplate.

7 Remove the contact breaker arm assembly.

8 From the lower end of the distributor shaft, drive out the tension pin which secures the gear to the shaft and then remove the gear using a suitable extractor.

9 Withdraw the distributor shaft complete with counterweights and springs through the top of the distributor.

10 Pick out the lubricating felt and remove the circlip and washer from the recess in the top of the distributor shaft. Check for wear in the moveable baseplate.

11 The mechanical advance mechanism may be dismantled and weak or worn springs or other components renewed as necessary.

12 If the shaft bearing in the distributor body is worn, drift it out by driving it into the interior of the distributor. Soak the new bearing in hot engine oil prior to fitting and press it into position until its lower edge is flush with the distributor body.

13 Reassembly is a reversal of dismantling.

Fig. 4.3. Location of the flywheel (left) and distributor (right) timing marks to ensure correct static ignition timing setting

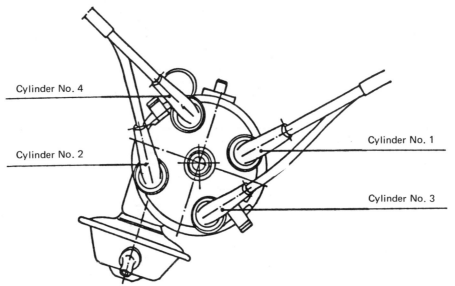

Fig. 4.4. Location of distributor cap and plug leads

8 Ignition timing

1 Prior to checking the ignition timing, check the contact breaker gap, and adjust, if necessary. See Section 3.

2 Remove the little plastic inspection cover from the rear crankcase end cover so that the flywheel can be seen.

3 Connect a small test-lamp (a 12 volt pilot bulb with two appropriate leads) across the distributor low tension terminal and earth. Switch on the ignition.

4 Rotate the crankshaft in its normal rotational direction until the static advance mark (a cut in the flywheel face) on the flywheel is in line with the pointer (static) on the rear cover. No 1 cylinder should be at Top Dead Centre, ie: both valves on that cylinder fully closed and on the compression stroke.

5 Check that in this exact position the contact points are *about* to open (the test bulb about to light) and that the rotor arm is in alignment to the small cut on the rim of the distributor body. (Fig. 4.3).

6 If the bulb is just about to light and all is aligned, then the ignition setting is correct. If the bulb lights up too early or is nowhere near it, then adjust as follows:

7 Slacken the fixing bolt on the distributor body clamp. Rotate the distributor body in an anticlockwise (advance) or clockwise (retard) direction to achieve the correct position. Once achieved, tighten the clamp bolt. Turn off the ignition, remove the test-lamp and replace the distributor cap. Replace the inspection cover over the flywheel.

8 Whilst static ignition timing is important ignition advance at speed is more important on this engine. A strobe light is necessary to check this.

9 Connect the strobe light contacts according to the instructions given on the equipment.

10 Disconnect the vacuum advance pipe. Switch on the ignition and start the engine, Remove the inspection cover on the crankcase end cover.

11 Check that at 2000 rpm and at 4500 rpm the reference pointer on the rear cover aligns with the second and third cut, respectively, on the flywheel (see Fig. 4.5). If this is not so, go through the procedure as just described for static timing, until it works.

12 This will cause static adjustment to move - high speed and intermediate speed advance are more important.

13 If vast movement results on the distributor are necessary to achieve proper 'speed' advance, then the distributor is faulty. Consult your Alfa Romeo agent.

14 Remove the strobe, replace the rear cover inspection cap and turn off the ignition. Replace the vacuum advance pipe.

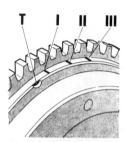

Fig. 4.5. Ignition timing

T   TDC of cylinder No 1
I   Static advance at idle
II Advance at 2000 rpm
III Advance over 4500 rpm

Fig. 4.6. Advance and retard direction on distributor body

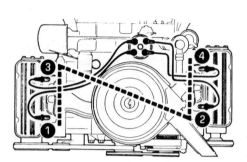

Fig. 4.7. Firing order

9 Spark plugs and HT leads

1 With the development of modern technology and materials, spark plugs are generally very reliable and require minimal attention. When they are due for checking and cleaning it is good practice to have them thoroughly sand blasted, gapped and checked under pressure on the machine that most garages have installed. They can also be used as good indications of engine condition, particularly as regards the fuel mixture being used and the state of the pistons and cylinder bores. Check each plug as it is possible that one cylinder condition is different from the rest. Only use the recommended plugs - **never** fit any other type. Your engine could ruin itself on the incorrect plugs. Under normal running conditions a correctly rated plug in a properly tuned engine will have a light deposit of brownish colour on the electrodes. A dry black sooty deposit indicates an over-rich fuel mixture. An oily blackish deposit indicates worn bores or valve guides. A dry hard whitish deposit indicates too weak a fuel mixture. If plugs of the wrong heat ranges are fitted they will have similar symptoms to a weak mixture together with burnt electrodes (plug too hot) or to an over-rich mixture caked somewhat thicker (plug too cold). Do not try and economise by using plugs beyond 15000 km (9000 miles). Unless the engine remains in exceptionally good tune, reductions in performance and fuel economy will outweight the cost of a new set.

2 The HT leads and their connections at both ends should always be clean and dry and, as far as possible, neatly arranged away from each other and nearby metallic parts which could cause premature shorting in weak insulation. The metal connections at the ends should be a firm and secure fit and free from any signs of corrosive deposits. If any lead shows signs of cracking or chafing of the insulation it should be renewed. Remember that radio interference suppression is required when renewing any leads. **Note:** It is advisable when removing spark plugs from this engine to use a fully cranked 'short' spark plug remover. Be especially careful when refitting plugs to do so without force and screw them up as far as possible by hand first. Do not overtighten. The aluminium heads do not take kindly to thread crossing and extra force. The proprietary non-cranked plug caps should always be used to ease fitting and to ensure against HT lead shorting.

10 Coil   general

1 The coil needs an equal amount of attention to the rest of the ignition system. Testing the coil is dealt with in Section 12.

2 Keep it clean. Do not abuse and do not move it from its original position. If faulty, replace with the correct type given in the specifications.

11 Ignition/starter switch

See Chapter 10, Section 18.

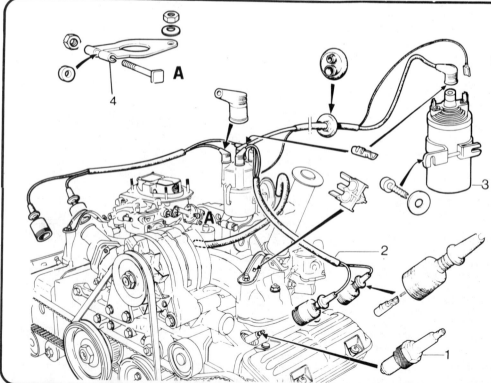

Fig. 4.8. Plug leads, coil and plugs

1 Special Alfasud spark plugs
2 Leads and caps
3 Coil
4 Distributor clamp

A Location of clamp

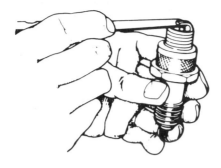

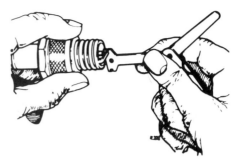

Checking plug gap with feeler gauges

Altering the plug gap. Note use of correct tool

Fig. 4.3a Spark plug maintenance

White deposits and damaged porcelain insulation indicating overheating

Broken porcelain insulation due to bent central electrode

Electrodes burnt away due to wrong heat value or chronic pre-ignition (pinking)

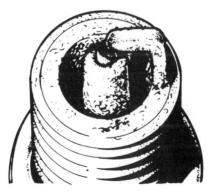

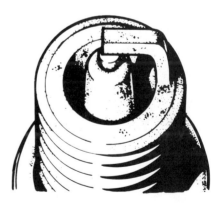

Excessive black deposits caused by over-rich mixture or wrong heat value

Mild white deposits and electrode burnt indicating too weak a fuel mixture

Plug in sound condition with light greyish brown deposits

Fig. 4.3b Spark plug electrode conditions

12 Ignition faults - symptoms, reasons and remedies

1 *Engine will not start*

a) The engine is so enclosed that the normal wet condition after leaving the car in the open overnight is not so prevalent. However, before running down the battery when the car will not start after being left in the open, have a look to see that everything is dry. If mist has penetrated then dry the moisture off, either with a cloth or with a proprietary type spray.

b) If the engine will not start when everything is dry, pull off a plug lead, and hold the end of the plug lead about 3 mm (0.13 in) from the crankcase. With the ignition switched on spin the engine with the starter. If there is a spark, a good fat one, then the ignition system is working. Check that the distributor body is held tight in the clamp ring, then check ignition timing setting. Take off the distributor cap. Set the ignition timing mark on the crankshaft pulley to the correct point on the scale and check that the rotor arm is pointing to No 1 cylinder plug lead. If the spark is correct and the timing has not altered then the fault is not in the ignition system.

c) If there is not a fat spark then the ignition system is at fault. Begin by checking the LT circuit in the following order:

i)   *Are the points opening correctly? Are they clean?*
ii)   *Check the voltage at coil terminal. It should be at least 9 volts (ignition on). If no voltage then the wiring or the switch is at fault.*
iii) *Check the voltage at coil terminal - points closed - no volts, points open - reading on the meter. If no reading on the meter with points open the coil has an open circuit.*
iv)   *With the ignition switched on check the voltage across the contact breaker points; points closed - no volts, points open meter reads. Points open - no reading, then the condenser is faulty.*

d) Check all the LT wiring and connections carefully and if the LT circuit is functioning correctly then proceed to the HT circuit. Check the following in the order given (ignition switched on):

i)   *Pull the HT lead from the centre of the distributor and hold the end about 3mm (0.13 in) from the crankcase. Spin the engine. There should be a spark. No spark means a faulty HT winding in the coil.*

ii)   *Turn off the ignition switch, put the lead back in the centre of the distributor cap and examine the carbon brush carefully. Is it making contact with the rotor arm spring? Examine the cap for cracks and tracking. Check that the segments are clean and that the rotor arm leading edge is not corroded. Clean these points if they are.*

iii) *Replace the rotor arm; check the drive by turning the rotor gently. There should be a slight movement. Anything more than a slight movement means that the drive is suspect or the automatic advance and retard has disintegrated. The latter is rare but it has happened.*

e) Finally remove a plug and check its condition. If it is oily, wet with petrol, or corroded, then clean it, and the other three. Oily or corroded plugs mean an engine overhaul or at least a checking of the exhaust gas composition by an expert. Wet plugs may be flooding during starting.

2 *Engine runs sluggishly but does not misfire*
a) Check the contact breaker points
b) Check the ignition timing
c) Check the octane rating of the fuel.

3 *Engine misfires, runs unevenly and cuts out at low revolutions*
a) Check contact breaker gap (CB gap too large?).
b) Check the distributor shaft for wear.
c) Check the fuel system.

4 *Engine misfires at high revolutions*
a) Check contact breaker gap (CB gap too small?)
b) Check the distributor shaft for wear.
c) Check the fuel system.

5 *General*
Ignition faults are quite often exasperating. Work steadily through the system checking all leads and connections methodically. Test the components, check the battery, and if finally the fault cannot be located then go to the expert. He has instruments specially designed to locate faults. But if his respect is to be obtained do not go about testing in a haphazard manner; that will only result in more faults being installed and the original one may never be located.

Chapter 5 Clutch

Contents

Specifications

Type	Diaphragm spring-operated single dry-plate, pedal operates release mechanism hydraulically
Release bearing	Ball bearing thrust bearing
Clutch diameter	
Outer	180mm (7.1in)
Inner	124mm (4.9in)
Maximum lining wear	2mm (0.08in)
Master cylinder diameter	19.05mm (0.75in)
Slave cylinder diameter	25.4mm (1.0in)
Adjustment	None

Torque wrench setting

	lb f ft	kg f m
Clutch cover bolts to flywheel	10.8 - 17.3	1.5 - 2.4

---

1 General description

The clutch is of the single dry-plate design and incorporates a driven plate, a pressure plate assembly of coil spring type and a ball bearing release bearing.

Clutch operation is hydraulic by means of a foot pedal-operated master cylinder and a slave cylinder.

Maintenance consists of maintaining the clutch-pedal free movement and keeping the master cylinder reservoir topped-up to the correct level.

---

2 Clutch adjustment

1 Because of the hydraulic operation of the clutch release mechanism adjustment is not necessary nor available. One measurement is possible but its alteration is only possible by bleeding the hydraulic system.

2 The clutch slave cylinder pushrod stroke should be between 16 to 18 mm; ie when operating the clutch pedal the pushrod should move 16 to 18 mm. If it does not, bleed the clutch hydraulic system and check throughout.

---

3 Clutch pedal - removal and refitting

The clutch pedal is dealt with in Chapter 8, the braking system, because the clutch pedal hinges on the same pivot as the brake pedal.

---

4 Clutch - removal, servicing and refitting

1 It is necessary to remove the engine and gearbox from the car before access can be gained to the clutch.

2 Split the engine and gearbox. See Chapter 1.

3 Place the engine on the bench and support it on wooden blocks so that it will not rock. To remove the clutch cover, lock the flywheel. This can be carried out carefully, with a large screwdriver or tyre lever on the teeth of the starter ring gear through the casting of the end cover.

4 There are six bolts which fix the clutch cover to the flywheel. Start to loosen each one progressively, and then remove them gradually. Remove the clutch cover and catch the driven plate, or clutch plate, as it falls away.

62

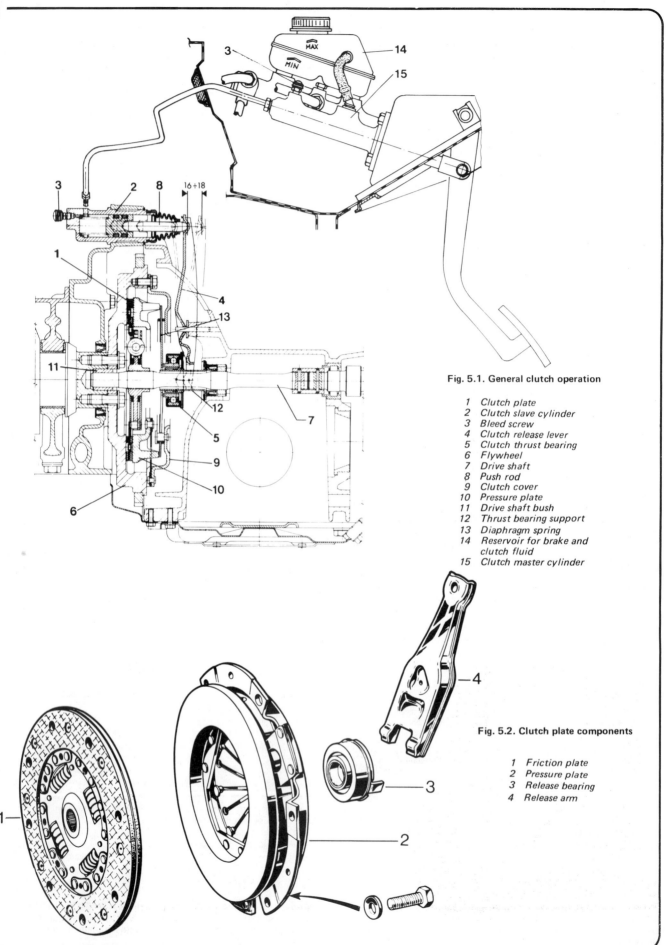

Fig. 5.1. General clutch operation

1 Clutch plate
2 Clutch slave cylinder
3 Bleed screw
4 Clutch release lever
5 Clutch thrust bearing
6 Flywheel
7 Drive shaft
8 Push rod
9 Clutch cover
10 Pressure plate
11 Drive shaft bush
12 Thrust bearing support
13 Diaphragm spring
14 Reservoir for brake and
    clutch fluid
15 Clutch master cylinder

Fig. 5.2. Clutch plate components

1 Friction plate
2 Pressure plate
3 Release bearing
4 Release arm

5   Left behind on the gearbox will be the clutch release or thrust bearing. Also, behind it, the clutch release lever. Pull off the release bearing and then the release lever from its locating pin on the gearbox casing.

6   The slave cylinder of the clutch hydraulic system can also be removed from the gearbox casing; it is held by a circlip only, unless it has been left in the car as instructed in Chapter 1.

7   Now check the various components. Ensure that the clutch plate friction linings are free from burns and oil and that the rivets are in good condition. Check wear in the friction linings and that the thickness is over 6.5 mm (0.26 in.), the minimum wear limit. Ensure that the splined hub is unworn and that it slides smoothly along the primary shaft splines, still in the gearbox, without excessive play. Renew the plate if in any doubt. (The engine and gearbox is out of the car - do not find yourself having to do it again through the oversight of not renewing the clutch plate!).

8   Check the smooth operation of the clutch release bearing. Any sign of seizure between it and the clutch lever must result in its renewal.

9   Inside the end of the crankshaft, through the flywheel, is the primary shaft bush. Pick it out of the crankshaft and inspect for wear. If in doubt, renew it.

10 If the clutch release lever is worn, cracked or distorted, renew it.

11 Now inspect the clutch cover. If it appears to be unevenly worn, shows signs of overheating or is otherwise damaged, renew it. If it is 'weakened or worn out', presumably the reason you have disassembled it, renew it anyway.

12 You should also check the flywheel face. See Chapter 1.

13 Remember, if oil is present on the clutch, either the crankshaft or gearbox oil seal, or both, need renewing.

14 Replacement is the reverse procedure of removal. First grease the crankshaft bush with a little high melting point grease. Centralise the clutch plate behind the clutch cover as you tighten the cover to the flywheel. Use an 'old' gearbox shaft or dowel of wood, to fit. Tighten the cover to the specified torque wrench setting.

15 Connect the engine to gearbox. Replace in the car.

16 If the hydraulic system has been disconnected, bleed the system. See Section 8.

5   Clutch release bearing - renewal

See Section 4.

6   Master cylinder - removal, servicing, refitting

1   Disconnect the fluid pipe from the clutch slave cylinder and depress the clutch pedal several times until all the hydraulic fluid is ejected into a clean vessel.

2   Disconnect the operating pushrod from the clutch pedal by removing the circlip and cotter pin.

3   Unscrew and remove the two flange securing bolts and remove the master cylinder from the engine rear bulkhead.

4   Peel the rubber dust cap from the end of the master cylinder and extract the circlip. Withdraw the pushrod.

5   The piston assembly will now be ejected. Carefully prise up the tongue of the spring retainer and dismantle the piston components.

6   Discard all rubber seals.

7   By compressing the piston return spring, the valve spindle can then be slipped through the keyhole shaped hole in the spring retainer and separated. Unscrew the bleed nipple. Pull out the slave cylinder pipe with its rubber holder.

8   Wash all components in methylated spirit or clean hydraulic fluid and examine for wear. If any 'bright' wear areas are evident on the surfaces of the piston or cylinder bore, renew the complete master cylinder.

9   Obtain a repair kit and refit all the parts supplied making sure that the new seals are manipulated into position using the fingers only and that their lips and chamfers are correctly located.

10 Reassembly and refitting are a reversal of removal and dismantling.

11 Refill the master cylinder reservoir with clean fluid which has been stored in an airtight container and has remained unshaken for the previous 24 hours.

12 Bleed the clutch hydraulic system as described in Section 8.

7   Slave cylinder - removal, servicing, refitting

1   Disconnect the fluid line from the slave cylinder and plug the line to prevent loss of fluid.

2   Remove the slave cylinder circlip; and then remove the whole unit from the crankcase end cover.

3   Peel back the dust cover from the end of the cylinder and extract the circlip.

4   Withdraw the piston/seal assembly and return spring, with the pushrod.

5   Wash all components in methylated spirit or clean hydraulic fluid and examine the surfaces of the piston and cylinder bore for scoring or 'bright' wear areas. If any are evident, renew the cylinder complete.

6   Discard the seal and fit a new one, manipulating it into position using the fingers only.

7   Refit the piston to the cylinder having first dipped it in clean hydraulic fluid.

8   Fit the circlip and then pack the dust cover with rubber grease and locate it over the end of the cylinder.

9   Refit the slave cylinder to the clutch bellhousing by first passing the pushrod through the rubber dust cover. Reconnect the fluid line.

10 Bleed the clutch hydraulic system as described in the following Section.

11 Check the full movement of the pushrod. See Section 2.

4.4a A new clutch friction plate is installed

4.4b Use the gearbox shaft to centralise the friction plate

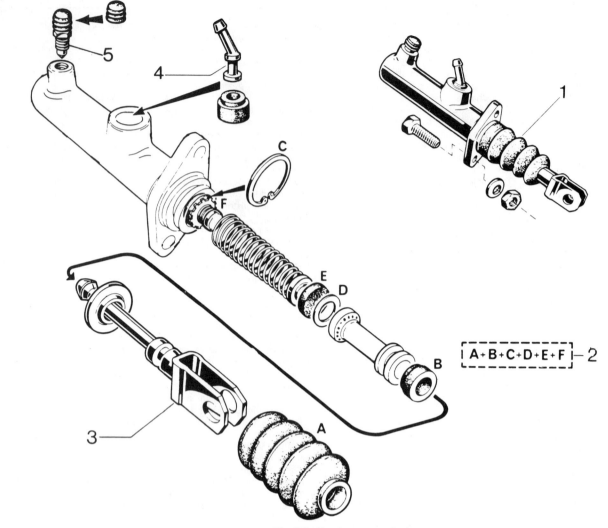

Fig. 5.3. Clutch master cylinder

1 Complete cylinder   3 Push rod   4 Feed off pipe   5 Bleed valve
2 Repair kit components

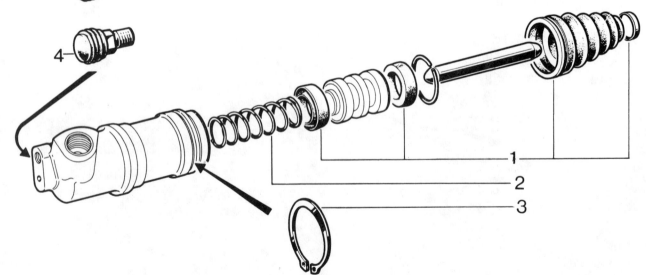

Fig. 5.4. Clutch slave cylinder

1 Repair kit components   2 Spring   3 Circlip   4 Bleed valve

8 Clutch hydraulic system - bleeding

1 Attach a plastic or rubber bleed tube to the nipple on the slave cylinder and to the one on the master cylinder.
2 Place the open end of each bleed tube in a jar which has been filled to a depth of about 38 mm (1.5 in.) with hydraulic fluid. Ensure that the ends of the tubes are kept below the surface of the fluid throughout the bleeding operation.
3 Unscrew the bleed nipples half a turn and have an assistant depress the clutch pedal to the full extent of its travel and then remove the foot quickly so that the pedal returns unimpeded. Repeat this operation until air bubbles cease to be expelled from the ends of the bleed tubes.
4 Tighten the bleed nipples while the pedal is in its fully depressed position, using a spanner of short length.
5 The master cylinder reservoir must be kept topped-up throughout the bleeding operation with hydraulic fluid which has been stored in an airtight container and remained unshaken for at least 24 hours. Failure to keep the reservoir topped-up will cause air to be drawn into the system and the bleeding process will have to start all over again.

9 Clutch faults - diagnosis and rectification

1 Provided the clutch is not intentionally slipped excessively, or the pedal used as a footrest, which may possibly keep the release bearing spinning due to permanent contact with the diaphragm spring, the only malfunction of the clutch one may expect would be due to wear of the friction plate. This normal wear will become obvious when the clutch starts to slip, that is, the engine turns normally but the car fails to accelerate properly or it slows down on hills. In such cases the clutch must be examined and repaired immediately. Delay could be costly.
2 Squealing noises from the clutch (and make sure the squeals *are* from the clutch and not the fan belt or water pump) are most likely to come from a worn out clutch release bearing. The actual efficiency of the clutch may not be immediately affected but if the bearing is not repaired in good time the wear will increase. This will lead to excessive and uneven wear of the clutch disc. Another cause of squealing could

be due to the friction plate being worn out or contaminated. In either case the inspection and repair will involve removal of the engine.
3 Clutch spin, or failure to disengage completely when the pedal is fully depressed, can be caused by one or more of several reasons. The symptoms are that it is either impossible, or the gearbox makes a very noisy 'crunch' when trying to engage bottom gear in the usual manner. First of all check the hydraulic system operation and condition to ensure that the clutch release lever is moving as necessary. If this is satisfactory then the clutch disc is sticking to the pressure plate or flywheel, or the release bearing is so badly worn that it is incapable of moving the diaphragm spring evenly or adequately. This will almost invariably be indicated by squeals and noises when the clutch pedal is operated. Check by stopping the engine, engaging a gear, depressing the clutch and putting on the handbrake. Then try starting the engine. If it refuses to turn, the clutch is stuck solid and should be removed and examined. If the engine is started without difficulty try using the clutch in the normal manner. If the drive continues to 'creep' a little when the pedal is fully depressed carry on slipping the clutch for a few moments to try and rub off whatever may have been on the friction surfaces, as a temporary measure. If no improvement of any kind results there must be a serious internal defect which will require engine removal and examination of the clutch.
4 The other fault which is associated with the clutch but not necessarily caused by a clutch defect is judder, particularly noticeable when moving away from rest. First check the security and condition of the engine mountings and the transmission rear mounting. Examine the driveshaft joints for wear and service them as described in Chapter 7.
5 If diagnosis indicates that the judder is due to a clutch fault it will be caused by 'snatching' between the friction surfaces and possibly associated with concurring problems of clutch spin or clutch slip. In this case the engine will need removal for further inspection of the clutch.
6 Faulty clutch operation can sometimes be caused by flexing of the master cylinder when the clutch pedal is depressed. This is caused by cracking due to metal fatigue of the bulkhead mounting directly behind the master cylinder flange. If inspection proves this to be the case, weld the cracks or fit a reinforcing plate.

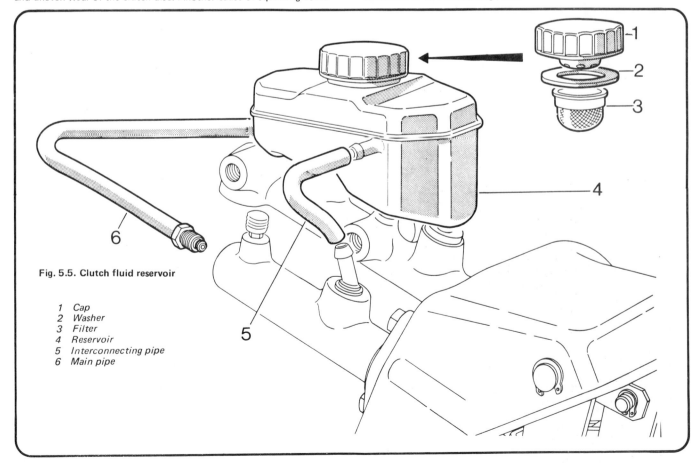

Fig. 5.5. Clutch fluid reservoir

   1 Cap
   2 Washer
   3 Filter
   4 Reservoir
   5 Interconnecting pipe
   6 Main pipe

Chapter 6 Gearbox and final drive

Contents

Specifications

Type	Alfasud	Alfasud TI and 5M
	Aluminium cased unit integral with the final drive unit, in place behind engine. Synchromesh on all forward gears.	
	4 forward speeds	5 forward speeds

Ratios (internal) and mph per 1000 rpm

1st	3.545 : 1/4.5	3.545 : 1/4.6
2nd	1.941 : 1/8.1	2.062 : 1/7.9
3rd	1.292 : 1/12.3	1.434 : 1/11.4
4th	0.966 : 1/16.3	1.115 : 1/14.6
5th	—	0.931 : 1/17.5
Reverse	3.091 : 1	

Final drive	Hypoid bevel
Ratio	4.111 : 1

Torque wrench settings

	lb f ft	kg fm
Rear mounting to support bolt	10.8 - 17.3	1.5 - 2.4
Rear cover to gearbox bolts	10.8 - 17.3	1.5 - 2.4
Mounting (bell housing to body) bolt	39 - 62.9	5.4 - 8.7
Mounting to bell housing bolt	28.9 - 35.4	4 - 4.9
Hub to driveshaft bolt	10.8 - 17.3	1.5 - 2.4
Crown wheel bolts	57 - 62.9	7.9 - 8.7
Differential side support bearing carrier nuts	28.9 - 35.4	4 - 4.9
Driveshaft to differential shaft Allen screws	26 - 28	3.6 - 3.9
Rear primary shaft spacer to casing bolt	50.6 - 62.9	7 - 8.7
Interior gearbox cross brace bolts	28.9 - 35.4	4 - 4.9
Pinion bearing retaining nut	162.7 - 180	22.5 - 25
Reverse gear shaft locking bolt	13.7 - 17.3	1.9 - 2.4
Engine to gearbox bolts	28.9 - 35.4	4 - 4.9
Gearbox sump pan bolts	3.6 - 5.7	0.5 - 0.8
Primary shaft bearing locking bolt	10.8 - 17.3	1.5 - 2.4
Flywheel guard panel bolts	4.3 - 7.2	0.6 - 1
1st/2nd gear selection fork locking bolt	16.6 - 18	2.3 - 2.5
3rd/4th gear selection fork locking bolt	13.7 - 15	1.9 - 2.1
Gear lever to control lever bolt	5.7 - 7.2	0.8 - 1
Gear lever fork to casing pivot bolt	4.3 - 7.2	0.6 - 1
Gear lever guide bolts	4.3 - 7.2	0.6 - 1
Flywheel to clutch cover bolts	10.8 - 17.3	1.5 - 2.4
Gearbox drain and filler plugs	10.1 - 13	1.4 - 1.8
Reverse lamp switch	28.9 - 36.1	4 - 5

1 General description

The Alfasud uses a fairly conventional gearbox and final drive in the same casing. It is mounted behind the engine and, of course, drives the front wheels. The front disc brakes are mounted in-board, the calipers being mounted to the top of the gearbox casing. It is necessary to remove the engine with the gearbox under every circumstance.

The Alfasud has four forward speeds, all using synchromesh, and reverse.

The Alfasud TI and 5M has five forward speeds, also with synchromesh, and reverse. Fundamentally these two gearboxes are the same. Drive comes from the engine via the clutch to the primary shaft situated in the 'top' of the gearbox. Drive is transmitted from a number of gears on the primary shaft to the pinion shaft 'below' it in the gearbox casing; the direction of motion changing as it goes 'back' along the pinion shaft to the crownwheel and pinion and so 'out' to the final drive flanges, and thence the driveshafts. The various forward gears slide along the pinion shaft and engage individually via control from the remotely mounted gear lever. There is a reverse idler gearshaft which is utilised only when reverse is engaged. The remote control gearlever which is 'floor' mounted is sited on a tailshaft, bolted to the end of the gearbox.

The Alfasud gearbox is a difficult unit to work upon; it is not recommended that you plunge into it if you have had no previous gearbox experience. Special tools are necessary for setting up purposes. The term 'gearbox' is used when meaning the whole casing holding the differential as well.

2 Transmission unit - removal and replacement

As it is necessary to remove the engine at the same time even though it may only be desired to remove the gearbox, no special description is given here as to how the gearbox is removed and replaced. See Chapter 1, Sections 4, 5, 6, 52 and 53 which cover total removal and separation, and then attachment to the engine and replacement.

3 4-speed unit - dismantling

1 Put the gearbox on a stout bench if possible. Clean it down so that before any work starts, it is as clean as possible. Jizer or Gunk and then water work well although a petrol/paraffin mix are equally as good. You should, of course, have drained the gearbox oil at the removal from the car procedure - if not, do it now. Have plenty of room to work and clean rags available. Do not clutter your tools around you.
2 Remove the front brake calipers and discs. First It is essential to remove the discs before the calipers can come away. This may sound strange but it is so. The discs are bolted to the final drive flanges by four bolts on each side. See Chapter 8, Sections 2 and 3 and slacken the adjustment of the front disc pads, remove the pads. Now loosen the four disc to flange bolts by locking the hub with a screwdriver. Remove the four bolts and then gently tap the disc away from the flange. It should then drop down from the caliper. The discs are brittle - look after them.
3 Once the disc is removed the studs which locate the caliper to the gearbox casing are exposed. There are two per caliper. With a socket spanner located on the nuts, release the pressure. It will be necessary to turn the flange to allow the socket spanner to fit 'through' for each nut. When the nuts are loose, remove them and pull off the caliper. Repeat for the other side.
4 Place the gearbox on its sump and then disconnect the remote gearchange rod which runs along the tail shaft of the gearbox. Pull off the retaining clip and washers, and then lift over the remote control rod sleeve. Lift off the rubber collar from the gear selector lever.
5 Remove the remote control lever and rod by undoing the cross pivot bolt through the tail shaft. This will enable the pivot bolt to be withdrawn and the mechanism to be lifted off.
6 The gear selector lever is pinned to the external part of the main selector rod. With a pin punch, punch the retaining pin through and then slide off the gear selector lever.
7 There are two types of tail shaft fitted. One is integral with the gearbox end-cover whilst the other is simply a welded (as opposed to

cast) tail shaft which bolts onto the end-cover. For the latter type undo the six retaining bolts which should enable the tail shaft to be lifted off but which leaves the end-cover still firmly attached to the gearbox. You can treat the former, cast type of tail shaft, as if it were simply an end-cover and nothing more.
8 Slacken and remove the reverse gear lamp switch together with its washer.
9 Remove the three bolts (end-cover only) or six bolts (tail shaft and end-cover together), fixing the end-cover to the gearbox. Pull off the cover and then clean off the gasket.
10 Look into the end of the gearbox and pull out the guide pin which is adjacent to the main selector rod. Lift the return spring to pull it out. The return spring stays on the selector rod.
11 Close to the final drive flanges, on the top of the gearbox, you will see the speedometer drive gear (this is the tube from which the speedometer drive cable was withdrawn when the engine/gearbox was removed from the car). Lift it out.
12 Turn the gearbox up the other way, so that the sump plate is on the top. From now on the sump plate will indicate the top of the gearbox, although when installed the plate would be at the 'bottom'. Slacken and remove the sump plate bolts. Remove the sump plate and gasket.
13 Slacken and remove the bolts fixing the cross brace to the gearbox casing. Remove the cross brace.
14 Now, on each side of the gearbox, remove the nuts fixing the differential housing carrier to the case. You will have to turn the drive flanges to gain access to each nut. Move each housing out slightly from the case to enable access to the housing spacers. These are 'split'. They should fall out. Record where they fit for correct replacement. At the same time note the spacer washers on the caliper fixing studs.
15 Dot punch the housings to the case so that correct replacement may be made. These parts are 'fitted' on assembly. Complete dismantling by withdrawing the differential housing carrier from each side. Do this carefully as there is a large circular oil seal around the housing which can be damaged quite easily.
16 Now look into the top of the gearbox casing. Have the bellhousing to your right as you start further dismantling. Remove the three bolts (whose heads you can easily see), which fix the selector forks to the selector rods. The bolt furthest to the left fixes the selector fork to the 3rd and 4th gear selector shaft. The middle bolt fixes the 1st and 2nd speed operating lever. Once this bolt is removed the operating lever can be lifted away. The bolt to the right fixes the 1st and 2nd selector fork to the selector shaft.
17 Nearest to you now are two further selector forks which are held to the selector shaft with pins. With a pin punch, punch out the pin on the left selector fork. Allow the pin to fall into the case. Now slide the selector shaft to the left. This should then allow you to punch the other pin holding the right-hand selector fork to the same shaft. Allow the pin to fall into the casing. You should now have two free selector forks on that one shaft.
18 On the other side of the gearbox, on the far shaft, punch out the pin holding that selector fork to its shaft. You can now tap out the selector shafts.
19 Gently tap the selector shaft nearest but one to you through to the rear. Use a copper-headed hammer and a drift. Be careful. You will need to twist the shaft as you go so that the detent ball does not lodge in the cut-outs in the shaft. This is obvious as the shaft passes through the end of the casing. Retain the detent ball once the shaft is through and out. Be very, very careful with the detent balls and springs.
20 Then tap through the next two shafts furthest from you, to the rear. Watch the interlock plunger pin in the nearer of these two shafts. Retain the detent balls. All three detent springs can now be picked out of the three drillings from where the detent balls came.
21 Now punch out the remaining selector shaft, again to the rear.
22 Pick out all the selector forks from the gear clusters where possible. This should leave the reverse gear selector fork still in the casing.
23 Now turn the gearbox casing the other way up again. This affords good support. First, however, lock the pinion shaft gears to those on the primary shaft. Neither shaft should turn. Effectively engage two gears.
24 Through the end of the gearbox, opposite the bellhousing, you can see the pinion shaft and primary shaft end nuts. The primary shaft has an oil deflector tube fitted over it. First loosen and remove the pinion shaft nut. This is very difficult, it is a large nut and is done up very tightly. You will need an appropriate socket and a long piece of pipe to obtain enough force. Two other people will be required to hold down

the gearbox casing. Go gently but expect to have to use a lot of force.
25 Now loosen the bolt which holds the deflector tube to the pinion shaft. A socket will be necessary. Remove the bolt and tube, with its washer.
26 Take the two shafts out of gear. Tap the pinion shaft slowly towards the bell housing end and catch the gear clusters as they loosen. Note that the gears split into two clusters. Remove the pinion shaft.
27 Now, to remove the primary shaft it has to be split into its two parts. In the differential housing is a splined tube joining each half with a roll pin hidden by a spring clip, which keeps it within its drilling. Prise out each spring clip and then punch through each roll pin.
28 From inside the bell housing using circlip pliers remove the circlip from the primary shaft and extract the thrust bearing support from behind it. Behind that is an oil seal which can be extracted. If complete dismantling is taking place, pick it out and throw it away as its renewal becomes automatically necessary.
29 Withdraw the front half of the primary shaft.
30 Remove the set bolt which holds the outer race of the front primary shaft bearing. There should now be only one bolt left in the casing. Now remove the bearing by tapping the other end of the primary shaft with a drift and hammer. Go carefully. Now extract the bearing from the differential housing and the primary shaft from the gearbox proper.
31 The reverse gear selector fork can now be withdrawn from the gearbox.
32 If so desired it is possible now to remove the reverse gear shaft by withdrawing its bolt from the outer casing and pulling the shaft and gear away.
33 All that is left in the casing is the primary shaft rear bearing. To remove this remove the circlip which holds it in place and tap the bearing away.

4 4-speed unit - reassembly

1   Read Sections 7 and 8.
2   In a nutshell the reassembly of this gearbox is a straightforward reverse procedure of its disassembly. Follow the photographs carefully.
3   Replace the primary shaft rear bearing and circlip if removed. Put the rear half of the primary shaft into the casing without its front bearing. Place it into its rear bearing and then tap in the front bearing.
4   Lock the front primary shaft bearing with its locking bolt from outside.
5   Now place the splined joint onto the front of the primary shaft.
6   Punch in the first roll pin and replace the first spring clip. Then replace the oil seal in the bell housing.
7   Push through a well-oiled front primary shaft with the spring clip over it. Make sure in advance that the roll pin holes will align.
8   Punch in the second roll pin and cover it with its spring clip.
9   Replace the reverse gear and its shaft. Lock the shaft with its bolt through the outer casing.
10 Replace the reverse gear selector fork as shown in the photo now. To forget will mean disassembly again or no reverse gear.
11 This is a difficult part. Place the front half of the maingear cluster into the gearbox. Hold it there, then add the second half. Then juggle both halves a little in order to mesh the gears with those on the primary shaft. Finally hold the gears together through the rear end.
12 Now begin to feed in the pinion shaft through the case and gears from the differential end. In the first photo the second half of the maingear cluster has been removed to show the pinion shaft as it passes through. The second shows the pinion shaft in properly.
13 Push onto the free end of the pinion shaft, at the rear of the casing,

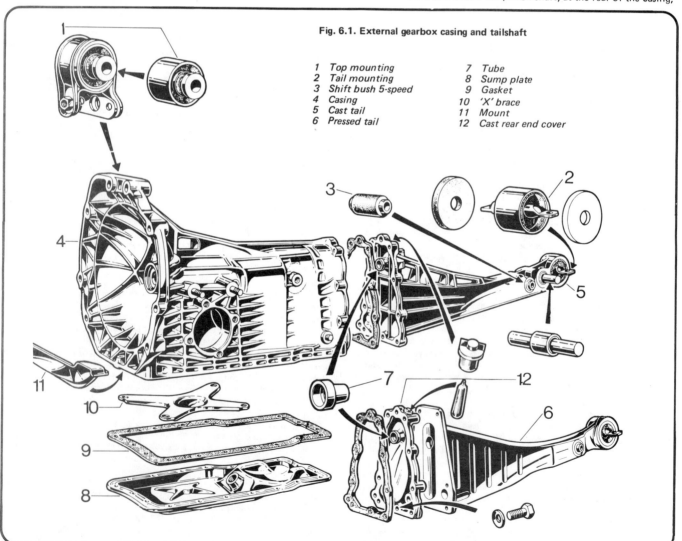

Fig. 6.1. External gearbox casing and tailshaft

1	Top mounting	7	Tube
2	Tail mounting	8	Sump plate
3	Shift bush 5-speed	9	Gasket
4	Casing	10	'X' brace
5	Cast tail	11	Mount
6	Pressed tail	12	Cast rear end cover

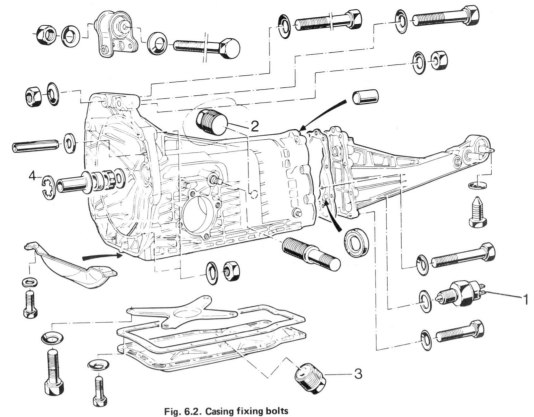

Fig. 6.2. Casing fixing bolts

1 Reverse light switch
2 5-speed plug
3 Drain plug
4 Thrust washer and oil seal circlip

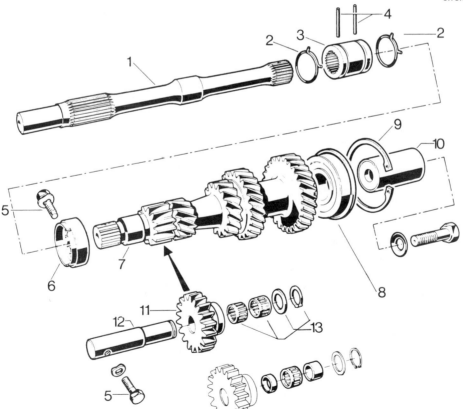

Fig. 6.3. 4-speed primary shaft

1 Front primary
2 Spring clip
3 Joint
4 Roll pins
5 Locking bolt
6 Bearing
7 Geared primary shaft
8 Bearing
9 Circlip
10 Deflector tube
11 Reverse gear
12 Reverse gear shaft
13 Bearing

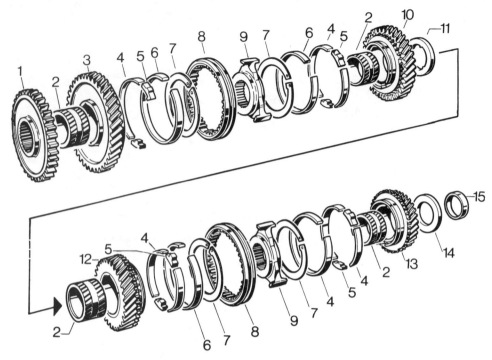

Fig. 6.4. 4 speed pinion shaft gear cluster

1	Reverse motion gear	5	Locking sector
2	Bearing	6	Bush
3	First gear	7	Circlip
4	Retainer	8	Synchro hub

9	Spider	13	Fourth gear
10	Second gear	14	Spacer
11	Spacer	15	Bearing race
12	Third gear		

the spacer and the pinion bearing inner race. Follow it with its nut. Tighten the nut, then lock two gears and tighten it fully to the specified torque wrench setting. Punch it to lock it.

14 Turn the gearbox up the other way. Replace the oil deflector tube and its bolt and washer to the rear end of the primary shaft. Tighten to the specified torque wrench setting.

15 Insert the main selector rod close to the side of the casing through the rear end. Have the proper selector lever ready for it to pass through. Note the spring which is attached to the rod end fits into the end of the casing. Punch the roll pin through the lever and shaft.

16 Replace the selector forks onto their appropriate selector/synchro hubs and feed in the first detent spring and ball to the drilling used by the selector rod nearest the main selector rod already installed. See Fig. 6.8, look at (4) and then at the photograph.

17 Now fix the selector fork to that rod with the bolt. Then feed in the next detent spring and ball and then hold them there with the next selector shaft. Do not fix the selector fork to it yet. Make sure that the third shaft has its interlock plunger in the drilling first.

18 Fit the operating lever which connects this third shaft to the lever on the first shaft. Bolt it. Then bolt the selector fork to that third shaft.

19 Now place the second interlock plunger through the side of the casing. Replace the bolt.

20 Carefully place the last detent spring and its ball into the gearbox and slide in the last selector shaft. Check that the interlock plunger is still in its proper place.

21 Locate the two selector forks to the last selector shaft and punch their roll pins home.

22 Place the differential into the differential housing.

23 Replace each final drive flange housing. Watch the large circular oil seals for they are easy to damage. A punch mark was made to aid replacement in the correct position and make sure the exact 'split' housing spacers are returned to their correct position. Mesh with the differential and tighten each housing diagonally to the specified torque wrench setting.

24 Now replace the 'X' cross brace to the differential housing and tighten to the specified torque wrench setting.

25 Turn to the rear end of the case and fix the main selector rod spring into location with its steel locking pin.

26 Using a new gasket and cement afix the end cover. Make sure the oil

seal for the selector shaft is good.

27 Fit the reverse lamp switch into the rear of the casing. It is prone to failure because of road dirt. It works from the end of the reverse gear selector shaft.

28 Replace the speedometer drivegear into the casing. A roll pin locates into the casing.

29 Use a new gasket and cement and locate the sump pan.

30 Replace the lever on the selector arm once the tail shaft has been located. Punch a roll pin in. Obviously on gearboxes with cast tail shafts there will be no temptation to fit it before!

31 Replace the rest of the gear change mechanism.

32 Replace the thrust washer and circlip to the primary shaft.

33 Replace the clutch release bearing and lever arm.

34 Replace the calipers and discs.

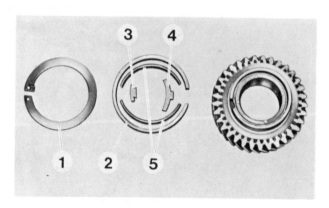

Fig. 6.5. Synchromesh repair kit

1	Circlip	4	Locking sector
2	Bearing	5	Retainer
3	Guide sector		

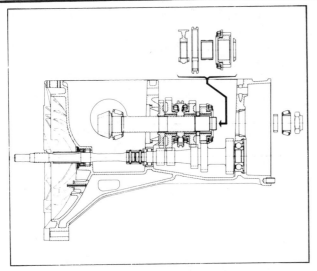

Fig. 6.6. Removal of the pinion gear cluster

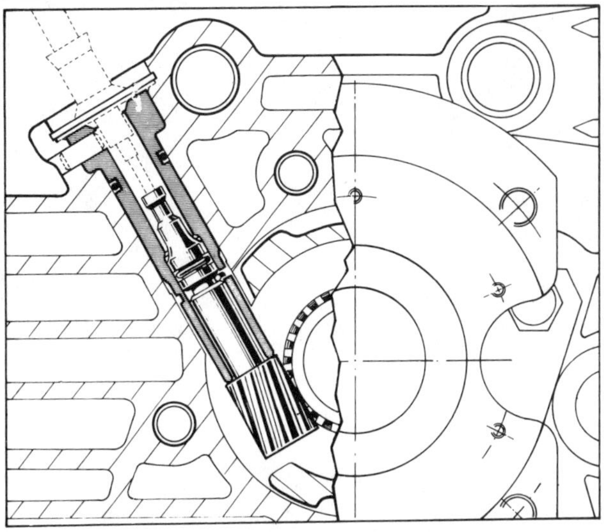

Fig. 6.7. Speedometer cable/drive retainer in cross section

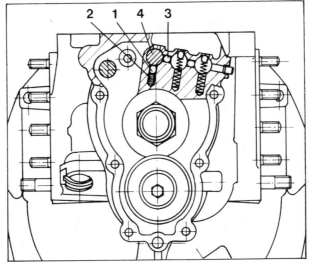

Fig. 6.8. Cross-section of the detent ball and springs, and interlocking balls on the 4-speed

1 Detent ball	2 Detent springs	3 Interlocking plunger	4 Selector rod

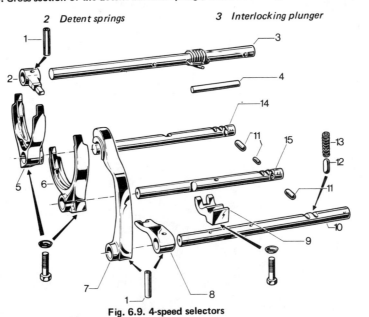

Fig. 6.9. 4-speed selectors

1	Roll pin	5	1/2 selector fork	9	Connector	13	Detent spring
2	Lever	6	3/4 selector fork	10	Reverse selector rod	14	1/2 selector rod
3	Main selector rod	7	Reverse selector fork	11	Interlocking plunger	15	3/4 selector rod
4	Pin	8	Cross lever	12	Detent ball		

4.3 This is the start of the rebuild

4.4 Make sure the bearing is fully in first

4.5 Obviously this shot is taken through the differential case

4.6 Security comes from replacing all the oil seals

4.7 Note the alignment of the roll pin holes

4.8 Use new roll pins and spring clips

4.9a Mesh the gears and slide the shaft in

4.9b Do not forget the washer under the locking bolt

4.10 Allow the selector fork simply to rest

4.11a This is the easiest way to hold in the gears.

4.11b Notice how this is done

4.12a This is a special photo for explanation only It is not a stage of assembly

4.12b The pinion shaft is fully in. Note the reverse gear selector is still in position

4.13a The outer race now needs to be inserted onto the shaft

4.13b It is now in and the nut is finger tight

4.13c Once torqued lock the nut this way

4.14 The casing is now up the other way

4.15a See how the lever fits loose at this stage, soon to be locked

4.15b The spring limits its to and fro travel

4.16 The rod is all the way in

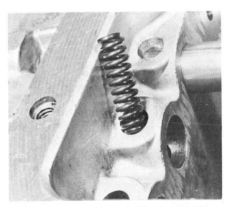

4.17a Note the detent spring bearing feed in

4.17b The third shaft is now installed

4.17c The interlock plunger is shown here ready to fit

4.18 So far so good. Note the location of everything

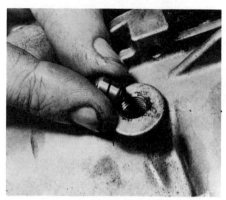
4.19 The interlock plunger has to go in here

4.20a The last detent spring and ball

4.20b The last shaft is nearly in place

4.21a Always use new roll pins

4.21b This is what the selectors should look like

4.22 Note the proper way round for the crownwheel

4.23 Oil the housings and be careful

4.24 Note the proper way up of the 'X' cross brace

4.25 An essential final detail

4.26a Oil the shaft for ease on the oil seal

4.26b Tighten the three bolts shown here first

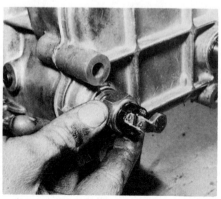
4.27 Make sure a washer is fitted

4.28 Several types have been fitted

4.29 Note how clean everything still is

4.30 A new roll pin is always necessary

4.32 It is easy to forget this at this stage

4.33 Note how the lever arm pivots

5 5-speed unit - dismantling

1   For the purposes of this manual the d-i-y home mechanic can forget this gearbox. If something major has gone wrong with one of these units it is going to be beyond the scope of even an experienced home mechanic. Something like 35 special tools are necessary to set one up properly should a major overhaul be necessary. Unlike the 4-speed, on which it is obviously based, special tools are more than desirable even to dismantle it because of the addition of the 5th speed. Here we shall describe the fundamental differences, provide hints on dismantling. and show the appropriate illustrations but nothing more.

2   The differential and the basic gearcluster inside the main casing are much as they are for the 4-speed, and dismantling procedures are close enough to the 4-speed to be the same. It is the 5th speed gear and selector which are attached to extended pinion and primary shafts outside the main case and inside the tail shaft or rear case, which provide the dismantling complication. The two appropriate figures illustrate how the gears lie.

3   On the primary shaft, (see Fig. 6.9) the 5th speed gear and a shorter deflector tube are inside the rear cover and fixed in the same way except that the 5th gear and the 4th gear just inside the main case are now on Woodruff keys. It means that the 5th gear has to be pulled off the shaft with a special tool with little space to work.

4   For the pinion shaft the 5th gear sits outside the main case with its synchro hub and spider but with one added complication: the gear is fixed to the shaft by a large circlip inside the synchro hub with the spider outside it. Removal of this circlip is extremely difficult. Its replacement is even worse.

5   The worst is still to come. On the selector side the problems compound themselves. Outside the case is the 5th gear selector fork held to its shaft by a roll pin. Once this roll pin is punched out, the selector fork can be removed (with the gear cluster and synchro hub removed before) That is simple enough, but then the selector rod has another set of detent balls (2) and a spring at its other end on the reverse gear selector. These are hard to remove successfully; if lost in

the case, a new casing may be necessary!

6   This is a gearbox, therefore, which looks as simple as the 4-speed, but which, in fact, has enough added complications to make it an impractical d-i-y task. It is not that it is impossible, it is that successful repair and overhaul will not be certain. see Section 7, and small component replacement (such as a synchro hub) too difficult. A fully equipped, experienced Alfa Romeo dealership, once presented with the gearbox out of the car should be able to pull a 5-speed gearbox apart in around an hour by virtue of the special tools.

6 5-speed unit - reassembly

1   Once apart the 5-speed unit provides no additional pitfalls to the obviously, by now, experienced d-i-y gearbox mechanic than those which will have beset him on disassembly. Of course, if he follows the assembly sequence for the 4-speed but using his additional, specific experience gained on the 5-speed the chance of success will be reasonable. Again read Sections 7 and 8 now.

2   The major difference on assembly concerns the detent balls and spring used on the reverse gear selector. If misplaced during assembly the gearbox casing could be 'written off'. Extreme care is needed in replacing them - once stuck in the case nothing can be done to remove them. Beware! Similar care is needed for the other detent balls and springs.

3   Great difficulty will be experienced in replacing the circlip onto the 5th gear on the pinion shaft. Be prepared to spend a long time fitting this.

4   It will be necessary to press on the 5th gear to the primary shaft because of the Woodruff key. Added complications arise because the 4th gear on that shaft also sits on a Woodruff key.

Note: Great emphasis has been given here on the lack of enthusiasm for 5-speed gearbox dismantling. This is intentional - it is very much more difficult than the 4-speed. Be very sure of your own ability before attempting any work. It may be cheaper to see an Alfa Romeo agent first. 35 special tools do not come cheaply.

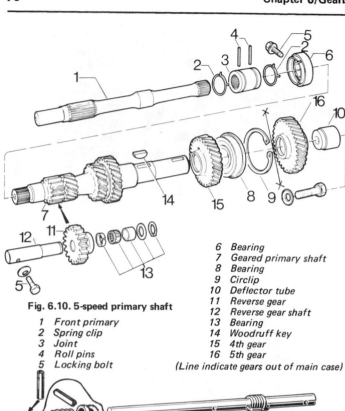

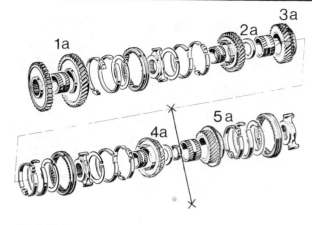

Fig. 6.11. 5-speed pinion shaft gear cluster

See Fig. 6.4 but note the numbered gears and the line indicating the point where gears to the right appear outside the main case

6   Bearing
7   Geared primary shaft
8   Bearing
9   Circlip
10 Deflector tube
11 Reverse gear
12 Reverse gear shaft
13 Bearing
14 Woodruff key
15 4th gear
16 5th gear
(Line indicate gears out of main case)

Fig. 6.10. 5-speed primary shaft

1   Front primary
2   Spring clip
3   Joint
4   Roll pins
5   Locking bolt

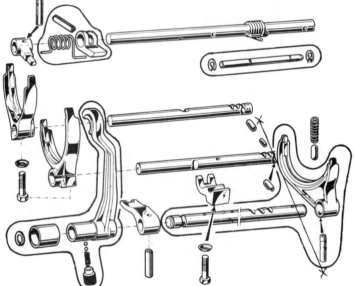

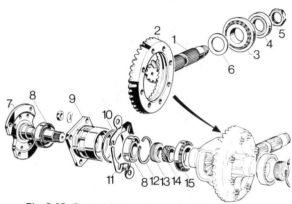

Fig. 6.13. Crownwheel, pinion and hub

1   Pinion shaft   9   Flange
2   Crownwheel   10   Flange seal
3   Bearing   11   Flange shim
4   Seal   12   Circlip
5   Nut   13   Thrower
6   Spacer   14   Speedo drive
7   Hub   15   Bearing
8   Bearing

Fig. 6.12. 5-speed selectors

Components circled denote special parts to the 5-speed gearbox. Line indicates 5th gear selector fork outside the main case. See Fig. 6.9

7 Differential and gear clusters

1   Little has been said about the differential and the actual gear clusters except in Section 8. Such is the precision of the traditional Alfa Romeo gearbox that, happily, gearbox and final drive shimming is not possible by the d-i-y mechanic. Special dial gauges and measuring tools are necessary to successfully measure up for end-float should major components require changing. Even pinion shafts come in sizes and the average home mechanic will not stand a chance in achieving a proper action with a change of pinion shaft or differential without recourse to the proper special tools.

2   By all means replace a synchro hub, even a gear (provided the proper tools are available) but do not replace a pinion shaft or differential without help from your Alfa Romeo agent. If in doubt consult him first, it could save you a lot of heartache and money!

3   Dimensions, shimming procedures and special tool numbers are not mentioned here for that reason.

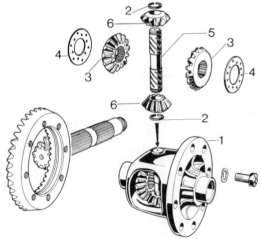

Fig. 6.14. Differential

1   Casing   4   Spacer
2   Spacer   5   Pinion
3   Side gear   6   Pinion gear

7.1 The pinion shaft number

7.2a The primary shaft with its machined-on gears

7.2b The complete pinion shaft and gear cluster

8 Inspection of components

Once decided that the transmission unit will have to be stripped down because of some minor irritant or major fault it is still not necessary to strip the unit completely. For example there is no need to remove the reverse gear cluster shaft if the synchromesh is being replaced on an otherwise properly functioning gearbox. Consequently you should go slowly once the three major components are removed from the unit because you may be doing unnecessary work. You may also have to face the fact that even when once dismantled you will do better to reassemble the box there and then (do it properly though) and exchange it for a replacement unit from Alfa Romeo. The economics of replacing large components is not always on when compared to a complete exchange unit. Remember also that exchange units are likely to be more readily available than individual component parts and that they will carry a guarantee.

Once dismantled into its three major components, the primary shaft, pinion shaft and final drive, inspection should be detailed. Clean the inside of the unit thoroughly first with a mixture of petrol and paraffin and wipe dry.

1   Check the casing for cracks or damage, particularly near the bearing housings and on the mating surfaces.
2   Check all the gears for chips and possible cracks and replace where necessary. You should be able to tell whether this should be so from the initial diagnosis before dismantling.
3   Check all the shafts and splines for wear and flat spots and replace if necessary. The gears through which the shafts pass should be a good slide fit and not rock about.
4   Check the synchromesh rings and assembly. Check for failure and if in doubt, replace. The springs should also be renewed at the same time.
5   Check the bearings: Primary shaft bearings are, generally speaking, very reliable and long lived and these are the only bearings apart from the bearings on the pinion shaft which can be replaced. Check them for scoring and 'wobble'. Pinion shaft bearings: The bearing at the opposite end from the final drive is easily replaced although generally long lived. Replace it if in any doubt. The pinion bearing next to the pinion wheel will have to be replaced at a cost of approximately one third of an exchange unit. If this has 'gone' and there are other necessary replacements within the transmission unit, then reassemble (properly) the gearbox and exchange the whole unit for a replacement transmission. It is not economic to do otherwise. The two outer differential bearings should be inspected in the same way. These may be replaced by the home mechanic but he will have difficulty in setting up the final drive in the casing afterwards. Again these bearings are usually reliable.
6   Any failure within the final drive unit will mean replacement of the whole crownwheel assembly unit in total. Under certain circumstances it will mean changing the bearing and speedo drive gear. See the specifications at the start of the Chapter. We did not dismantle the crownwheel and pinion because it is not a task which can be undertaken, at least at the reassembly stage, by the home mechanic. The cost of purchasing a new crownwheel without a new pinion, madness anyway, is again approximately half that of a new exchange

transmission unit. Purchasing the two together, crownwheel assembly and pinion assembly, to enable them to mesh and set-up correctly, is approximately the cost of the exchange transmission and you will not get the guarantee.
7   Check that the speedometer drive is in good condition and running easily in its bush.
8   Check the selector forks for wear. Measure them with a pair of calipers and compare their ends with the thickest point; if in doubt replace. They should be only fractionally worn.
9   Check the gear shift mechanism. The tongue which also slots into the top of the selectors wears quite rapidly, often resulting in non-selected gears and sloppy action.
Special Note: Such is the construction of these transmission units that they are generally speaking very reliable but often noisy. They all whine from new to some degree and this should not frighten owners. Obviously, it is not possible to detect any increase in whine over a period of time, only to think suddenly that is doing it more than perhaps it should. However, this is not good reason in itself to remove and disassemble the unit. The usual reason for discontent is the gradual failure of the synchromesh, particularly on first and second gears. This again is not really good reason for disassembly until it is completely non-functioning and the whine is excessive, from a mechanical point of view. Provided the unit still selects its gears, keeps them there and functions smoothly there is no mechanical reason for worry. Only at a point where it becomes unbearable for the individual owner should this action be taken. See the 'Fault diagnosis' at the end of this Chapter before jumping to conclusions.

9 Gearchange

1   The gearchange mechanism is a simple affair which is situated on the cast or sheet steel tail shaft. Its operation is self explanatory once the gearbox is removed from the car. See Fig. 6.15.
2   Four components can wear to cause floppy, rattling changes. The first is the bush on the selector lever on the gearbox itself. It sits inside a tube on the lever rod and is effectively nothing more than a cushion. Replacement is simple.
3   The lever rod and the shift lever are connected by a bush between the forked end of the lever rod on the through bolt. This wears. Again its replacement is straightforward.
4   The third 'wear' factor occurs in the bush in the top of the shift lever base. This bush suffers the vibration of the whole system and the positive change factor as well. Dismantle the whole system then punch out the bush, and push in a new one.
5   Finally, the two bushes on which the fork of the shift lever base sits, wears. Again, dismantling is necessary but once the lever base is off the bushes can be removed.
6   It is intentional that the whole system is fairly flexible. Do not be over alarmed if there is more than a correctable amount of movement, for the tail of the gearbox carries two very flexible rubber mountings which are not possible to replace at home. Take the tail shaft to your Alfa Romeo dealer who should be able to renew them. Wear on these mountings may affect gear shifting.

9.2 The bush is inside the 'tube'   9.3 The top bolt encloses the second wear factor   9.5 The bush is visible

10 Reversing lamp switch

1   The reversing lamp switch is located at the tail end of the gearbox casing. It is a screw-in type. It is easy to locate from beneath the car.
2   To remove, take off the two wires and then unscrew. A little oil may drip but if a replacement is very handy virtually none will be lost.
3   There is no repair facility, renewal being the only answer.

11 Speedometer cable

1   The speedometer cable is thoroughly conventional. It has an inner and outer cable driving from the crownwheel of the differential. It goes through a simple direct route from the gearbox to the speedometer.
2   Access to the underside of the speedometer is available from under the bonnet in the inner bulkhead. It is a standard screw type fitting.
3   At the gearbox end the outer cable fixes to the speedometer drive with a spring clip like a circlip.
4   The cable removal and replacement is very simple. When failure occurs it is usually the inner which has broken or stretched.

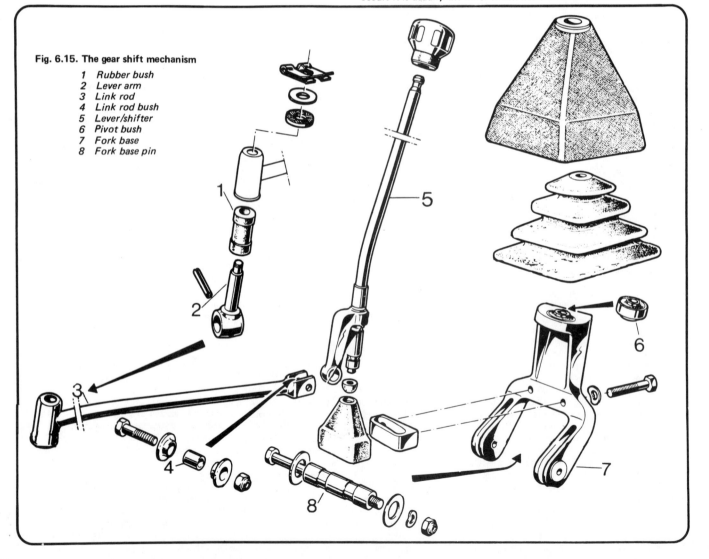

Fig. 6.15. The gear shift mechanism

1   Rubber bush
2   Lever arm
3   Link rod
4   Link rod bush
5   Lever/shifter
6   Pivot bush
7   Fork base
8   Fork base pin

12 Fault diagnosis

It is sometimes difficult to decide whether it is worthwhile removing and dismantling the gearbox for a fault which may be nothing more than a minor irritant. Gearboxes which howl, or where the synchromesh can be 'beaten' by a quick gearchange, may continue to perform for a long time in this state. A worn gearbox usually needs a complete rebuild to eliminate noise because the various gears, if re-aligned on new bearings, will continue to howl when different wearing surfaces are presented to each other.

The decision to overhaul therefore, must be considered with regard to time and money available, relative to the degree of noise or malfunction that the driver has to suffer.

Symptom	Reason/s	Remedy
Ineffective synchromesh	Worn baulk rings or synchro hubs	Renew.
Jumps out of one or more gears (on drive or over-run)	Weak detent springs, worn selector forks, worn synchro hubs or all three	Dismantle and renew.
Noisy, rough, whining and vibration	Worn bearings, (initially) resulting in extended wear generally due to play and backlash	Dismantle and renew.
Noisy and difficult engagement of gear	Clutch fault	Examine clutch operation.

Chapter 7 Driveshafts, hubs, wheels and tyres

Contents

Specifications

Driveshafts ... ... Two solid shafts transmit drive from the gearbox/final drive unit to the front wheels. Each shaft is fitted with constant velocity joints at each end. The inner ends of the shafts slide to compensate for suspension movement.

Front hubs ... ... Pre-lubricated double ball race located in a vertical slide

Rear hubs ... ... Two taper roller bearings integral with rear hub/discs. Adjustable

Wheels

	Alfasud	Alfasud TI
Type	Steel (plain)	Steel (sculptured)
Width	4½J or 5J	5½J
Diameter	13 inch	13 inch
Fixing	4 stud	4 stud

Tyres

Type and size	4½J 145SR13 Radial (tubeless)	165/70SR13 Radial (tubeless)
	5J 165/15SR13 Radial (tubeless)	

Pressures:

Front:		
4½J	27 psi (1.9 kg sq. cm)	
5J	26 psi (1.8 kg sq. cm)	
5½J	26 psi (1.8 kg sq. cm)	
Rear:		
4½J	20 psi (1.5 kg sq. cm)	
5J	20 psi (1.4 kg sq. cm)	
5½J	20 psi (1.4 kg sq. cm)	

Torque wrench settings	lb f ft	kg fm
Hub to driveshaft retaining bolt	10.8 - 17.3	1.5 - 2.4
Wheel nuts	47 - 57.8	6.5 - 8

1 General description

The driveshafts fitted to the Alfasud drive the front wheels direct from the final drive in the transmission casing. They also undergo the steering movement of the car with the front wheels. Consequently they are fitted with totally universal joints at the outer (wheel) end and sliding joints at their inner (transmission) end.

Little maintenance is practical. If wear occurs, the shafts can be removed and dismantled, at least, up to a point. Great care is needed. See the component illustration.

The front wheel hubs are reasonably conventional and can, in fact, be separated from the front suspension without trouble. Rear wheel hubs are absolutely conventional although they are integral with the rear brake discs.

Alfa Romeo use steel disc wheels, with four bolt fixings. Each model has a different style of wheel, some have hub caps, others are

'sculptured'. Radial tyres are fitted as standard and must be considered obligatory.

2 Driveshaft - disconnection and connection

1   It is necessary to disconnect both driveshafts from the gearbox/differential to enable the engine/gearbox to be removed. This is covered in Chapter 1, Section 6.

3 Driveshaft - removal and replacement

1   It is a complicated business to remove a driveshaft, at least at the outer, suspension end. It becomes more so as soon as you start to work on the shaft. Some special tools *will* have to be borrowed.

2   Jack-up and chock the front of the car. Remove the appropriate roadwheel.

3   Disconnect the driveshaft at the inner end (see the previous Section) which will lead you to Chapter 1, Section 6.

4   Remove the front anti-roll bar. See Chapter 10, Section 2.

5   Disconnect the outer end of the transverse link at the hub. This is bolted through a rubber bush on the semi-trailing link.

6   Now put a heavy ring spanner, or socket wrench, onto the four bolts which fix the hub to the suspension strut. A lot of force will be necessary to undo them. Loosen the bolts and remove.

7   From beneath the hub, undo the bolt which connects the semi-trailing link to the hub carrier which should now be separated from the suspension strut. Once undone, the hub carrier, hub and driveshaft can be removed from the car.

8   Now the problem is to remove the shaft from the hub and hub carrier. We advise that you don't do it. Take the whole thing to an Alfa Romeo agent of some experience; alternatively take it to a competent automotive engineer.

9   However, a brief description of driveshaft hub removal is given here. Remove the bolt, washer and oil ring from the end of the shaft. Using a press, puller and Alfa Romeo special tool 'A.2.0240' release the driveshaft stub from the front wheel hub. Extract the hub oil seal.

10 Replacement is the reverse procedure of removal. Make sure that the wheel hub and driveshaft stub splines have been cleaned using a special cleaner: 'Omnifit Activator'. (See your Alfa Romeo dealer). Before pressing have the splines into the hub and apply 'Omnifit 150 H compound' to the splines.

11 Torque the respective bolt and screw fixings according to the specifications.

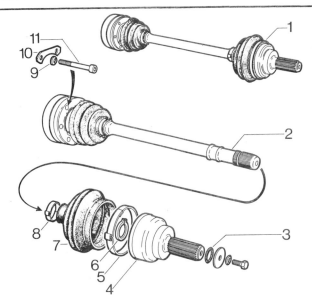

Fig. 7.1. Driveshaft components

1 Driveshaft complete	6 Circlip
2 Actual shaft	7 Boot
3 Washer	8 Outer clip
4 Joint outer	9 Washer
5 Outer clip	10 Tab washer
	11 Allen bolt

3.1 The driveshaft installed correctly

3.6 Two of the four hub carrier bolts

7   Replace the other components in a reverse order of their dismantling. Make sure the rubber bellows are good, and that their clips are in full strength.

4   Driveshaft joints - general

1   There are two driveshaft joints, both are described by Alfa Romeo as "yokes". Inner and outer yokes are different, each can be removed from the driveshaft but cannot be repaired. Replacement is the only answer.

2   If a driveshaft yoke is suspect - it may be noisy, slack or stiff. The chances are that the protective bellows which cover each one will have become cracked or perished and the weather has entered.

3   Remove the driveshaft from the car. See Section 3.

4   Remove the rubber bellows hose clips and slide the bellows along the shaft.

5   Clean away the grease from the yoke with your fingers (only) and release the circlip which attaches the yoke to the shaft. Now pull off the yoke.

6   Seek advice from your Alfa Romeo dealer. Push on the new yoke having packed it with 2.8202 (80g) of 'Molykote 2461C' or 'Optionol Olistamoly 2LN 548'. (Do not use solvents to clean the yoke). Afix the circlip.

5   Front hub bearings - removal and replacement

1   Front hub bearings cannot be removed and replaced whilst the hub is still affixed to the car. Rear Section 3, and proceed to the point where the front hub is removed from the driveshaft.

2   Your front hub is still in the hub carrier and is with your Alfa Romeo dealer because he has the special tools to take you so far. Because further special tools are necessary, leave the problem with your dealer - ask him to replace the hub bearing for you, it will be most efficient in the end.

3   The basic method is described here. Place the hub flange on the bench and clamp it. Using special tool 'A.5.0179', remove the hub retaining nut having released the locking tab. Using special tools 'A.2.0240' and 'A.3.0358' extract the hub from the housing. Now using special tool 'A.3.0356' extract the hub bearing inner race. Remove

the housing cover retaining screws and remove the cover. Push out the bearing.

4   Replacement and reassembly is a reverse procedure.

5   Check the bearing in the conventional manner for fit and smooth running.

6   Always renew the locknut and oil seals. Lubricate the two races with Castrol LM Grease. Special tool 'A.3.0330' is required to press in the oil seals. Use special tool 'A.3.0457' to press in the hub flange.

7   As can be seen from the above, a number of special tools are necessary. If they are not used damage will take place - this will be more costly in the end. It is obvious that the time necessary to use these tools is not long, and it is time which costs the most money.

6   Rear hub bearings - removal and replacement

1   The rear hubs are much more conventional. See Chapter 8, Section 6 to remove the rear calipers, then see Chapter 10, Section 11 to remove the hubs.

2   The hub is off the stub axle. The outer bearing inner race is loose. Extract the outer bearing outer race from the hub. Alfa Romeo recommend special tool 'A.3.0349' although it is possible to tap it out carefully using a suitable drift and copper head hammer. The inner bearing outer race can be removed from the hub in the same way (this time Alfa Romeo special tool A.3.0355) once the oil seal has been picked out. The inner bearing inner race is still on the stub axle. Pull this off with a conventional 2-legged puller.

3   Check the bearings carefully in the usual manner. If in doubt, replace. Always use new oil seals.

4   Replacement is a reverse procedure to removal. Use fresh Castrol LM Grease to grease the bearings. Special tools are not strictly

necessary to refit the bearing races. Use a suitable drift with care.

5   Hub replacement is dealt with as mentioned in paragraph 1, of this Section.

7   Wheels - general

1   Because the design of the suspension of the car, the strength and the trueness of the roadwheels is critical, particularly at the front. A great deal of excessively fast wear on the wheel bearings and universal joints can be attributed to buckled and deformed wheels. Check every 3000 miles or when there is a sudden difference of feeling at the steering wheel, that the wheels are not buckled or dented. Check also that the front wheels are balanced. If any deformity is noticed the wheel concerned should be replaced by new. Do not attempt to 'repair' wheel rims.

2   Do not overtighten the wheel bolts for this can deform the rim. Always check that the inner side of the wheel is free from mud and grit, for the accumulation of these can create im-balance.

8   Tyres - general

In the same way that the condition and suitability of the wheels fitted is critical so it is with the tyres. Because of the type of suspension it is always wise to fit radial tyres on all wheels of these cars. Tyre wear is not great under any circumstances but the front tyres wear faster than the rear. Do not fit oversize tyres. The wheel rims are not readily able to take a larger section tyre than that recommended. See Specifications for suitability of tyres. Tyre pressures are critical too.

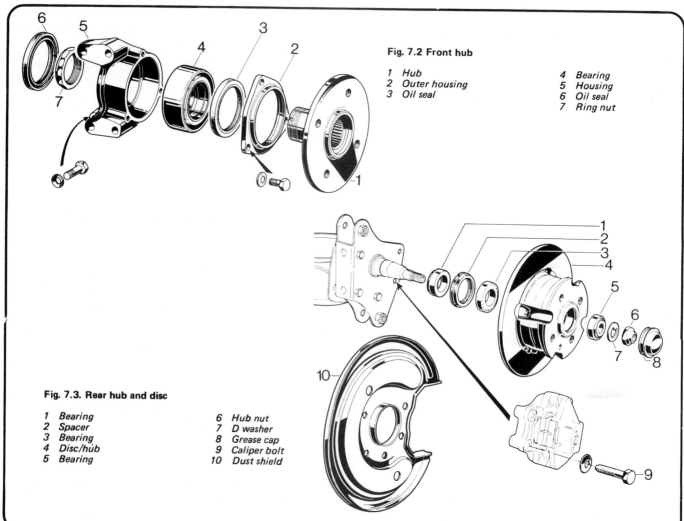

Fig. 7.2 Front hub

1 Hub	4 Bearing
2 Outer housing	5 Housing
3 Oil seal	6 Oil seal
	7 Ring nut

Fig. 7.3. Rear hub and disc

1 Bearing	6 Hub nut
2 Spacer	7 D washer
3 Bearing	8 Grease cap
4 Disc/hub	9 Caliper bolt
5 Bearing	10 Dust shield

Chapter 8 Braking system

Contents

Specifications

Type	ATE disc brakes on all four wheels. Front discs are in-board on each side of the gearbox/final drive. Rear discs are out-board. Dual circuit with pressure regulating valve in the rear line. Handbrake operates on calipers on front wheels from centrally mounted lever (floor)

Disc diameter:

Front	259 mm (10.2 in.)
Rear	234 mm (9.2 in.)
Maximum disc runout (at diameter 254 mm)	0.15 mm
Maximum regrind	1 mm (0.5 mm on each side)

Maximum thickness of disc

Front	9.3 mm
Rear	8.2 mm

Servo	Fitted as optional equipment on Alfasud. Standard Alfasud TI

Pad thickness:

New	15 mm (0.591 in.)
Minimum	7 mm (0.275 in.)
Running clearance for disc/pad (front)	1 mm

Torque wrench settings

	lb f ft	kg f m
Pedal housing to body nuts	11.5 - 14.4	1.6 - 2
Disc dust cover to gearbox bolts	4.3 - 7.2	0.6 - 1
Disc dust cover to caliper bolts	4.3 - 7.2	0.6 - 1
Brake master cylinder to pedal housing	10.8 - 17.3	1.5 - 2.4
Front calipers to gearbox	69.4 - 75.9	9.5 - 10.5
Disc to differential half-shaft	40.5 - 49.9	5.6 - 6.9
Rear caliper and wheel bearing to axle	28.9 - 35.4	4 - 4.9

1 General description

The Alfasud braking system is somewhat unconventional. It consists of a dual-line hydraulic system, there being two independent circuits for the front brakes and one for the rear brakes. A servo is normally fitted. The front brakes consist of discs and adjustable calipers mounted in-board, at the inner end of the driveshafts, on the gearbox. A cable operated handbrake system also operates from the front calipers. The rear brakes are also discs and calipers but this

time affixed to the outer ends of the rear beam axle in a more conventional manner. A brake pressure limiter valve is fitted on the beam axle.

An explanatory diagram illustrates the system (Fig. 8.5). The system works well but requires a certain amount of maintenance, over and above that which is normal, to achieve longevity. Working on the front discs and calipers is very difficult because of the cramped working conditions when the engine and gearbox are fitted in the car. For this reason it is wise to check the front brakes when the engine and gearbox are removed for other reasons.

2 Front disc brakes - inspection, removal and refitting of pads

1   The Alfasud can use front brake pads at an alarming rate if the calipers are not looked after properly. Section 3 will tell you that the calipers are adjustable, and how and why it is necessary. This section will tell you what to look for in terms of wear and how to pull out and replace the pads. Read that section next should you contemplate pad replacement.

2   You can inspect the disc pad wear by simply opening the bonnet and with a torch looking at the top of the two calipers mounted inboard on top of the gearbox. You need the torch because they are somewhat hidden from any bright light.

3   The calipers should be relatively clean. The front pads do not seem to spread everything with dust. You should see a thickness of pad friction material on each side of the disc. If the pad friction material and its backing appears to be less than 10 mm, or there is uneven wear, you should remove the anti-rattle spring for a proper inspection. (The minimum thickness is 7 mm).

4   Unclip the anti-rattle spring by pinching the top loop and unhooking it. It is tough and will break your finger nails if you are not careful.

5   Now go through the procedure as described in Section 3 to enable the pads to be removed, noting its position, with your fingers gripping the top lifting eye. If it is loose but will not come out, use a screwdriver blade through the eye and lift it out that way.

6   Measure the thickness of each pad. If any are too thin (less than 10 mm), renew all four. If one is more than 2 mm thinner than the others, renew all four even if none are under the minimum size.

7   Replace the old pads, if they are satisfactory, in the same place as they came from. If new pads are to fitted ensure that the new pads are fitted with the direction arrows, printed on their sides, facing in the direction of rotation - to the front of the car.

8   Now read Section 3 and adjust the calipers.

9   It makes good sense to inspect the discs for wear and the calipers for leaks.

3 Front brake adjustment

1   The Alafsud is unusual in that it is fitted with 'adjustable' calipers for its front disc brakes. The reasons for this appear to be their location, at the inner end of the driveshafts, on the gearbox and the subsequent lack of working room and because the handbrake also operates the front brakes through the same calipers via a cable. Adjustment, suffice it to say, is not very easy without the right tools.

2   Brake adjustment is only necessary when replacing the disc pads. It is not necessary when bleeding the hydraulic system nor when adjusting the handbrake. Automatic adjustment still takes place in the conventional manner to take up running wear on the pads. This adjustment is necessary for pad removal and replacement.

3   Adjustment will mean that you should possess the appropriate Allen key and a tiny ring spanner. Open the bonnet and chock the wheels. Release the handbrake. To release the outer pad, remove the plastic cap by unscrewing it with your fingers (if tight use a spanner). This cap is on the outer side of each caliper. Having released the pad anti-rattle clip from the top of the caliper fit the spanner on the lock nut hidden

by the plastic cap and then insert the Allen key into the Allen screw or to which the lock nut fits. Release the lock nut, keep the spanner there to hold it, now turn the Allen key. Turn it in the direction which will release the outer pad in the caliper. What you need to do is draw the caliper outer piston 'outwards'. Continue to hold the lock nut and turning the Allen screw until the pad can be removed. See Section 2 for details of the front pads.

4   Now you need to release the other piston, the inner case one, of that caliper. The principle remains the same although the method used is slightly different. This time there is no lock nut and the Allen screw is a bolt. On top of the caliper, opposite the bleed screw, is the inner adjuster. Turn this bolt until the inner pad is released and you are able to remove it.

5   Now you have the pads removed. Before you can fit the new pads and adjust the calipers again, you may have to repeat each operation to the two pistons to pull both further out; to enable fitment of the new pads. Fit the new pads. Leave the anti-rattle clip off for the moment.

6   To adjust, repeat each operation again but in the opposite direction. Obviously you now need to draw the pistons in again. However, this time insert a 0.10 mm feeler blade between the pad face and the disc. When you can just pull the feeler blade out without undue resistance, your caliper is adjusted. Make sure you do this adjustment for each pad of both calipers. Never do half a job, if you touch one pad, you must then adjust all four. It is worth repeating that pads should always be replaced in sets. Read Section 2 to check for pad fitment.

7   Replace the plastic cap on each outer side of the calipers, having tightened the lock-nut.

8   Replace the anti-rattle springs.

4 Rear disc brakes - inspection, removal and refitting of pads

1   The rear disc brakes are conventional. To get at them jack up the rear of the car and chock it. Remove the road wheels. Leave the handbrake on.

2   The calipers are of the trailing type. To inspect the pads go to the rear of the caliper and pick out the dust cover. This clips into the caliper top and bottom and a screwdriver blade should help removal. Now look at the pads. A torch may again help. If the pad and backing appears to be less than 10 mm thick, remove all four pads and measure them.

3   To remove the pads is easy. Obtain a pin punch and tap the holding pin from the outside inwards. You will see a drilling in the outer side of each caliper; tap through this. The anti-rattle spring should then come out.

4   Hook out the pads, either with your fingers or with the blade of a screwdriver. If the wear is uneven renew all four pads, if the pads and backing are less than 7 mm, renew all four pads.

5   Replacement is a reverse procedure. If new pads are fitted it may be necessary to push the pistons back to give you the space to insert the new pads. Do this carefully with a screwdriver blade - watch the piston rubbers.

6   These calipers are totally automatic.

2.7a Note the direction of rotation arrow on the new pad

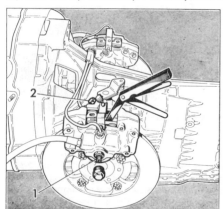

Fig. 8.1. Fitting front disc pads
1 and 2 Adjusting screws - two different tools are necessary

Fig. 8.2. Disc pad location with anti-rattle spring

2.7b The rear of the pads also has an arrow and a slot

3.3a An outer adjuster removed. Note the direction of rotation of the locknut relative to the Allen screw

3.3b Here the spanner and the Allen key are in use

3.3c This shot locates the other adjuster with the socket

4.5a A rear caliper awaits two pads

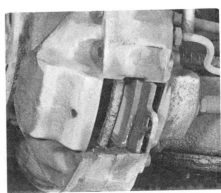

4.5b Place the inner pad into the caliper first ...

4.5c ... obviously followed by the outer one

4.5d The anti-rattle spring and pin is installed

4.5e A rear hub disc and caliper properly installed

5 Front caliper units - removal, servicing and refitting

1   It is unwise to contemplate work on a front caliper with the caliper still fitted, in fact, depending on the work involved, it is almost impossible. However, to remove the caliper it is necessary to remove the disc and to remove the disc it is necessary to disconnect the driveshaft - all these tasks are possible, if a little difficult, with the engine and gearbox still in the car. Obviously it is necessary to disconnect the handbrake cable.

2   To disconnect the driveshaft, see Chapter 7. To remove the disc see Section 8.

3   Remove the handbrake cable, see Section 15.

4   Remove the disc pads, see Section 2.

5   If the engine is still in the car disconnect the flexible hydraulic pipe to the caliper at the inner bulkhead. Plug the static pipe with a piece of wood or a pencil to stop excess fluid from flowing out. Now disconnect the front caliper interconnecting rigid pipes. It is best to disconnect them from each caliper so that they are not damaged. They are clipped together in their centre above the gearbox.

6   The caliper is fixed to the gearbox by two through bolts which are fitted from the outer side (behind the disc). Use a socket and extension and loosen both fixing bolts. Withdraw the bolts and then lift up the caliper. Repeat this operation for the other caliper - it is a good idea to overhaul the calipers in pairs.

7   The above instructions apply to the task when the engine is still in the car. If it is out then some of the tasks nave been completed in a different order.

8   Remove the flexible hose from the caliper.

9   It is possible to renew the pistons and the rubbers only. If the bores of the caliper are worn or scored then a new caliper will have to be fitted. It is not possible to split the caliper.

10 If failure or leakage has occurred then you should remove the pistons, and the rubbers and refit new ones. Renew the pistons if they

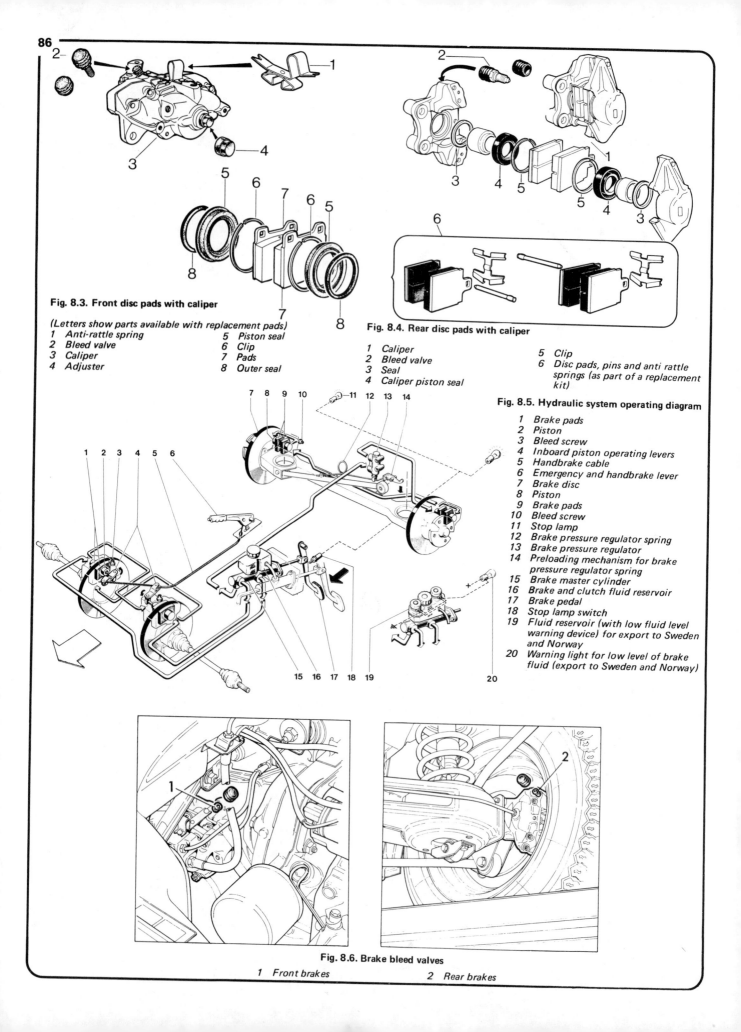

Fig. 8.3. Front disc pads with caliper

(Letters show parts available with replacement pads)

1	Anti-rattle spring	5	Piston seal
2	Bleed valve	6	Clip
3	Caliper	7	Pads
4	Adjuster	8	Outer seal

Fig. 8.4. Rear disc pads with caliper

1	Caliper	5	Clip
2	Bleed valve	6	Disc pads, pins and anti rattle springs (as part of a replacement kit)
3	Seal		
4	Caliper piston seal		

Fig. 8.5. Hydraulic system operating diagram

1 Brake pads
2 Piston
3 Bleed screw
4 Inboard piston operating levers
5 Handbrake cable
6 Emergency and handbrake lever
7 Brake disc
8 Piston
9 Brake pads
10 Bleed screw
11 Stop lamp
12 Brake pressure regulator spring
13 Brake pressure regulator
14 Preloading mechanism for brake pressure regulator spring
15 Brake master cylinder
16 Brake and clutch fluid reservoir
17 Brake pedal
18 Stop lamp switch
19 Fluid reservoir (with low fluid level warning device) for export to Sweden and Norway
20 Warning light for low level of brake fluid (export to Sweden and Norway)

Fig. 8.6. Brake bleed valves

1 Front brakes   2 Rear brakes

are damaged or scored.

11 To remove the outer piston remove the adjuster screw lock nut and then push the piston through with the adjuster Allen screw. Do much the same thing with the inner piston with the other adjusting screw. Pick out the cylinder piston rubbers, circlips etc. See Fig. 8.5 which will give the placing of the pistons and the rubbers.

12 Before refitting make sure everything is spotlessly clean. Methylated spirits should be used for cleaning, not petrol or paraffin.

13 Wipe the pistons and caliper bore with clean brake fluid, also the rubbers and circlips. Carefully replace them in the reverse order to their removal.

14 Refit the flexible brake hose to each caliper. Do not overtighten.

15 Replace the caliper onto the gearbox. Tighten its fixing bolts to the specified torque wrench setting.

16 Refit the disc and driveshaft in the reverse order of removal.

17 Adjust the pads. See Section 3.

18 Bleed the hydraulic system. See Section 7.

19 Test the car.

6 Rear caliper units - removal, servicing and refitting

1 Once again the complexity of the front disc brakes is offset by the simplicity of the rear disc brakes.

2 Follow the instructions given in Section 4, remove the disc pads.

3 Disconnect the flexible brake hose at the caliper and plug the end with a pencil to stop excessive fluid loss. Disconnect also the caliper rigid interconnecting pipe which is fixed to the beam axle.

4 On the outer side of the hub/discs are four drillings. Turn the hub/disc until one of the drillings allows you to insert a socket onto one of the caliper fixing bolts. Loosen and remove the bolt. Turn the hub/disc again and align the second caliper fixing bolt. Loosen and remove that bolt too.

5 Lift off the caliper.

6 Apply the same inspection and principles as to the front calipers. See Section 5, paragraphs 9 and 10. Pull out each piston in the conventional manner. Sometimes, if the pistons are not 'loose', a compressed air line will help blow out the pistons if fitted to the flexible hose and/or rigid pipe orifices.

7 Now read paragraphs 12 and 13 of Section 5.

8 Caliper refitting is an exact reverse sequence of removal.

9 Bleed the hydraulic system and road test the car.

7 Hydraulic system - bleeding

1 Strictly it is necessary to bleed all four brakes at the same time as there is a dual line system fitted. This is done through three bleed nipples. If you look at the schematic diagram you will see how the fluid should flow.

2 It is always important to use new fluid of the proper type.

3 Fix bleed tubes to each of the front caliper bleed nipples. Fix a third bleed tube to the right-hand rear caliper bleed nipple. Each tube should be fed in a glass jar. The end of the tube should be covered with a level of brake fluid.

4 Fill the brake fluid reservoir on the master cylinder.

5 Loosen each of the bleed nipples.

6 Depress the brake pedal several times allowing the pedal to return very slowly and waiting a few moments before pressing it again. Repeat this operation, constantly checking that the fluid reservoir is topped up, until each of the bleed tubes discharges fluid totally free from air bubbles. Once you are satisfied this is the case, finally have some one hold the brake pedal down and then tighten up all three brake bleed nipples. Remove the tubes and fluid jars and replace the bleed nipple rubber covers. Check that the fluid reservoir is up to its top level.

7 Test the car. After two or three applications of the brakes, the car should brake strongly, consistently and in a straight line.

Special note: Brake fluid ruins paintwork - bleed the brakes carefully and in an unrushed state.

The Alfasud has a brake fluid loss warning light fitted to the dashboard. It is interconnected with the choke light. If the choke light comes on (or stays on too long) check that the choke is fully home. If it is and the light remains on, stop the car immediately. Check the level of the brake fluid. If it is too low top it up immediately and check that the light is extinguished. If it remains on after several further applications of the brakes it means that there is a leak in the system. It will be unsafe to continue driving the car.

8 Discs - inspection and renovation

1 Front discs can be removed from the gearbox relatively easily with the engine in the car. Disconnect the driveshafts, see Chapter 7.

2 Remove the disc pads, see Section 2.

3 Each front disc is connected to the differential flanges by four securing set screws. Lock the hub with a large diameter drift, use a socket and long wrench from below to loosen the screws. Once loosened remove them and slip the disc downwards.

4 Replacement is an exact reverse procedure of removal. **Always** use new set screws for disc to flange fixing.

5 Rear discs are integral with the rear hubs. See Chapter 10, Section 11 for hub removal, once you have removed the rear calipers, see Section 6.

6 Now see Chapter 7, Section 6 to remove the rear hub bearings.

7 Replacement of rear disc/hubs is a reverse procedure of their removal.

8 Disc removal will be necessary if wear has become excessive or fracture has occurred. It is possible to regrind the surface of disc to 1 mm under size to a maximum of 0.5 mm per face. Minimum thickness of a reground disc should be 9.3 mm at the front and 8.2 mm on the rear. Maximum run out, to be measured with the disc installed should be 0.15 mm measured on the diameter 254 mm.

9 If in doubt consult your Alfa Romeo dealer.

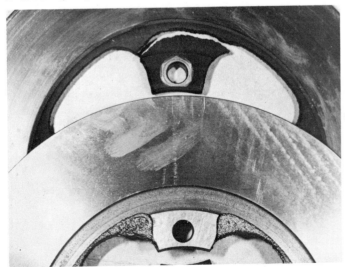

8.3 A flange broke from the early disc behind. The new disc has been re-inforced

8.4 Here a new disc has been installed

9   Master cylinder - removal, servicing and refitting

1   Removing the master cylinder is easy but messy. Try to remove as much of the brake fluid from the reservoir above the cylinder as you can before you set about the master cylinder. Remember however, that this reservoir serves the clutch system as well.
2   If the car is fitted with a servo unit ignore the next instruction. For cars not fitted with a servo unit, disconnect the push rod from the brake pedal inside the car. See Section 17.
3   With a large rag laid underneath the master cylinder to catch any surplus brake fluid, loosen the two nuts which fix the master cylinder to either the servo unit or the inner bulkhead. Remove the nuts.
4   Undo the rigid hydraulic pipes fixed to the master cylinder and the flexible fluid pipe leading to the clutch master cylinder.
5   Pull up and out gently the master cylinder and the reservoir together.
6   Now pull off the reservoir - it locates as a push-on fit into two rubber seals.
7   See the adjacent figure 8.8 which will show you the make up of the master cylinder seals, circlip and pistons.
8   Inspect the pistons and the cylinder. If the pistons are scored or otherwise damaged they can be renewed. If the cylinder is scored or otherwise damaged then it will be necessary to renew the whole master cylinder. If you have disassembled the cylinder you should renew the seals automatically.
9   Clean the cylinder with methylated spirits, never petrol or paraffin. Lubricate the new components with clean, new brake fluid and install in a reverse order of their dismantling.
10   Master cylinder replacement and installation is a reverse procedure of removal.
11   Bleed the brake hydraulic system and then bleed the clutch system. See Section 7 of this chapter and then Chapter 5.

10   Vacuum servo unit - removal, dismantling and refitting

1   To remove the servo, first remove the master cylinder. See Section 9.
2   Now disconnect the vacuum pipe at the servo. This is connected just below the master cylinder with a hose clip.
3   Inside the car disconnect the push rod from the brake pedal. See Section 17.
4   The servo is fixed to the main bulkhead by four studs and nuts.

These nuts should be undone from inside the car. Once removed, carefully juggle the servo out.
5   Nothing can be done to the servo in the way of repair should it be proven to be faulty. The only maintenance applicable is the changing of the filter and 'silencer'. These are fitted under the push rod gaiter. They are cut to enable you to slip them on and off, once the gaiter is pulled off.
6   Replacement is a reverse procedure to removal.
7   It will be necessary to bleed the brake system and the clutch system.
8   If in doubt as to the efficiency of your servo check with your Alfa Romeo dealer who should have the appropriate equipment.

11   Stop lamp switch - servicing

1   The stop lamp switch will either function or it will not, there are no half measures and no repair is available.
2   The switch is mechanical and operates on the brake pedal itself.
3   To remove, pull off the electrical lead, access to which is given under the steering column.
4   Undo the lock nut on the body of the switch and remove. The switch itself should then be free from the bracket in which it locates.
5   Replacement is straightforward, a reverse sequence of removal.

12   Rigid brake lines inspection and renewal

1   Periodically and certainly well in advance of the MOT test, if due, all brake pipes, connections and unions should be completely and carefully examined.
    The steel pipes must be examined carefully. They must be thoroughly cleaned and examined for signs of dents or other percussive damage, rust and corrosion. Rust and corrosion should be scraped off and, if the depth of pitting in the pipes is significant, they will need renewing. This is most likely in those areas underneath the chassis and along the rear suspension where the pipes are exposed to the full force of road and weather conditions.
2   If any section of pipe is to be removed, first of all take off the fluid reservoir cap, line it with a piece of polythene film to make it airtight and screw the cap back on. This will minimise the amount of fluid dripping out of the system when the pipes are removed.

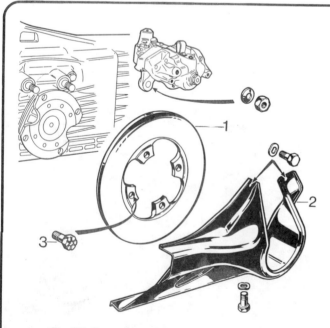

Fig. 8.7. Front disc and dust shield

1   Disc

2   Dust shield
3   Special disc bolt

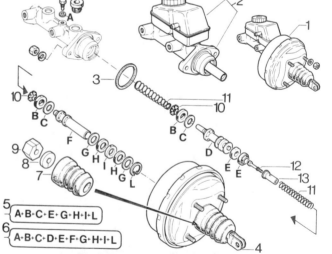

Fig. 8.8. Master cylinder and servo unit

1   Servo equipped master cylinder
2   Master cylinder without servo attached
3   'O' ring
4   Servo pushrod
5   Repair half kit for master cylinder
6   Repair kit for master cylinder complete
7   Gaiter
8   Spacer
9   Spacer
10 Star washer
11 Spring
12 Piston screw
13 Piston socket

3 Rigid pipe removal is usually quite straightforward. The unions at each end are undone and the pipe drawn out of the connection. The clips which may hold it to the car body are bent back and it is then removed. Underneath the car exposed unions can be particularly stubborn, defying the efforts of an open ended spanner. As few people will have the special split ring spanner required, a self-grip wrench (mole) is the only answer. If the pipe is being renewed new unions will be provided. If not then one will have to put up with the possibility of burring over the flats on the union and use a self-grip wrench for replacement.

4 Flexible hoses are always fitted to a rigid support bracket where they join a rigid pipe, the bracket being fixed to the chassis or rear suspension. The rigid pipe unions must first be removed from the flexible union. Then the locknut securing the flexible pipe to the bracket must be unscrewed, releasing the end of the pipe from the bracket. As these connections are usually exposed they are more often than not rusted up and a penetrating fluid is virtually essential to aid removal (try Plus-Gas). When undoing them, both halves must be supported as the bracket is not strong enough to support the torque required to undo the nuts and can easily be snapped off.

5 Rigid pipes which need renewal can usually be purchased at any local garage where they have the pipe, unions and special tools to make them up. All that they need to know is the pipe length required and the type of flare used at the ends of the pipe. These may be different at each end of the same pipe.

6 Replacement of pipes is a straightforward reversal of the removal procedure. It is best to get all the sets (bends) in the pipe made preparatory to installation. Also any acute bends should be put in by the garage on a bending machine otherwise there is the possibility of kinking them and restricting the bore area and fluid flow.

7 With the pipes replaced, remove the polythene from the reservoir cap and bleed the system as described in Section 7.

13 Flexible hoses - inspection and renewal

1 Run through the checks given in Section 12.
2 Examine first all the unions for signs of leaks. Then look at the flexible hoses for signs of fraying and chafing (as well as for leaks). This is only a preliminary inspection of the flexible hoses as exterior condition does not necessarily indicate interior condition, which will be considered later.
3 Once the flexible hose is removed examine the internal bore. If clear of fluid it should be possible to see through it. Any specks of rubber which come out, or signs of restriction in the bore, mean that the inner lining is breaking up and the pipe must be replaced.
4 Removal is straightforward, as is replacement. Make sure the pipes do not twist.

14 Handbrake - adjustment

1 The handbrake operates the two inner pistons of the two calipers of the front disc brakes through a conventional handbrake lever, single cable and system of levers as the calipers.
2 Adjustment is made at the handbrake lever in the car only. It is correct when both front wheels are locked when the handbrake lever is pulled-up four notches. When off, the front wheels should rotate freely.
3 To adjust, remove the plastic handbrake lever shroud, and then tighten or loosen the threaded adjuster on the cable, to achieve the correct adjustment.

15 Handbrake cable - renewal

1 This operation must be one of the most difficult to carry out. Do not attempt it unless you absolutely must. Two possible reasons might be excessive stretch or breakage.

16 Handbrake lever - removal, dismantling, reassembly and refitting

1 Read Section 15. Disconnect the handbrake cable at the lever end.
2 Now remove the one fixing bolt from the lever assembly on the floor. Unhook the other end of the lever and pull out.
3 The lever assembly is easy to dismantle. Undo and remove the pivot bolt. This allows the basic assembly to come apart. You can now remove the release spring and button by pushing off the clip under the inner end of the grip.
4 Reassembly and refitting is a reverse procedure of removal.

17 Pedals - removal and replacement

1 The brake and clutch pedals pivot on the same shaft, therefore you should expect to dismantle both pedals at the same time, in the same way.
2 Remove the brake stop lamp switch. See Section 11.
3 Disconnect the clutch and brake push rods from the pedals. These are fixed by a pivot and a circlip. Use circlip pliers (external) to remove. Pull off the pedal return springs first. Slip out the pivots.
4 So far you have been working under the dashboard. Now you should open the bonnet and remove the cross-duct in the bulkhead space. See Chapter 2. Behind the servo or master cylinder you should be able to see the pivot bolt for the pedals. On the inner end is a special clip. Pull this off, push the pivot outwards, and withdraw it from the bodyshell.

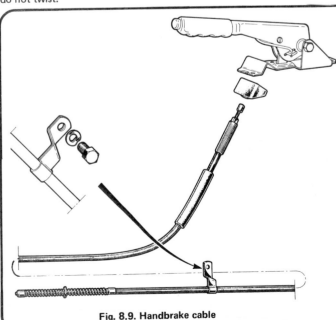

Fig. 8.9. Handbrake cable

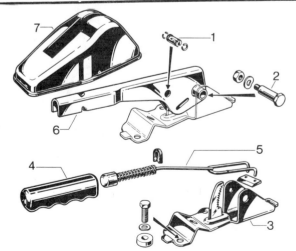

Fig. 8.10. Handbrake lever components

1 Cable ferrule	4 Handle
2 Pivot bolt	5 Spring release
3 Ratchet body	6 Outer handle
	7 Cover

5 From inside the car the pedals and their bushes should now be ready to pull away. See Figure 8.11. which gives the location of the bushes.

6 Replacement is a reverse procedure of removal. Grease the bushes before replacement. The pedals should be smooth in operation. The basic pivot bracket cannot be removed without dismantling the steering.

18 Pressure limiter valve

1 A pressure limiter valve is fitted into the rear brake hydraulic

circuit to avoid rear wheel lock-up under hard braking, which might occur when the rear of the vehicle lifts on its suspension. It is a single, conventional device usually fitted to vehicles of this type.

2 No repair or testing facility is available. If suspect operation is considered have an Alfa Romeo agent check your car. If it is necessary to renew the unit, this is something you can do. Treat the unit with the same care you would when renewing hydraulic pipes.

3 See Figure 8.12. A spring rod (with rubber band) is pivotted on a Panhard rod. Its free end works a lever which abuts a special valve. As the suspension goes up at the rear it starts to actuate the valve.

4 Removal and replacement of all the parts is straightforward. The units are normally very reliable.

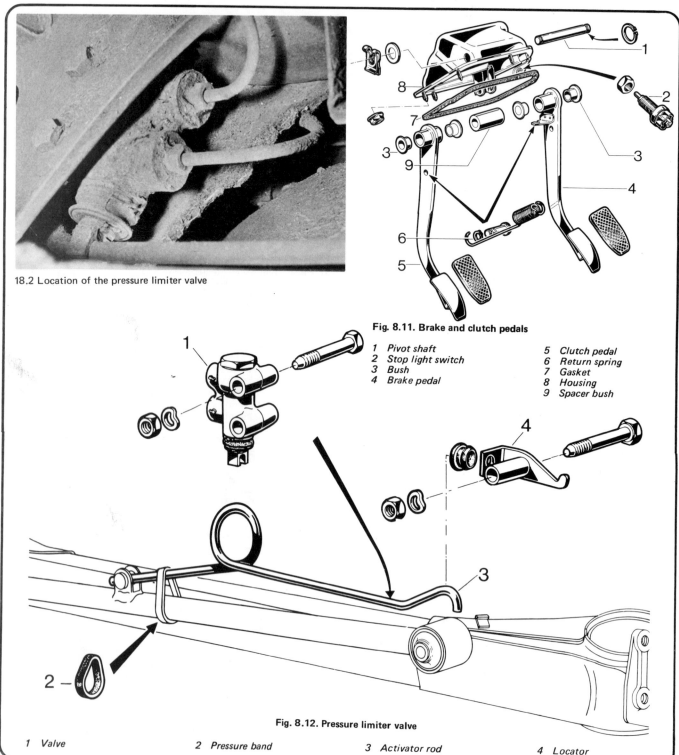

18.2 Location of the pressure limiter valve

Fig. 8.11. Brake and clutch pedals

1 Pivot shaft
2 Stop light switch
3 Bush
4 Brake pedal
5 Clutch pedal
6 Return spring
7 Gasket
8 Housing
9 Spacer bush

Fig. 8.12. Pressure limiter valve

1 Valve   2 Pressure band   3 Activator rod   4 Locator

19 Fault diagnosis - braking system

Symptom	Reason/s	Remedy
Pedal travels almost to floorboards before brakes operate	Brake fluid level too low	Top up master cylinder reservoir. Check for leaks.
	Caliper leaking	Dismantle caliper, clean, fit new rubbers and bleed brakes.
	Master cylinder leaking (bubbles in master cylinder fluid)	Dismantle master cylinder, clean and fit new rubbers. Bleed brakes.
	Brake flexible hose leaking	Examine and fit new hose if old hose leaking Bleed brakes.
	Brake line fractured	Replace with new brake pipe. Bleed brakes.
	Brake system unions loose	Check all unions in brake system and tighten as necessary. Bleed brakes.
	Pad linings over 75% worn	Fit replacement pads.
	Front brakes badly out of adjustment	Jack up car and adjust brakes.
Pedal travel normal after second or third rapid application	Air in system	Bleed brakes.
Brake pedal feels springy	New pads not yet bedded-in	Use brakes gently until springy pedal feeling disappears.
	Brake discs badly worn or cracked	Fit new brake discs.
	Master cylinder securing nuts loose	Tighten master cylinder securing nuts. Ensure spring washers are fitted.
Brake pedal feels spongy and soggy	Caliper leaking	Dismantle caliper, clean, fit new rubbers and bleed brakes.
	Master cylinder leaking (bubbles in master cylinder reservoir)	Dismantle master cylinder, clean and fit new rubbers and bleed brakes. Replace cylinder if internal walls scored.
	Brake pipe line or flexible hose leaking	Fit new pipeline or hose.
	Unions in brake system loose	Examine for leaks, tighten as necessary.
	Air in system	Bleed brakes.
Excessive effort required to brake car	Pad linings badly worn	Fit replacement pads.
	New pads recently fitted - not yet bedded-in	Use brakes gently until braking effort normal.
	Harder linings fitted than standard causing increase in pedal pressure	Remove pads and replace with normal units.
	Servo vacuum pipe leaking	Renew.
	Servo air filter clogged	Renew.
	Servo unit faulty	Remove and exchange.
Brakes uneven and pulling to one side	Pads and discs contaminated with oil, grease or hydraulic fluid	Ascertain and rectify source of leak, clean discs, fit new pads.
	Tyre pressures unequal	Check and inflate as necessary.
	Radial ply tyres fitted at one end of the car only	Fit radial ply tyres of the same make to all four wheels.
	Brake caliper loose	Tighten securing nuts and bolts.
	Brake pads fitted incorrectly	Remove and fit correct way round.
	Different type of linings fitted at each wheel	Fit the pads specified by the manufacturer all round.
	Anchorages for front suspension or rear suspension loose	Tighten front and rear suspension pick-up points.
	Brake discs badly worn, cracked or distorted	Fit new brake discs.
Brakes tend to bind, drag or lock-on	Front brake pads adjusted too tightly	Slacken off adjusters.
	Air in system	Bleed brakes.
	Seized caliper	Overhaul or renew.

Chapter 9 Electrical system

Contents

Specifications

System	12 volt, Negative (-ve) earth
Battery	12 volt, lead acid, six cell, 36 ampere hours
Alternator	Rotating field with static windings for output current, built in rectification by diodes mounted in the end plate. Bosch 564 G1 or Ducellier 5764. Bosch AD1 (14V) or Ducellier 8375A
Voltage control	Mechanical type single contact
Starter Motor	Solenoid operated pinion drive with over-run clutch Bosch EF12 - 0.7PS or Ducellier 622A
Output HP	0.7
Voltage	12
Fuses	8 in single fuse box, numbered
1	Left-hand dipped beam
2	Right-hand dipped beam
3	Left-hand main beam
4	Right-hand main beam
5	Parking lights
6, 7, 8	Other main components
Windscreen wiper motor	Two-speed Bosch WS4 197 AR2A or Giagia 510875
Heated rear window	Option only

Headlights

	Alfasud	Alfasud TI
Type	Special 'square' dual Carello or Bosch	4 headlight system
Wattage	45/40W pre-focus	QI 55W
Front direction indicator bulbs	21W in headlight	21W mounted on bumper
Front parking light bulbs	5W in headlight	5W mounted on bumper

								4W mounted on front wing	4W mounted on front wing
Side indicator bulb	...	...	...	...	...	...	...	5W	5W
Rear parking lights	...	...	...	...	...	...	...	21W mounted in unit	21W mounted in unit
Indicator bulbs, reversing light bulbs, stop light bulbs					...	...	...	3W	3W
Instrument bulbs	...	...	...	...	...	...	...	5W	5W
Interior light	...	...	...	...	...	...	...	5W mounted in rear bumper	5W mounted in rear bumper
Number plate bulbs	...	...	...	...	...	...	...		

1 General description

The electrical system is of 12 volt, negative earth type and includes an alternator and voltage regulator, a pre-engaged starter motor and a range of conventional lights and accessories.

All models have their electrical circuits protected by fuses.

2 Battery - removal and replacement

1 The battery is situated at the left-hand side of the engine compartment between the inner and outer bulkhead.
2 Disconnect the earth lead (negative) from the terminal by unscrewing the shackle and twisting the terminal cover off. Do not use any striking force or damage could be caused to the battery. Then remove the positive lead in the same way. Always remove the earth terminal first.
3 Slacken off the nut holding the battery clamp until the assembly can be disengaged sufficiently to lift the battery out. The battery clamp is the base plate of the battery - it is loosened through the centre bulkhead.
4 Lift the battery out, keeping it right way up to prevent spillage of the electrolyte.
5 Replacement is a reversal of this procedure. Replace the positive lead first and smear the terminal posts and connections beforehand with petroleum jelly (not grease) in order to prevent corrosion.

3 Battery - maintenance and inspection

1 Any new battery, if properly looked after, will last for two years at least (provided also that the generator and regulator are in correct order).
2 The principal maintenance requirements are cleanliness and regular topping up of the electrolyte level with distilled water. Each week the battery cell cover or caps should be removed and just enough water added, if needed, to cover the tops of the separators. Do not overfill with the idea of the topping up lasting longer - it will only dilute the electrolyte and with the level high the likelihood of it 'gassing' out is increased. This is the moisture one can see on the top of the battery. 'Little and often' is the rule.
3 Wipe the top of the battery carefully, at the same time removing all traces of moisture. Paper handkerchiefs are ideal for the job.
4 Every three months disconnect the battery terminals and wash both the posts and lead connectors with a washing soda solution. This will remove any corrosion deposits. Dry them off and smear liberally with petroleum jelly - not grease, before reconnection.
5 If a significant quantity of electrolyte is lost through spillage it will not suffice to merely refill with distilled water. Empty out all the electrolyte into a glass container and measure the specific gravity. Electrolyte is a mixture of sulphuric acid and water in the ratio of 2 parts acid to 5 parts water and the ready made solution should be obtained from battery specialists or large garages. The 'normal' solution can be added if the battery is in fully charged state. If the battery is in a low state of charge, use the normal solution, then charge the battery, empty out the electrolyte, swill the battery out with clean water and then refill with a new charge of normal electrolyte.

4 Battery - electrolyte replenishment

1 If the battery is in a fully charged state and one of the cells maintains a specific gravity reading which is 0.025 or more lower than the others, and a check of each cell has been made with a voltage meter to check for short circuits (a four to seven second test should give a steady reading of between 1.2 and 1.8 volts), then it is likely that electrolyte has been lost from the cell with the low reading, at some time.

2 Top the cell up with a solution of 1 part sulphuric acid to 2.5 parts of water. If the cell is already fully topped up draw some electrolyte out of it with a hydrometer.
3 When mixing the sulphuric acid and water **never add water to sulphuric acid** — always pour the acid slowly onto the water in a glass container. **If water is added to sulphuric acid it will explode.**
4 Continue to top up the cell with the freshly made electrolyte and then recharge the battery and check the hydrometer readings.

5 Battery charging and precautions when charging or starting from an external source

1 In order to protect the alternator, it is essential to observe the following whenever the electrical system is being attended to, or the battery charged from an external source or the engine started by means of a stand-by battery and 'jump' leads.
2 Always make sure that the negative terminal of the battery is earthed. If the terminal connections are accidentally reversed or if the battery has been reverse charged the alternator diodes will burn out.
3 The output terminal on the alternator marked 'B+' must never be earthed but should always be connected directly to the positive terminal of the battery.
4 Whenever the alternator is to be removed or when disconnecting the terminals of the alternator circuit always disconnect the battery earth terminal first.
5 The alternator must never be operated without the battery to alternator cable connected.
6 If the battery is to be charged by external means always disconnect both battery cables before the external charge is connected.
7 Should it be necessary to use a booster charger or booster battery to start the engine always double check that the negative cable is connected to negative terminal and the positive cable to positive terminal.
8 In winter time when heavy demand is placed upon the battery, such as when starting from cold, and much electrical equipment is continually in use, it is a good idea occasionally to have the battery fully charged from an external source at the rate of 3.5 to 4 amps.
9 Continue to charge the battery at this rate until no further rise in specific gravity is noted over a four hour period.
10 Alternatively, a trickle charger charging at the rate of 1.5 amps can be safely used overnight.
11 Specially rapid 'boost' charges which are claimed to restore the power of the battery in 1 to 2 hours are not recommended as they can cause serious damage to the battery plates through overheating.
12 While charging the battery note that the temperature of the electrolyte should never exceed 100°F (37.8°C).

6 Alternator - general description

1 The alternator is of Bosch or Ducellier manufacture and varies slightly in design according to date of vehicle manufacture but the operating principle is the same.
2 The advantage of the alternator over other types of generator is that it provides a charge at much lower revolutions even at engine idling speed.
3 No maintenance is required other than keeping the driving belt correctly tensioned.

7 Alternator - removal and refitting

1 Carefully disconnect the plug-in connector for the three lower leads.
2 Slacken the mounting and adjustment bolts and push the alternator in towards the engine so that the drive belt can be slipped off the pulley.

3 Remove the mounting and adjustment bolts and lift the alternator from the engine compartment.
4 Refitting is a reversal of removal but ensure that the leads are correctly connected and that the drive belt is correctly tensioned.

8 Alternator - servicing

1 It is not recommended that the unit is tested, or dismantled beyond the operations described in this Section. Due to the sensitive nature of the alternator internal diodes, it is better to have the unit tested by an auto-electrician having the necessary equipment rather than risk damage by the use of make-shift testing circuits.
2 Unscrew the nut from the alternator driving pulley. To prevent the pulley turning during this operation, locate an old belt in the groove of the pulley and grip it in a vice as near to the pulley wheel as possible. Do not grip the pulley itself either in a vice or with a Stilson type wrench or the pulley will be distorted or damaged, which will cause subsequent failure of the driving belt.
3 To renew the carbon brushes, mark the relative positions (to each other) of the drive end bracket, the bush end housing and rear protective ring and then remove the rear protective cap (three screws).
4 Unscrew and withdraw the brush holder plate.
5 If the brushes have worn to the minimum specified length of 9 mm (0.34 in), unsolder their leads and fit new brushes. When soldering the new brush leads, localise the heat and make sure that the solder does not run into the cable covering.
6 Refitting is a reversal of removal.
7 To renew the rotor bearings, proceed as for carbon brush renewal and then unscrew the drive end bracket bolts and withdraw the drive end bracket, stator and rotor.
8 Support the drive end bracket and carefully press out the rotor from it.
9 Remove the ball race at the slip ring end using a two or three-legged puller.
10 To remove the front bearing, press the rotor from the drive end bracket and then unscrew and remove the bearing retaining plate.
11 Check the condition of the slip rings; they should be clean and smooth, otherwise polish them with fine glass paper.
12 Reassembly is a reversal of dismantling but pack the bearings with recommended grease and ensure that the bearing which is pressed into the drive end bracket has its sealed side towards the driving pulley.
13 Align the marks made on the drive end bracket, brush end housing and rear protective cover, fit the securing bolts and then locate the driving pulley and tighten the securing nut securely.

9 Voltage regulator - fault testing

1 If the ignition warning lamp comes on and does not go out when engine speed increases, first check that the alternator drive belt is not slack and slipping and also that the cable connections are secure.
2 Pull out the plug from the rear of the alternator and bridge the 'D+' and 'DF' tags of the plug.
3 Start the engine and run it up to 2000 rev/min. If the ignition warning lamp goes out immediately, the voltage regulator is defective and must be renewed. Do not run the engine at a speed higher than 2000 rev/min with the plug leads bridged or the electrical accessories may be damaged due to current being produced with too high a voltage.
4 If the warning lamp stays on or flashes on and off then it is the alternator which is defective and should be repaired or renewed.

10 Starter motor - general description

The starter motor is of the pre-engaged type. When the ignition key is turned, the solenoid is energised and moves the forked engagement lever, which in turn, meshes the pinion assembly with the ring gear of the flywheel. It is then that the main starter motor contacts close and the flywheel is rotated to start the engine.
Incorporated in the pinion assembly is a clutch device which ensures that the drive pinion is disengaged from the flywheel ring gear as soon as the engine fires and the engine speed exceeds that of the starter motor.

11 Starter motor - removal and installation

1 Disconnect the lead from the battery negative terminal.
2 Disconnect the cables from the solenoid and starter terminals.
3 Unscrew the two starter securing bolts and withdraw the starter motor.
4 Installation is a reversal of removal.

12 Starter motor - dismantling, inspection and reassembly

1 Disconnect the lead from the motor field windings at the solenoid lower terminal nut.
2 Unscrew and remove the two screws which secure the solenoid to the drive end bracket.
3 Unhook the solenoid plunger from the pinion engagement lever and withdraw the solenoid switch.
4 From the commutator end, unscrew and remove the protective cap and extract the 'U' washer, the shims and rubber washer.
5 Unscrew the two tie-bolts and remove the commutator end cover.
6 Using a piece of bent wire, pull back the brush springs so that the brushes can be withdrawn from their holders.
7 Remove the brush holder plate, fibre and steel washers. If the brushes are worn, their leads should be disconnected from the brush holder plate and the field winding terminal tags by using a soldering iron. Refit the new brushes, taking care to localise the heat, particularly in the case of the field winding leads.
8 Separate the starter yoke from the drive end bracket and then unscrew the pinion engagement lever pivot bolt.
9 Extract the rubber plug and steel washer from the drive end bracket.
10 Withdraw the armature complete with drive pinion and engagement lever from the drive end bracket. Detach the engagement lever from the drive pinion assembly.
11 Examine the condition of the commutator at the end of the armature. If it is burned or blackened it should be polished with very fine glass paper (not emery). Do not undercut the mica separators between the commutator segments.
12 If the drive pinion is sticky in operation, wash it thoroughly in paraffin and apply a trace of light oil to the spiral threads on the commutator shaft. If the drive pinion must be dismantled for renewal of a component, drive the stop washer down the shaft to expose the circlips, using a piece of tubing. Extract the circlip and pull off the stop washer and drive pinion assembly.
13 Refitting the pinion assembly is a reversal of removal but use a new stop washer and circlip. Having driven the new stop washer down the shaft to enable the circlip to be located in its groove, the stop washer may be drawn back into position by using a two legged extractor.
14 Reassembly is a reversal of dismantling but the commutator endfloat must be between 0.05 and 0.3 mm (0.002 and 0.012 in). If it is outside this tolerance then the shim pack within the commutator protective cap should be adjusted.

13 Starter motor - testing in position

1 If the starter motor fails to operate then check the condition of the battery by turning on the headlamps. If they glow brightly for several seconds and then gradually dim the battery is in an uncharged condition.
2 If the headlights glow brightly and it is obvious that the battery is in good condition, then check the tightness of the battery wiring connections (and in particular the earth lead from the battery terminal to its connection on the body frame). If the positive terminal on the battery becomes hot when an attempt is made to work the starter this is a sure sign of a poor connection on the battery terminal. To rectify, remove the terminal, clean the mating faces thoroughly and reconnect. Check the connections on the rear of the starter solenoid. Check the wiring with a voltmeter or test lamp for breaks or shorts.
3 Test the continuity of the solenoid windings by connecting a test lamp (low wattage) and 12 volt battery between the solenoid main terminal nut nearest the starter motor and the solenoid body. If the two windings are in order, the lamp will light. Now connect the test lamp (high wattage bulb) between the two main terminals of the solenoid. Energise the solenoid by applying a 12 volt supply between the terminal

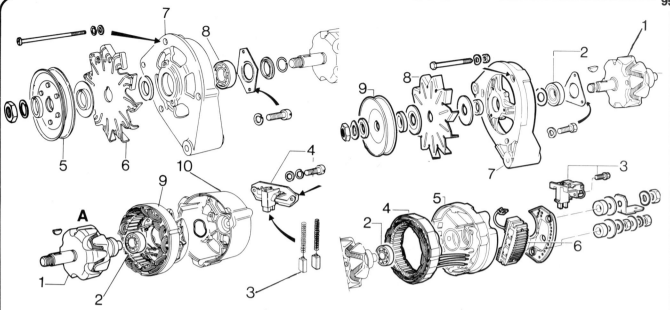

Fig. 9.1. Bosch alternator components

1	Rotor	6	Fan
2	Bearing	7	Front of body
3	Brushes	8	Bearing
4	Brush holder	9	Stator
5	Pulley	10	Body

Fig. 9.2. Ducellier alternator components

1	Rotor	6	Diodes
2	Bearing	7	Front of body
3	Brush holder	8	Fan
4	Stator	9	Pulley
5	Housing		

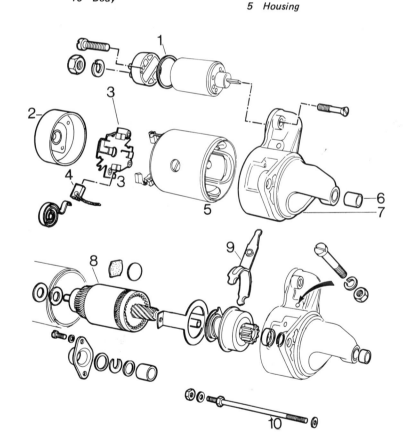

Fig. 9.3. Bosch starter motor components

1	Solenoid	4	Brushes	7	End cap	9	Yoke
2	End cover	5	Body	8	Armature	10	Through bolts
3	Brush holder	6	Bush				

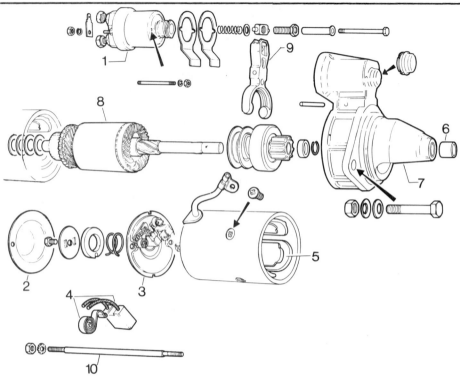

Fig. 9.4. Ducellier starter motor components
1   Solenoid
2   End cover
3   Brush holder
4   Brushes
5   Body
6   Bush
7   End cap
8   Armature
9   Yoke
10   Through studs

"3" and the solenoid body. The solenoid should be heard to operate and the test bulb will illuminate.

4   If the battery is fully charged, the wiring in order, and the starter/ignition switch working and the starter motor still fails to operate, then it will have to be removed from the car for examination. Before this is done ensure that the starter motor pinion has not jammed in mesh with the flywheel by engaging a gear and rocking the car to and fro. This should free the pinion if it is stuck in mesh with the flywheel teeth.

14 Fuses

1   A bank of 5 8-amp fuses and 3 16-amp fuses is located on the left-hand side inner wing just below the windscreen. It has a clear plastic cover.

2   Always renew a fuse with one of the same rating and if the same fuse blows twice in succession, thoroughly check the circuit for shorting, also the electrical accessories which are served by it.

15 Headlamps and switches

1   The twin headlamps of the Alfasud are 'special' to it. They are rectangular in shape, incorporating in them on their outer edges the side and indicator lenses. They use prefocus bulbs which are replaceable.

2   The round headlamps of the Alfasud TI are in pairs, four in number. Each one uses a quartz halogen bulb - the dip or inner lamps have single filament bulbs which remain ignited when the outer or main beam bulbs are switched through. The side lights are incorporated in one lamp, and the indicator lamps are separate fittings mounted on the bumper.

3   The lighting switches, on-off and dip switch are integral with the wiper and horn switches, are mounted on the steering column and operated by stalks. Their removal, servicing and replacement are dealt with in Chapter 10, Section 18 as they have become part of the steering mechanism.

16 Headlamp bulb renewal

Alfasud

1   From under the bonnet free the headlamp inner protective cover by pushing round the spring clip. Remove the cover and sealing rubber.

2   A spring clip holds the bulb in the lens. Pull off the electrical feed

plug from the back of the bulb and then twist the bulb/holder in an anticlockwise direction and remove the bulb.

3   Replacement is straightforward. Make sure the bulb is fitted into the 'correct' slots, replace the feed plug and refit the cover.

4   Bulb filaments break. Handle the bulb carefully.

Alfasud TI

5   A similar procedure exists. Pull off the rubber rear cover gently. Pull off the feed connectors.

6   Unhook the wire holding frame at the rear of the bulb and carefully hinge it downwards.

7   Grip the halogen bulb by the electrical connector and withdraw it, still with the round cap plate attached.

8   Replacement is a reverse procedure.

9   **Do not** touch the 'bulb' with your fingers (if you do, clean the 'bulb' with methylated spirits). Halogen bulbs are expensive; they become very hot, hence the moisture taken from one's fingers will fry and ruin the bulb.

10   The dipped beams come from the inner lamps.

17 Headlamp - unit renewal

Alfasud

1   It is not possible to replace any components of the headlamp (integral with side/indicators) unit - it must be renewed as a complete, expensive unit. Obviously bulbs are replaceable. Open the bonnet and remove the back cover, the headlamp bulb electrical connector and the side/indicator electrical connector.

2   Undo the one fixing nut, also the earth location, on the inner edge of the unit. Pull off the earth wire, then pull away the unit off the locating stud and remove the unit. The other edge of the unit tucks into the appropriately shaped location in the bodyshell.

3   Replacement is a reverse procedure. Adjust the headlamp beam direction.

Alfasud TI

4   Although each headlamp is separate, a pair must be removed at one time as they are mounted together.

5   Removal of the pair uses a similar procedure as for one of the Alfasud's. Once removed each lamp can be removed from the mounting by releasing the tension springs and adjusters which locate.

6   Replacement is a reverse procedure. Adjust the headlamp beam direction.

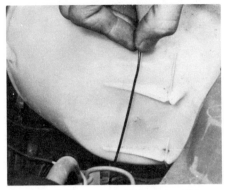

14.1 Location of the fuse box under the bonnet   16.1 The plastic cover and thin spring clip   16.2 A usual method of headlamp location

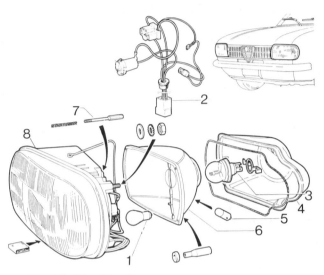

Fig. 9.5. Alfasud headlamps

1	Flasher bulb	5	Side light bulb
2	Complete headlamp harness	6	Shell
3	Headlamp bulb	7	Adjuster screw
4	Back cover	8	Glass complete

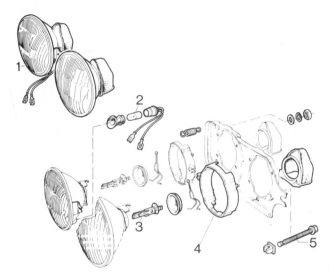

Fig. 9.6. Alfasud TI headlamps

1	Headlamp glass complete	4	Locking rim
2	Side light bulb	5	Adjuster screw
3	QI bulb		

18 Headlamps - Alfasud - alignment

1 Headlamp adjustment is best done using proper optical equipment at your local Alfa Romeo agency. Should you require to do-it-yourself, the car must be placed in an unladen condition, on level ground, at right angles to a wall some 25 feet from it. On main beam the centre of the two headlamp beams must be parallel to the centreline of the car, if drawn out to the wall. On dipped beam the height of the horizontal cut-off to the left of the illuminated area must be between 4 to 6 inches less than the headlight centres.

2 Adjustment is made from under the bonnet. Two adjuster screws are located on the rear of the headlamp, on opposite diagonals. Up-and-down and side-to-side adjustment is available - use both adjusters.

19 Headlamps - Alfasud TI - alignment

1 Although the Alfasud TI has four headlamps, mounted in pairs, they are not individually adjusted. They are adjusted in pairs, using the same method as the two headlamp Alfasud. See Section 18.

20 Front parking and direction indicator lamps - bulb renewal and lamp replacement

Alfasud

1 The front parking (or side) and direction indicator lamps are

integral with the headlamps. To replace the bulb, it is a double filament bulb remove the plastic rear cover of the whole headlamp unit - see Section 16.

2 Pull out the bulb socket - it is a push fit - and unscrew the bayonet type bulb from the socket. Leave the electrical connector connected.

3 Renew the bulb and replace in a reverse sequence.

4 If the parking/indicator part of the lens is broken, the **whole** headlamp has to be replaced.

Alfasud TI

5 The side light bulb is a push-in socket in one of two of the headlamps. It is removed and replaced in a strictly conventional manner. See the renewal of headlamp bulbs of the Alfasud TI, Section 16.

6 The indicator lamps are mounted on the front bumper below each outer headlamp. The bulbs are removed and replaced once the screws fixing the lens to the lamp housing are undone and the lens and its rubber surround removed. The bulbs are bayonet fixing.

7 The lamps themselves are fixed to the bumper by two integral studs and nuts. Undo the nuts from below the bumper, disconnect the wiring to the indicator from inside the bonnet under the headlamps at the junction.

8 Replacement is straightforward.

Both models

9 Both models have front/side indicator lamps, one on each front wing. Each lamp is a simple push-in fit. It is necessary to release the whole lamp to replace a bulb. Pull off the socket from the unit/lens once it is released. The bulb is a bayonet fixing.

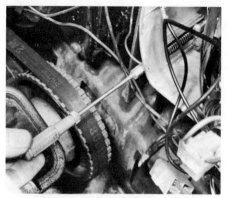
18.2 One of the adjuster screws. A short screwdriver is essential

20.1a The side light bulb is usually pushed up into the holder

20.1b The flasher bulb, on RHD version, is located this way ...

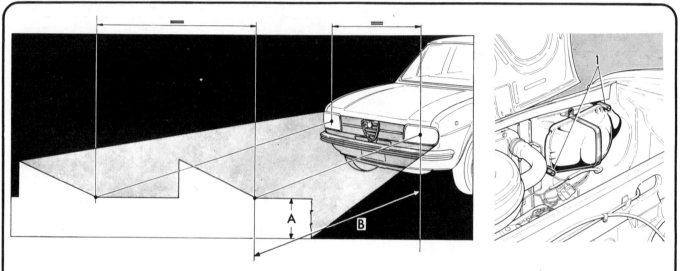

Fig. 9.7. RHD headlamp beam pattern

A = 37 cm
B = 10 metres
For LHD cars the pattern is equal and opposite

Fig. 9.8. Headlamp beam adjusting screws

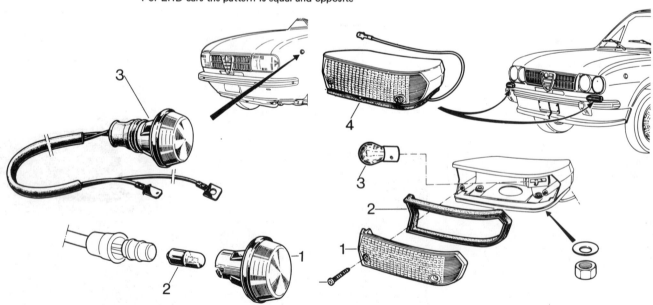

Fig. 9.9. Side light components

1 Lens   2 Bulb   3 Light complete

Fig. 9.10. Front flasher lights - Alfasud TI - components

1 Lens   3 Bulb
2 Rubber surround   4 Light complete

21 Rear stop, tail, direction indicator and reversing lamps - bulb renewal and lamp replacement

1   Each rear lamp cluster contains a single lens for the stop, indicator and reversing lamps. The registration number lamp is a separate unit mounted on the rear bumper. A separate reflector is stuck to the bodywork beneath each cluster.
2   To replace any of the bulbs in the cluster, remove the four lens screws. Each of the bulbs is a bayonet fixing.
3   The cluster unit is fixed to the bodywork by bolts, not screws. These have square heads - their hexagonal nuts must be undone from inside the rear wing.
4   An electrical wiring junction box is inside the rear wing. This should be disconnected before the cluster is removed.
5   Replacement is straightforward. Make sure the lens seal is in place.
6   The registration number lamp has two single-filament bulbs. The lens and lens cover are removed once the single fixing screw is removed. The bulbs are bayonet fixing. The unit itself is a push-in fit on the bumper.
7   The electrical connections for this lamp are inside the boot.

22 Direction indicators (flashers) - servicing

1   Flasher units either work or they don't. If you experience trouble, first check that each bulb in the circuit is functioning. If not, replace it. If the circuit still doesn't work properly, this time in either 'direction', seek out the flasher unit. It is located on the inner bulkhead.
2   Remove the unit and replace it. If it still doesn't function and you are certain the circuits are complete, investigate the switch at the steering column. If this needs to be renewed, for no repair is available, it will be expensive. See Section 15 about the switch.

23 Interior light

1   The interior light is in the centre of the roof panel. It is operated either automatically from switches in the front door pillars or manually from a switch on its lens.
2   To replace the bulb, unscrew the two screws which fix the lens. The lens comes away easily. The bulb is a torpedo type.
3   The unit itself is fixed to the roof panel by the lens screws.
4   The 'courtesy' switches are located in each front door hinge pillar by a screw. These are easily removed.

24 Horn

1   The horn switch is dealt with in Section 16.
2   The horn is located under the front of the car behind the small grille beneath the left hand headlamp. It is fixed by one stud and nut.
3   If the horn is inoperative, see Section 30, it is easily replaced. Make sure that the 'horn' does not point upwards so as to fill with water.

25 Instruments - removal and refitting

1   It is not necessary to remove the dashboard to remove the instrument cluster. This is done easily by removing the four screws, two set diagonally on each circular instrument, and carefully easing the 'cluster' away from the dashboard.
2   Disconnect the speedometer drive cable from behind the speedometer. Do this with a pair of grips. Carefully note the wiring connections and delicately disconnect them.
3   The instruments are located from behind by small screws. If you wish to remove them, do so carefully. It is simple but delicate. The instrument bulbs are push-in fits, from behind.
4   Little can be done to any of the instruments at home. See Figs. 9.13 and 9.15 for the breakdown.
5   Replacement is a straight reverse process to their removal.

26 Windscreen wipers - description, maintenance and adjustment

1   The wiper mechanism comprises an electrical motor mounted on the engine compartment rear bulkhead driving mechanical linkage through a crank secured to the wiper motor spindle.
2   Maintenance is minimal as the motor bearings and gears are grease packed in production. Occasionally check the security of the connecting wiring.
3   Every two years, or earlier if they fail to wipe clean, renew the wiper blades.
4   Obviously wiper blade parking is adjusted by 'replacing' the wiper arm on the spindle once the wipers are 'parked'.

27 Windscreen wiper motor and linkage - removal and refitting

1   The wiper motor is fixed to the wiper linkage. Do not attempt to work on either the motor or the linkage without removing the whole unit first.
2   To remove the whole unit, first remove the wiper blades and arms, from their driving spindles.
3   Unscrew and remove the spindle housing nuts, washers and distance pieces from the front of the scuttle. Disconnect the wiper motor electrical connection. Remove the motor fixing plate setscrew from the bulkhead having first removed the cross-ducting parallel to the scuttle.
4   Now juggle out the complete wiper motor and linkage.
5   Once free, to remove the motor, remove the circlip from the motor crank to linkage connection. This is rather inaccessible being located below the motor mounting plate.
6   Carefully retain the mounting plate rubber insulators, and remove the motor.
7   The linkage has to be "pulled" apart, and new washer/bushes refitted.
8   The whole unit is reassembled in a reverse sequence.
9   Wiper motors are not repairable.

21.1 The complete lens comes away this way ...

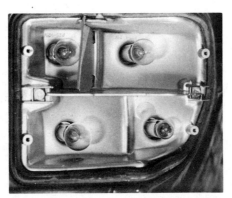

21.2 ... and reveals four bulbs like this

21.6 The number plate light has two bulbs

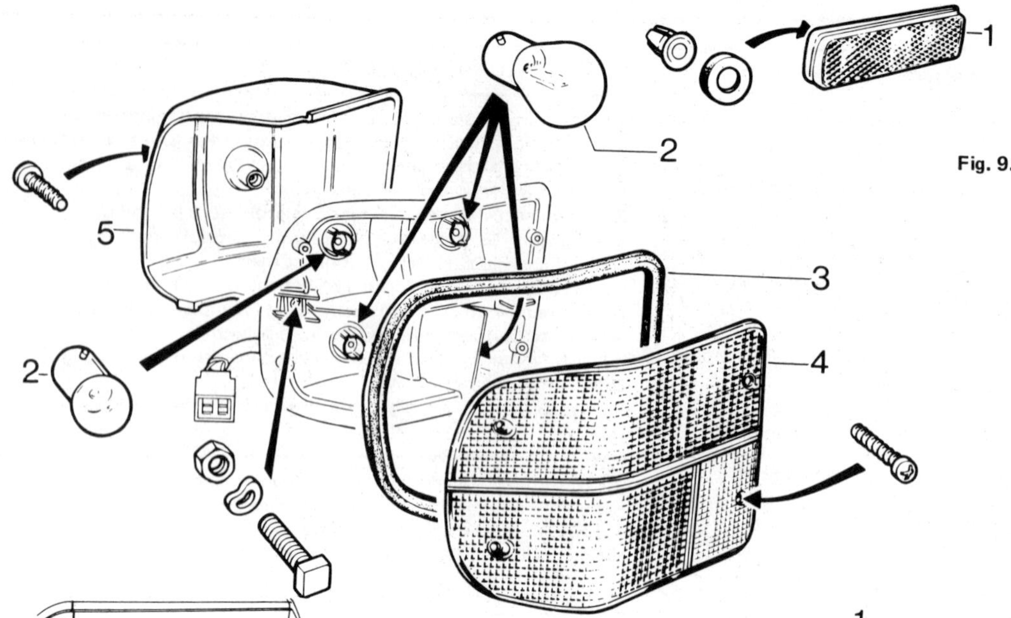

Fig. 9.11. Rear lights and reflector

1 Stick-on reflector
2 Bulbs
3 Rubber surround
4 Lens
5 Shell

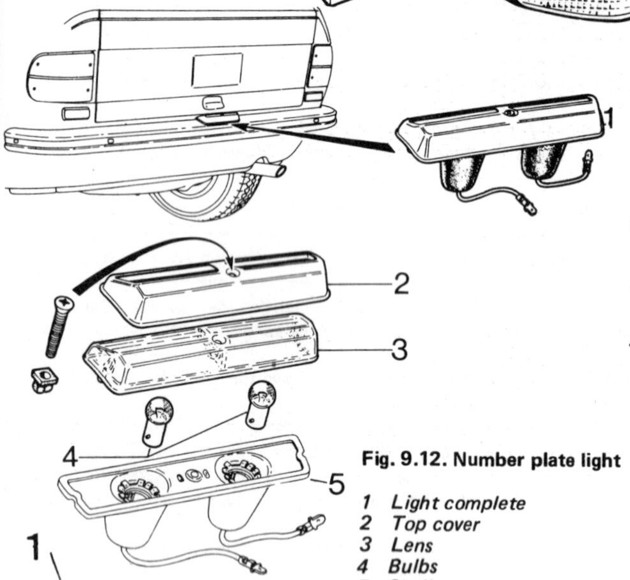

Fig. 9.12. Number plate light

1 Light complete
2 Top cover
3 Lens
4 Bulbs
5 Shell

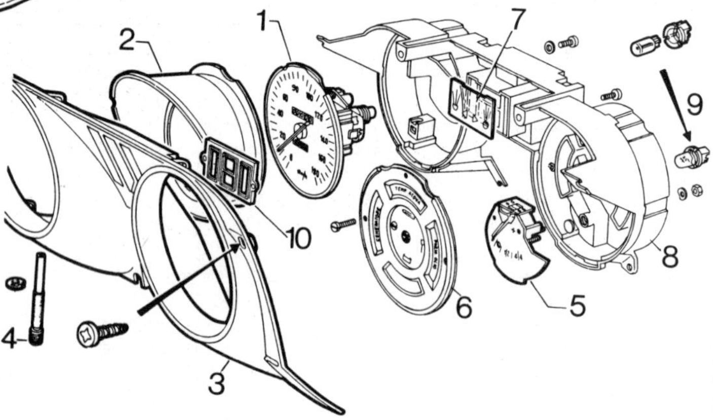

Fig. 9.13. Alfasud instruments

1 Speedometer
2 Cowl
3 Outer cowl
4 Trip adjuster
5 Fuel gauge
6 Outer face
7 Lens
8 Inner housing
9 Bulbs
10 Outer face

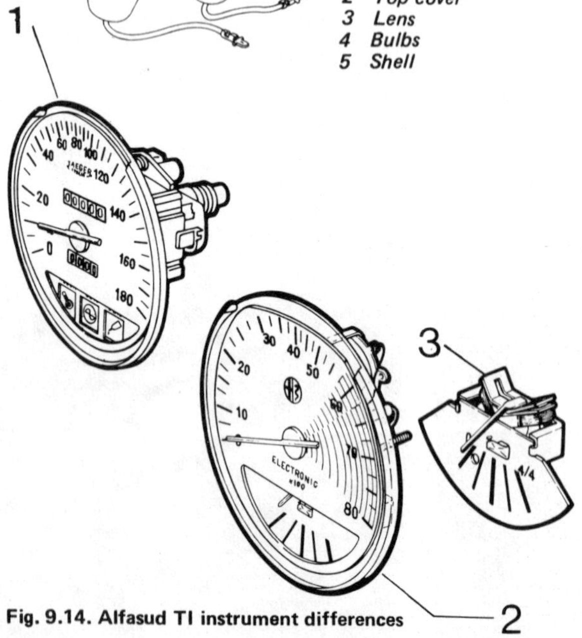

Fig. 9.14. Alfasud TI instrument differences

1 Different speedometer head
2 Rev counter with fuel gauge
3 Fuel gauge for use with rev counter

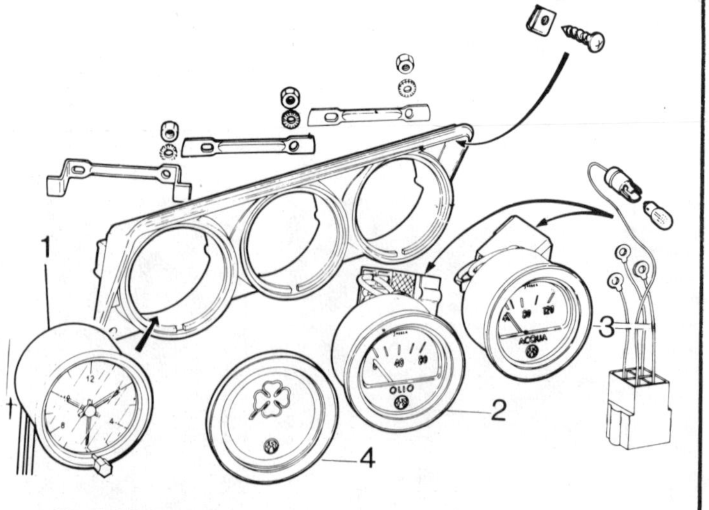

Fig. 9.15. Additional instruments for Alfasud TI

1 Clock
2 Oil pressure
3 Water temperature
4 Cover for cars not fitted with a clock

26.3 New blades are easy to fit. Press up the clip

26.4 Park the wipers first, then spline on the arm

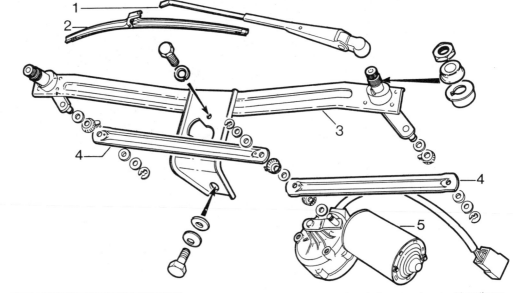

Fig. 9.16. Typical windscreen wiper arrangement

1 *Arm*
2 *Blade*
3 *Mechanism frame*
4 *Outriggers*
5 *Motor*

28 Windscreen wiper motor - repair and overhaul

1 It is not possible to overhaul wiper motors at home as parts are not readily available.
2 Take your wiper motor to an auto-electrician or to an Alfa Romeo agency.

29 Radio - guide to installation

1 Installation of a car radio is really a job for a professional but where the fitting is being undertaken by the home mechanic, then the following guide lines should be borne in mind.
2 The receiver should be located in the instrument panel or glove compartment.
3 The recommended position for the aerial is on the left-hand front wing or above the windscreen in the centre, as remote as possible from the ignition coil.
4 Connect the receiver to the ignition switch or the spare terminal of the fuse block.
5 Always include a cartridge type fuse in the feed line to the receiver.
6 Check that the receiver is of negative earth type or is suitable for conversion to this polarity.
7 Ensure that the ignition system is adequately suppressed and be

prepared to add suppressors to the windscreen wiper and headlamp wiper motors if they cause interference once the radio receiver is installed.

30 Auxiliary lamps - guide to fitting

1 The Alfasud has reasonable headlamps of the conventional type because the lens are large. The Alfasud TI has four quartz halogen lamps - these are much better. It would be expensive to use these lamps in the Alfasud. It is not recommended that quartz halogen bulbs be fitted to the Alfasud (for they will 'fit') because the beam becomes mis-shapen. It is possible to fit extra lamps to both models.
2 Choose lamps which have brackets designed for the vehicle or are of universal fitting pattern.
3 Locate the operating switches conveniently to hand where they will not be masked by other controls or the steering wheel.
4 Connect the supply cable through the fuse box and ensure that all electrical leads are of suitable diameter to carry the required current.
5 Remember UK regulations demand that lamps are fitted as a pair and mounted so that their centres are at least 61 cm (24 in) but not more than 106 cm (42 in) from the ground and not more than 40 cm (16 in) from the outer extremities of the vehicle. Failure to observe the mounting conditions means that the lamps can only be used in fog or falling snow.

31 Fault diagnosis - electrical system

Symptom	Reason/s
Starter motor fails to turn engine	
No electricity at starter motor	Battery discharged.
	Battery defective internally.
	Battery terminal leads loose or earth lead not securely attached to body.
	Loose or broken connections in starter motor circuit.
	Starter motor switch or solenoid faulty.
Electricity at starter motor: faulty motor	Starter motor pinion jammed in mesh with flywheel gear ring.
	Starter brushes badly worn, sticking, or brush wires loose.
	Commutator dirty, worn or burnt.
	Starter motor armature faulty.
	Field coils earthed.
Starter motor turns engine very slowly	
Electrical defects	Battery in discharged condition.
	Starter brushes badly worn, sticking, or brush wires loose.
	Loose wires in starter motor circuit,
Starter motor operates without turning engine	
Mechanical damage	Pinion or flywheel gear teeth broken or worn.
Starter motor noisy or excessively rough engagement	
Lack of attention or mechanical damage	Pinion or flywheel gear teeth broken or worn.
	Starter motor retaining bolts loose.
Battery will not hold charge for more than a few days	
Wear or damage	Battery defective internally.
	Electrolyte level too low or electrolyte too weak due to leakage.
	Plate separators no longer fully effective.
	Battery plates severely sulphated.
Insufficient current flow to keep battery charged	Battery plates severely sulphated.
	Fan belt slipping.
	Battery terminal connections loose or corroded.
	Alternator not charging.
	Short in lighting circuit causing continual battery drain.
	Regulator unit not working correctly.
Ignition light fails to go out, battery runs flat in a few days	
Alternator not charging	Fan belt loose and slipping or broken.
	Brushes worn, sticking, broken or dirty.
	Brush springs weak or broken.
	Commutator dirty, greasy, worn or burnt.
	Alternator field coils burnt, open, or shorted.
	Commutator worn.
	Pole pieces very loose.
Regulator or cut-out fails to work correctly	Regulator incorrectly set.
	Cut-out incorrectly set.
	Open circuit in wiring of cut-out and regulator unit.
Horn	
Horn operates all the time	Horn push either earthed or stuck down.
	Horn cable to horn push earthed.
Horn fails to operate	Blown fuse.
	Cable or cable connection loose, broken or disconnected.
	Horn has an internal fault.
Horn emits intermittent or unsatisfactory noise	Cable connections loose
	Horn incorrectly adjusted.
Lights	
Lights do not come on	If engine not running, battery discharged.
	Sealed beam filament burnt out or bulbs broken.
	Wire connections loose, disconnected or broken.
	Light switch shorting or otherwise faulty.

Symptom	Reason/s
Lights come on but fade out	If engine not running battery discharged. Light bulb filament burnt out or bulbs or sealed beam units broken. Wire connections loose, disconnected or broken. Light switch shorting or otherwise faulty.
Lights give very poor illumination	Lamp glasses dirty. Lamp badly out of adjustment.
Lights work erratically - flashing on and off, especially over bumps	Battery terminals or earth connection loose. Light not earthing properly. Contacts in light switch faulty.

Wipers

Symptom	Reason/s
Wiper motor fails to work	Blown fuse. Wire connections loose, disconnected, or broken. Brushes badly worn. Armature worn or faulty. Field coils faulty.
Wiper motor works very slowly and takes excessive current	Commutator dirty, greasy or burnt. Armature bearings dirty or unaligned. Armature badly worn or faulty.
Wiper motor works slowly and takes little current	Brushes badly worn. Commutator dirty, greasy or burnt. Armature badly worn or faulty.
Wiper motor works but wiper blades remain static	Wiper motor gearbox parts badly worn.
Wipers do not stop when switched off or stop in wrong place	Auto-stop device faulty

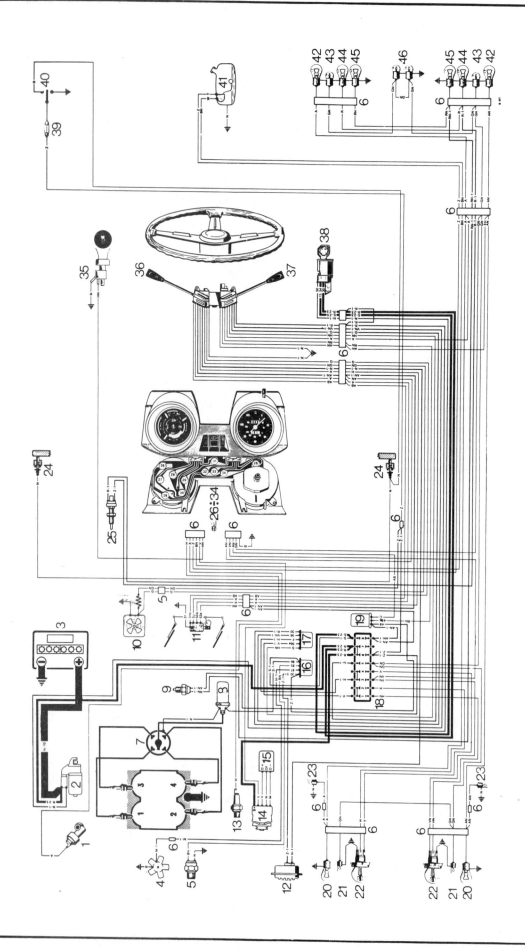

Fig. 9.17. Wiring diagram - Alfasud (RHD cars)

Fig. 9.17. Wiring diagram - Alfasud (RHD cars)

1	Thermostatic switch	25	Stop lights switch
2	Starting motor	26	Instrument light bulb 3W
3	Battery	27	Oil pressure warning light bulb 3W
4	Electric fan	28	Coolant temperature warning light bulb 3W
5	Thermal switch for electric fan	29	Alternator warning light bulb 3W
6	Junction boxes and connectors	30	Fuel reserve warning light bulb 3W
7	Distributor	31	Choke warning light bulb 3W
8	Coil	32	High beam warning light bulb 3W
9	Reversing light switch (optional)	33	Direction indicator warning light bulb 3W
10	Blower motor (two speed)	34	Parking light warning bulb 3W
11	Windscreen wiper (two speed)	35	Choke warning light switch
12	Horn	36	Switch for blower motor, windscreen wiper motor, horn control
13	Oil pressure switch	37	Direction indicators, parking lights, headlamps and flashing switch
14	Alternator	38	Ignition and starting switch
15	Voltage regulator	39	Courtesy light bulb 5W
16	Relay for electric fan	40	Courtesy light toggle switch in light unit
17	Relay for headlamp	41	Fuel level sender
18	Fusebox	42	Rear direction indicators bulb 21W
19	Flasher unit	43	Rear parking lights bulb 5W
20	Front direction indicators bulb 21W	44	Stop lights bulb 21W
21	Front parking lights bulb 4W	45	Reversing lights bulb 21W
22	Headlamp Hi/Low bulb 45/40W	46	Number plate light bulb 5W
23	Side direction indicator bulb 4W		
24	Microswitch on door jambs for courtesy light		

Cable colour code

A	blue	VI	violet
G	yellow	AB	blue/white
Gr	grey	AN	blue/black
M	brown	BN	white/black
N	black	GN	yellow/black
Rs	red	GrN	grey/black
R	pink	RsN	red/black
V	green	VN	green/black

The figure following the colour code on the diagram shows the wire gauge in mm^2. Where not shown the wire gauge is 0.5 mm^2.

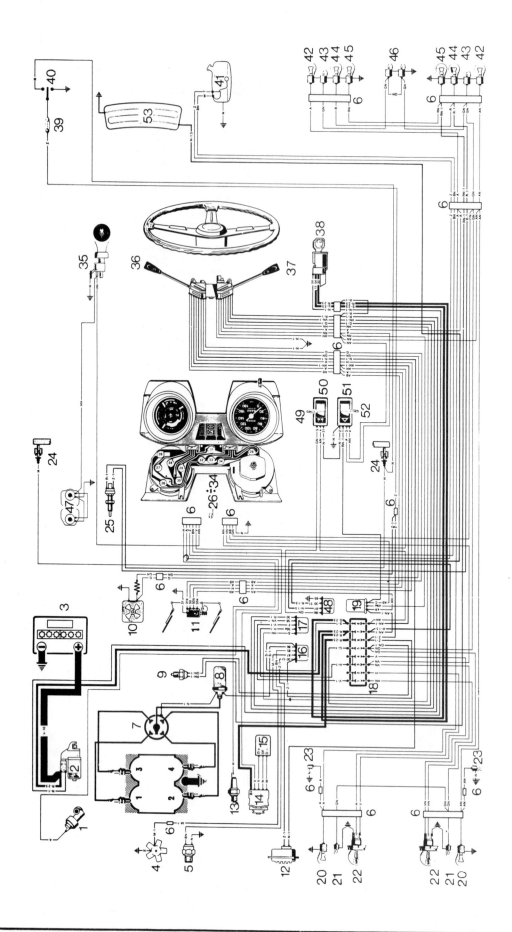

Fig. 9.18. Wiring diagram — Alfasud (LHD cars)

Fig. 9.18. Wiring diagram - Alfasud (LHD cars)

1	Thermostatic switch
2	Starting motor
3	Battery
4	Electric fan
5	Thermal switch for electric fan
6	Junction boxes and connectors
7	Distributor
8	Coil
9	Reversing light switch (optional)
10	Blower motor (two speed)
11	Windscreen wiper (two speed)
12	Horn
13	Oil pressure switch
14	Alternator
15	Voltage regulator
16	Relay for electric fan
17	Relay for headlamp
18	Fusebox
19	Flasher unit
20	Front direction indicators bulb 21W
21	Front parking lights bulb AW
22	Headlamp Hi/Low bulb 45/40W
23	Side direction indicator bulb 4W
24	Microswitch on door jambs for courtesy light
25	Stop lights switch
26	Instrument light bulb 3W
27	Oil pressure warning light bulb 3W
28	Coolant temperature warning light bulb 3W
29	Alternator warning light bulb 3W
30	Fuel reserve warning light bulb 3W
31	Bulb for low brake fluid level and choke warning light
32	High beam warning light bulb 3W
33	Direction indicator warning light bulb 3W
34	Parking light warning bulb 3W
35	Switch for choke warning light
36	Switch for blower motor, windscreen wiper motor, horn control
37	Direction indicators, parking lights, headlamps and flashing switch
38	Ignition and starting switch
39	Courtesy light bulb 5W
40	Courtesy light toggle switch in light unit
41	Fuel level sender
42	Rear direction indicators bulb 21W
43	Rear parking lights bulb 5W
44	Stop lights bulb 21W
45	Reversing lights bulb 21W
46	Number plate light bulb 5W
47	Switches for low brake fluid level warning light (export to Sweden and Norway)
48	Bulb for road hazard light telltale
49	Switch and telltale unit for road hazard light (Sweden and Norway)
50	Relay for heated rear window
51	Switch for heated rear window
52	Heated rear window (Sweden and Norway)
53	Bulb of heated window telltale in push button switch

Cable colour code

A	blue		VI	violet
G	yellow		AB	blue/white
Gr	grey		AN	blue/black
M	brown		BN	white/black
N	black		GN	yellow/black
Rs	red		GrN	grey/black
R	pink		RsN	red/black
V	green		VN	green/black

The figure following the colour code on the diagram shows the wire gauge in mm^2. Where not shown the wire gauge is 0.5 mm^2.

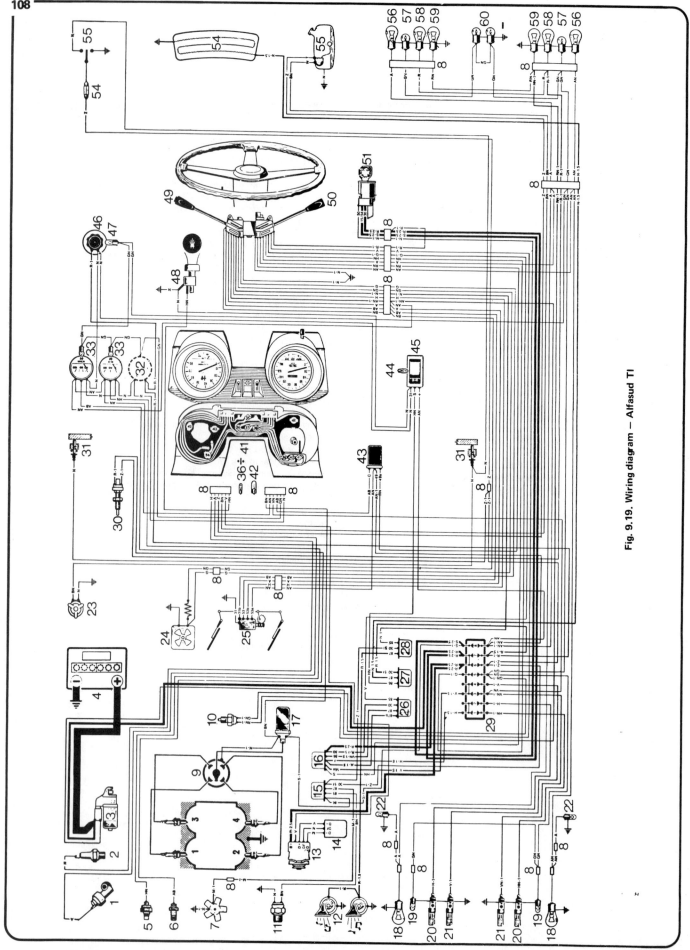

Fig. 9.19. Wiring diagram – Alfasud TI

Fig. 9.19. Wiring diagram - Alfasud TI

1 Thermostatic switch
2 Oil pressure switch
3 Starting motor
4 Battery 12V 43 Ah
5 Oil pressure gauge sender
6 Coolant thermometer sender
7 Electric fan
8 Junction boxes and connectors
9 Distributor
10 Reversing light switch
11 Thermal switch for electric fan
12 Horn
13 Alternator
14 Voltage regulator
15 Relay for electric fan
16 Relay for headlamp
17 Coil
18 Front direction indicators bulb 21W
19 Front parking lights bulb 4W
20 Headlamp low beam bulb 55W halogen
21 Headlamp high beam bulb 55W halogen
22 Side direction indicator bulb 4W
23 Screen washer electrical pump
24 Blower motor (two speed)
25 Windscreen wiper (two speed)
26 Relay for flashing and dipping
27 Relay for heated rear window
28 Horn relay
29 Fusebox
30 Stop lights switch
31 Microswitch on door jambs for courtesy light
32 Provision for electric clock

33 Coolant thermometer and oil gauge light bulb 3W
34 Fuel reserve warning light bulb 1,2W
35 Bulb for choke warning light 1,2W
36 High beam warning light bulb 1,2W
37 Direction indicator warning light bulb 1,2W
38 Parking light warning bulb 1,2W
39 Oil pressure warning light bulb 1,2W
40 Alternator warning light bulb 1,2W
41 Coolant temperature warning light bulb 1,2W
42 Tachometer and speedometer light bulb 3W
43 Relay for direction indicators
44 Bulb of heated window telltale 1,2W
45 Switch for heated rear window
46 Cigarette lighter
47 Cigarette lighter lamp bulb 4W
48 Switch for choke warning light
49 Switch for blower motor, windscreen wiper motor, horn control, screen washer
50 Direction indicators, parking lights, headlamps and flashing switch
51 Ignition and starting switch
52 Courtesy light bulb 5W
53 Courtesy light switch
54 Heated rear window
55 Fuel level sender
56 Rear direction indicators bulb 21W
57 Rear parking lights bulb 5W
58 Stop lights bulb 21W
59 Reversing lights bulb 21W
60 Number plate light bulb 5W

Cable colour code

A blue
G yellow
H grey
M brown
N black
R red
S pink
V green

Z violet
AB blue/white
AN blue/black
BN white/black
GN yellow/black ·
HH grey/black
RN red/black
VN green/black

The figure following the colour code on the diagram shows the wire gauge in mm^2. Where not shown the wire gauge is 0.5 mm^2.

Plate on fusebox

1 LH low beam
2 RH low beam
3 LH high beam
4 RH high beam
5 Parking lights
6,7,8 Main devices

Chapter 10 Suspension and steering

Contents

Specifications

Wheelbase	2464 mm (8ft 1in)
Front track	1372 mm (4ft 6in)
Rear track	1346 mm (4ft 5in)
Minimum ground clearance	140 mm (5.5 in)
Front suspension	Independent by MacPherson strut, transverse link, coil springs and anti-roll bar
Rear suspension	Beam axle, non-independent, Watt linkages, Panhard rod and coil springs and telescopic shockabsorbers

Spring length
Front	173.5 mm (6.76 in)
Rear	231.5 mm (9.02 in)

Steering
Steering	Rack and pinion with steering wheel adjustable for height
Number of turns, lock-to-lock	3.69

Steering geometry
Front toe-out	2 ± 1 mm
Front camber	$20^o 12' \pm 30'$
Castor	$0^o 22' \pm 30'$
Rear toe-in	Parallel $\pm 25'$

Torque wrench settings
Steering

	lb f ft	kg f m
Steering track arms to rack nuts	28.9 - 35.4	4 - 4.9
Track arm to suspension leg nuts	28.9 - 31.7	4 - 4.5
Track rod adjuster nut	40.4 - 50.6	5.6 - 7
Rack to body bolts	10 - 17	1.4 - 2.4
Steering column pinch bolt	10.8 - 17	1.5 - 2.4
Steering wheel to column nuts	8.6 - 10.8	1.2 - 1.5
Steering column bracket to body bolt	10.8 - 17	1.5 - 2.4

Torque wrench settings (contd)

	lb f ft	kg f m
Front suspension		
Stabilizer bar to suspension arm bolts	10.8 - 17	1.5 - 2.4
Crossmember to body	50.6 - 62.8	7 - 8.7
Wheel nuts	46.9 - 57.8	6.5 - 8
Bearing carrier to strut bolts	40.4 - 49.8	5.6 - 6.9
Bottom ball-joint clamp bolt	28.9 - 35.4	4 - 4.9
Bearing carrier oil seal cover bolt	13.7 - 17.2	1.9 - 2.4
Front hub bearing ring nut	20.9 - 25.2	2.9 - 3.5
Suspension arm to crossmember	38.9 - 62.8	5.4 - 8.7
Suspension arm to control arm	38.9 - 62.8	5.4 - 8.7
Control arm to body	38.9 - 62.8	5.4 - 8.7
Front shockabsorber bottom retaining nuts (inside strut)	10.8 - 17	1.5 - 2.4
Front suspension retainer bracket nuts	8.6 - 10.8	1.2 - 1.5
Shockabsorber top to retainer bracket nuts	14.4 - 23.0	2 - 3.2
Rear suspension		
Rear hub bearing locknut	18 - 21.6	2.5 - 3
Shockabsorber to axle bracket bolt	10.8 - 17	1.5 - 2.4
Shockabsorber bracket to axle	10.8 - 17	1.5 - 2.4
Panhard rod to axle and body	50.6 - 62.8	7 - 8.7
Hub bearing carrier to axle	21.6 - 35.4	3 - 4.9
Watts linkage to body	21.6 - 35.4	3 - 4.9
Shockabsorber to body locknut	10.8 - 17	1.5 - 2.4

1 General description

The independent front suspension uses two lower links (a tranverse arm and a semi-trailing link) in conjunction with a coil spring MacPherson strut. All the links are rubber mounted. Bump stops are used inside the strut.

An anti-roll bar is attached to the semi-trailing links and mounted to the front bodyshell crossmember.

All front suspension swivels are pre-lubricated and do not require regular maintenance.

Rack and pinion steering is used, the rack is mounted to the bodyshell, under the inner bulkhead.

The rear suspension uses a 'dead' beam axle - it is non-independent. The axle is located by a Watts linkage (two longitudinal rods on each side), coil spring and hydraulic telescopic shockabsorbers and bump stops, and a Panhard rod (transverse rod).

2 Anti-roll bar - inspection, removal and replacement

1 To inspect the anti-roll bar is easy, for they do not tend to 'wear out', as a torsion factor at least. Look at the straightness of the tranverse section and then look at the mountings. It is the four rubber bush mountings which wear. If these appear to have perished or are cut or compressed, renew all four. Check also the mounting brackets - if these are damaged, renew them also.
2 To remove the anti-roll bar, drive the car up on a pair of ramps. From below, loosen the four setscrews of the 'U' brackets on the front crossmember. Now loosen the nuts at each of the anti-roll bar end mountings on the suspension arm or transverse link. When all four mountings are loose, remove the two front 'U' brackets. Now remove the rear end 'U' brackets. The anti-roll bar should come away.
3 Cut the old rubber bushes off. Then clean up the anti-roll bar with a petrol/paraffin mix. Dry it.
4 Using rubber lubricant or liquid soap (sparingly) lubricate the new rubber bushes and slide them onto the anti-roll bar.
5 Replacement of the anti-roll bar is a reverse procedure to its removal.

3 Front crossmember - removal and replacement

1 This helps to support the engine. It is easiest to remove if it is removed with the anti-roll bar and the two semi-trailing links as described in Chapter 1, for engine removal.
2 Therefore, read Section 4, paragraphs 35, 36 and 37. This will enable you to remove the crossmember most easily for subsequent replacement.
3 Remove the anti-roll bar, See Section 2.
4 Remove the semi-trailing links, see Section 4.

5 Replacement is a reverse sequence to its removal.

4 Front semi-trailing link and transverse arm - removal and replacement

1 If you wish to replace both front semi-trailing links and/or their bushes, remove the front crossmember, anti-roll bar and semi-trailing links complete. See Section 3.
2 To remove one semi-trailing link only, proceed as follows: Jack up and support the **front** of the car, both wheels off the ground and removed. Disconnect the anti-roll bar end mounting from the centre of the link. See Section 2.
3 Now disconnect each end of the link. At the crossmember end use a socket on the single setscrew, from above, which passes through the link bush. Then undo and remove the bolt from the other end of the link on the transverse arm.
4 Now knock out the semi-trailing link. It is not possible to simply tap out the bush from the transverse arm; that is the bush for the rear yoke end of the semi-trailing link. See paragraph 8 which discusses all the bushes.
5 To remove the transverse arms is a similar operation. If you are rebushing all the suspension links/arms, remove the crossmember, anti-roll bar and semi-trailing links, as in Section 3, first; then tackle the tranverse arms. If not, and you wish to remove one or both of the tranverse arms, proceed as follows. (Rember the tranverse arm has to be removed to replace the end bush for the semi-trailing link!).
6 Jack up the front of the car, both sides, and remove the wheels. Loosen the setscrew which locates the inner end of the arm first, then loosen the bolt which locates the rear end of the semi-trailing link to the transverse arm. Now loosen the clamp on the front hub housing which grips the tranverse arm outer end bush 'stud'. All should be loose.
7 Remove the semi-trailing link to the tranverse arm bolt, remove the inner transverse arm locating setscrew and then fully release the hub housing clamp. Juggle the transverse arm away.
8 There are three 'silent bloc' bushes and one balljoint for each side of the front suspension. The bushes are replaceable, the balljoint is not - you have to purchase a new suspension arm. Therefore, once the semi-trailing links and the transverse arms are off the car, inspect the bushes, more closely. Obviously you have removed the arms because you suspect wear or damage. If the bushes are perished, cut or 'floppy' renew them. You cannot do this yourself. Take the arms/links to your Alfa Romeo agency or a competent engineering works and have them press-out the old bushes, and press-in the new ones. (Alfa Romeo special tools required are A.3.0241, A.3.0359, A.3.0351 and A.3.0352 for all three bushes). Check the smooth operation of the balljoint. If it is 'rough', restricted or 'floppy' replace the transverse arm complete. Check the suspension arm/link damage. Have your Alfa agency check these for you.
9 Replacement is a straightforward reverse sequence to removal.

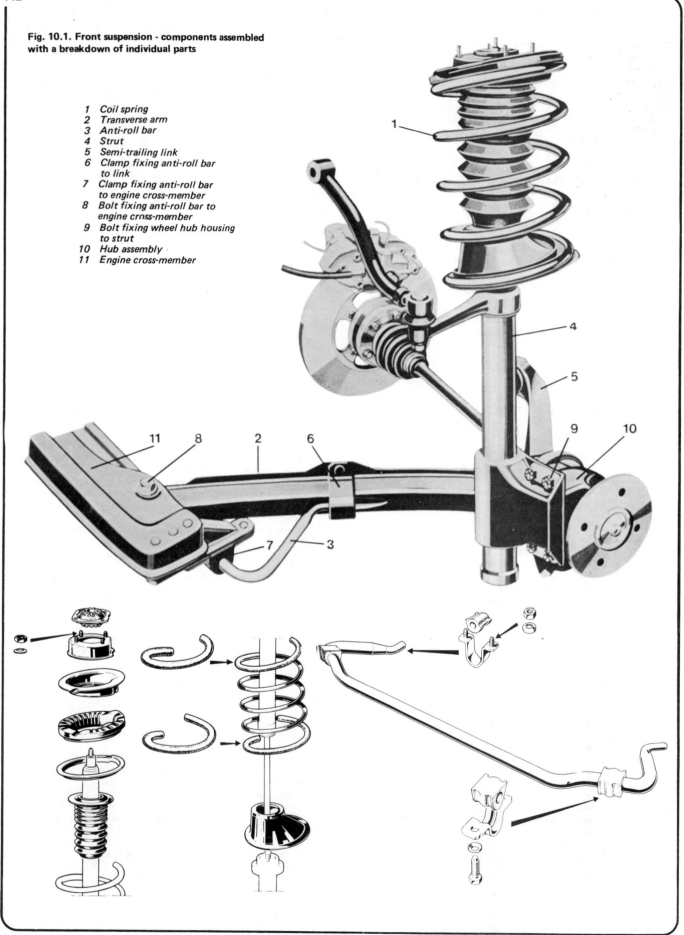

Fig. 10.1. Front suspension - components assembled with a breakdown of individual parts

1 Coil spring
2 Transverse arm
3 Anti-roll bar
4 Strut
5 Semi-trailing link
6 Clamp fixing anti-roll bar
   to link
7 Clamp fixing anti-roll bar
   to engine cross-member
8 Bolt fixing anti-roll bar to
   engine cross-member
9 Bolt fixing wheel hub housing
   to strut
10 Hub assembly
11 Engine cross-member

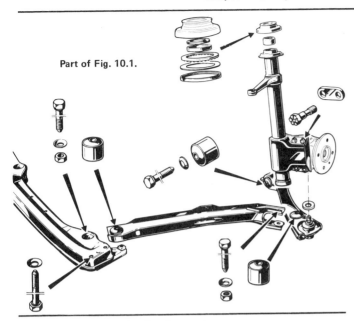

Part of Fig. 10.1.

5 Front strut - removal and replacement

1 Strut removal is not too difficult. You must do this then to be able to remove the shockabsorber and/or coil spring.
2 Jack up the front of the car and support. Remove the road wheels.
3 Remove the anti-roll bar, see Section 2.
4 Disconnect the driveshaft as if you would be removing it from the differential, see Chapter 7.
5 Disconnect and remove the semi-trailing link and the transverse arm (of the strut that you wish to remove), see Section 4. The strut should now only be fixed at the top, and by the steering arm just below the coil spring.
6 Using a proprietary balljoint separator or a pair of suitable wedges, separate the steering arm joint from the arm on the strut.
7 Now open the bonnet and loosen all four strut top plate fixing nuts. Have someone hold the strut and driveshaft, remove the nuts and push the strut downwards. Pull the whole unit away. Now separate the driveshaft from the strut on the bench, see Chapter 7 for instructions.
8 Replacement is a reverse sequence to removal.
9 Note: dismantling of the strut is dealt with in two sections of this Chapter, Section 6 deals with the coils spring and Section 7 deals with the shockabsorber. The strut itself does nothing more than 'hold' these two.

6 Front coil spring - removal and replacement

1 To release the coil spring you require a spring compressor, Alfa Romeo recommend special tool number A.2.0251 but most proprietary spring compressors of the right size will work. You must remove the strut from the car, see Section 5, and you must release the spring to release the shockabsorber.
2 Put the strut in a suitable vice. Position the spring compressor,

tighten and stop when the spring is 'loose'.
3 Remove the nut at the top of the shock absorber in the centre of the top plate fixing. Pull off the washer, cup washer, rubber mounting, bellows, and bottom cup washer. With the spring still in compression remove the upper spring retainer, the housing and cap, then the spring itself (still compressed), spring lower retainer and its support. (If you have used the Alfa Romeo tool the lower retainer will still be on the spring). Now release the compression tool.
4 Replacement is a straight reverse process of its removal.
5 Note: do not play with the spring under compression - it has a lot of power.

7 Front shock absorber - removal and replacement

1 Study Sections 5 and 6 and proceed as far. The shock absorber will still be located in the strut but will be released at the top.
2 Your best move at this stage is to take the strut in the state it is in now to your Alfa Romeo agent, because the dismantling of the lower end is difficult and requires a number of special tools which are difficult to fabricate. Any Alfa Romeo agent with special tools A.2.0221, A.3.0360, and A.3.0332 will be able to remove the shock absorber from the strut and replace it without difficulty, quickly and therefore reasonably cheaply. Do not tackle this job without these tools - danger exists and failure is inevitable.
3 It goes without saying that once removed, the shock absorber will have to be replaced into the strut in a reverse method of its removal.

8 Front suspension components - inspection

1 As has been mentioned elsewhere the Alfasud is one of the best steering and handling cars to be purchased anywhere in the world and at any price! Whilst obviously the design has been executed superbly it must not be taken as read that the car will continue to function properly without careful attention to the steering and suspension. In the previous sections maintenance and dismantling and reassembly of the front suspension components has been described in terms of what you can do yourself; also you have been recommended to take certain tasks to an Alfa Romeo agent because he has the necessary tools. Likewise, in terms of inspection and measurement, he has the proper jigs and probably more experience. Look at the suspension as follows, but if in doubt, consult him afterwards.
2 There is supposed to be a short 'warm-up' period in the front suspension. When you start from cold there will be a certain harsh, almost noisy suspension movement which goes away or smooths out quickly. If it does not then inspect the struts and consult your agent.
3 Look at the coil springs for sagging or breakage. Test the movement of the shock absorbers by pressing hard on the wing. They should depress and then return to rest with one up and one down movement. Any fluid leakage from the strut means shock absorber failure.
4 Check the anti-roll bar bushes and the silentbloc bushes in the suspension links/arms as described in their relevant sections. Check the balljoints in the tranverse arms.
5 Finally check that the arms and links are not 'bent' or split.
6 Read Section 20, and have your agent check your car for side height if any new components, apart from pairs of springs and shock absorbers have been used.

4.1a This shows the front suspension well from behind

4.1b A close-up of the lower swivel

5.7 The top mounting of the front shock absorber

9 Rear Watts linkage - removal and replacement

1   The rear Watts linkage controls the backward and forward motion of the rear beam axle. To remove one of the four rods is very simple. It is necessary to disconnect both ends of one rod to remove it and then inspect its bushes, one at each end. This Section will describe the removal and replacement of one of the four rods and its bush. The other three rods follow the same procedure.
2   Jack up the rear of the car with the handbrake on. Support both sides of the car at the rear adjacent to the jacking points. Remove the road wheel on the side to be worked upon.
3   Using two ring spanners loosen the bush end on the bodyshell. Remove the bolt and washer.
4   Remove the bush with the rod having undone and removed the fixing bolt on the beam axle.
5   Replacement is a direct reverse procedure. Tighten the bolts to the specified torque wrench setting.
6   Bushes are replaceable by pushing out the old one in a vice and the new one being pushed in the opposite way. If in doubt have your Alfa Romeo agent do the change for you.

10 Rear panhard rod - removal and replacement

1   Proceed as for the Watts linkage to remove the panhard rod which crosses the car laterally. Undo the bush end attached to the bodyshell first, once the car is jacked up and supported.
2   Proceed to the beam axle end, and remove the rod fixing bolt. On the panhard rod there is a fixing for the rear brake pressure limiter valve mechanism. Disentangle the mechanism from the little bracket on the rod; it is very simple.
3   Reassembly is a reverse procedure of the dismantling. The bushes are replaced as per the Watts linkage rods. Read Section 14.

11 Rear shock absorber - removal and replacement

1   Jack up the rear of the car and support it. Remove the road wheels.

Open the boot lid.
2   Remove the top locknut inside the boot then the fixing nut, bevel washer and top rubber bush which is inside the boot.
3   From below the car spray the bottom of the shock absorber with releasing fluid. Undo the two bolts which locate the fixing bracket to the beam axle, remove them and then pull the shock absorber from below, out and away.
4   Now remove the eye bolt which holds the shock absorber to the lower fixing bracket.
5   Replacement is a reverse procedure of removal.

12 Rear beam axle - removal, dismantling and replacement

1   To remove the beam axle jack up the rear of the car, support the car and remove the road wheels. Place a hydraulic jack under the centre of the beam axle.
2   Disconnect the Watts linkage and the panhard rod bushes on the beam axle, as described in Sections 9 and 10. Leave them on the bodywork.
3   Remove both shock absorbers. See Section 11.
4   Disconnect the brake pipe at the union on the axle and free the hose from the bracket. Plug the hydraulic feed pipe to avoid fluid loss with one of the caliper bleed screw caps. Tie the hose out of the way.
5   Slowly lower the hydraulic jack and pull the control mechanism for the pressure limiter, off the panhard rod.
6   Lower the axle to the ground with the springs still attached.
7   The axle will have to be further dismantled now that it is off the car. How far you go will depend upon what component you need to reach. To remove the hub/discs see Chapter 7.
8   The rear springs will now pull out of their seats. See Section 13.
9   The stub axles are affixed to stub axle plates which are bolted to the ends of the beam axle by three bolts. Their removal is obvious.
10 Read Section 14.
11 Replacement of the components to the axle and the axle to the car are a straightforward reverse sequence. Once the car is rebuilt it will be necessary to bleed the hydraulic brake system.

9.1a The front location on the bodywork of the front watts link rod

9.1b The rear location of the rear watts link rod

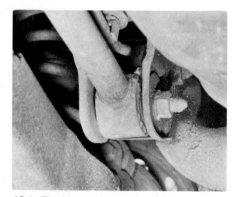

10.1a The bodyshell mounting of the Panhard rod

10.1b Panhard rod on the beam axle and the rear shock absorber lower mounting

11.2 Inside the boot - everything should be clean

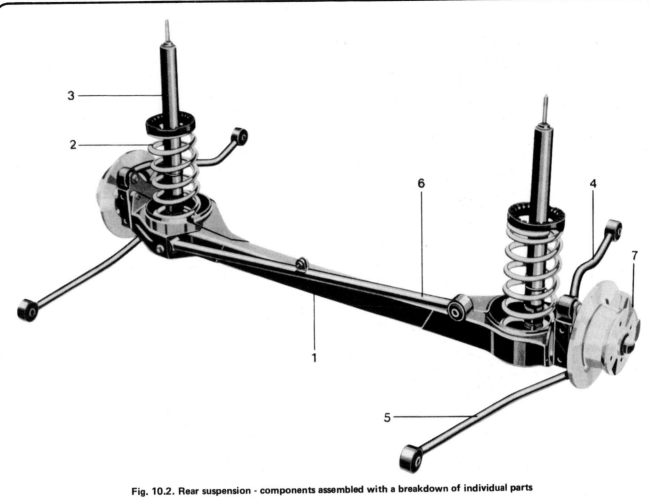

Fig. 10.2. Rear suspension - components assembled with a breakdown of individual parts

1   Beam axle
2   Spring
3   Shock absorber
4   Watts linkage, rear
5   Watts linkage, front
6   Panhard rod
7   Wheel hub assembly

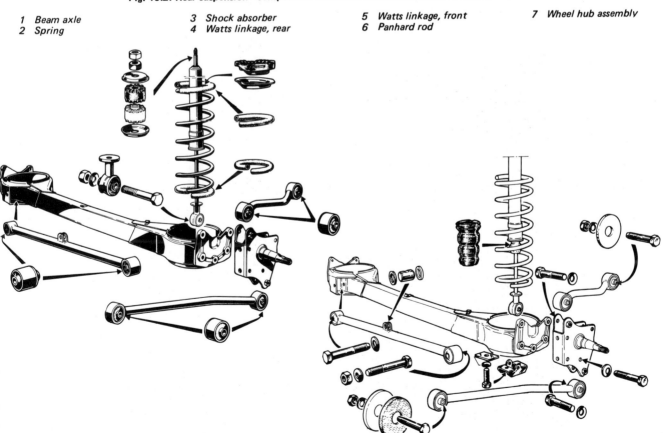

13 Rear coil spring - removal and replacement

1   It is necessary to remove the beam axle to remove the rear coil springs. Read Section 12.
2   The top of the coil spring sits in a rubber buffer and cup located up in the rear wheel arch. Both ends of the coil spring have a rubberised tube fitted over the coil.
3   Read Section 14.

14 Rear suspension components - inspection

1   Read Section 8, paragraphs 1 to 3 inclusive.
2   Check the Watts linkage, panhard rod and beam axle casing for corrosion, distortion and cracks. Check the silentbloc bushes in all these components for perishing, tearing and corrosion. If in doubt consult an Alfa Romeo agent; repair may be available.
3   Check the spring for cracking and the shock absorbers for leakage. If in doubt, replace, but do so in pairs only.
4   Read Section 20 and have your agent check the car for ride height if any new suspension components, not parts of springs and shock absorbers alone, have been used.

15 Steering wheel - removal and replacement

1   The steering wheel is easy to remove. Pull off with your fingers the plastic boss which sits in the centre of the steering wheel.
2   The centre boss of the steering wheel sits on three studs on a plate on the end of the steering column. Undo the three nuts now visible and pull off the steering wheel.
3   Replacement is a direct reverse procedure. Tighten the wheel properly.

16 Steering rack - removal and replacement

1   Raise the front of the car and support it on stands near the jacking points. Chock the rear wheels.
2   Remove the road wheel on the same side as the steering column. Disconnect the balljoint on the suspension strut/steering arm joint on that side. See Section 5, paragraph 6.
3   Apply full 'opposite' lock (for rhd car left lock, lhd car right lock). From under the bonnet remove the inner end of the track rods from the steering rack. Remove the other road wheel, and disconnect the other track rod balljoint. Now pull away both track rods through the wing apertures.
4   Remove the bolt securing the lower column universal joint to the pinion shaft on the steering rack. Remove the plastic sleeve protecting the rack.
5   Remove the two bolts fixing the steering rack to the bodyshell.
6   Now pull the rack away from the bodyshell and loosen away from the lower column universal joint. Remove the rack through the aperture of the left hand wheel arch.
7   Replacement is a direct reverse procedure. Remember all the shims etc. Read Section 18 and 19.

17 Steering track rod end balljoint - removal and replacement

1   Read Section 16, paragraphs 1, 2 and 3.
2   Balljoints are screwed into the ends of the track rods and secured by a locknut. They are adjustable, to enable track to be widened or narrowed.
3   To remove a balljoint from the track rod undo the locknut and then unscrew the balljoint. Mark the distance between the inner end of the track rod and the outer edge of the balljoint. This will allow a new track rod balljoint (or track rod) to be approximately the same length before replacement.
4   The inner end of the track rod has a replaceable silentbloc type bush.
5   Read Section 20.

18 Steering column and joints - removal and replacement

1   The steering column and joints can be divided into two sets of components as it is in the Alfa Romeo spare parts catalogue; those components inside the car which simply consist of the column covers and electrical switch gear for the lights/horn/wipers etc, and the major steering column components.
2   To expose the steering column proper and the major switch cluster, remove the four screws from the lower, under plastic cover. Pull the cover away, then pull the top cover off. Remove the steering wheel as in Section 15.
3   The light/horn/wiper switch can now be removed by undoing the fixing screw exposed and disconnecting the electrical earth and junction box.
4   Undo the locking screw which holds the ignition/starter switch into its location, disconnect the electrical connections and pull the switch out should you desire to dismantle the steering further.
5   The next stage is to remove the top column and the height adjustment components. Remove the plastic height lock screw by tapping out the roll pin lock from below the top steering boss, and then unscrewing it , pull it out. Retain the serrated ratchet components.
6   Remove the pinch bolt on the bottom universal joint in the footwell inside the car so that the top column can be freed. Now remove the pilot bolt on which the top column 'hinges' for height adjustment. A certain amount of juggling should now free the adjustable column.
7   It is now possible to remove the top column from inside the adjustable column outer. However, should only the top column need removing, it is possible when leaving the adjustable column in the car by ignoring the dismantling of the height adjustment facility. The top column runs in needle rollers which need retaining.
8   The major column support bracket is on the bulkhead at three points; the forked bracket with one bolt, the cross brace with two and the base with five. Removal of all these will enable this bracket to be removed.
9   The steering shaft with the two universal joints, one at each end, can be removed through the inside of the car by undoing the joint on the steering rack, see Section 16 and inside the car as just described. Pull up the top column and extract the shaft.
10 Replacement is an exact reverse procedure of its dismantling. Read Section 19.

19 Steering components - inspection

1   Efficient service and safety can be achieved if the steering is inspected properly. Much of the performance of the Alfasud is obtained through its excellent steering.
2   Ensure that the balljoints and the track rods pivot smoothly and with sufficient clearance in front seats. Look at the gaiters on the balljoints and on the steering rack for splitting, cracking and leakage. If in doubt, renew. Before worrying about the condition of the steering rack have the car inspected by an Alfa Romeo agent.
3   Check the universal joints at both ends of the shaft and the bearings in the upper column for smoothness of operation. If in doubt, change them.
4   Remember always to tighten the steering column height adjusting nut so that it holds properly.
5   In the light of poor steering performance check the suspension.

20 Steering rack - dismantling and reassembly

1   Dismantling the steering rack itself is fairly easy, however, five special tools are necessary to reassemble and adjust it. For the d-i-y mechanic it will be a fairly pointless task. It would be best to remove the rack from the car and have an Alfa Romeo agent do any disassembly or assembly work on it.
2   Dismantling is described here in brief: cut the clip securing the RH gaiter to the sliding coupling and the clip fixing LH gaiter to the rack body. Remove the end cap, RH gaiter and support bracket. Remove the spacer and plate. Remove the studs.
3   Extract the coupling from the rack guide tube. At the same time release the sliding member from the tube. Remove the upper cap, adjusting screw, spring and plunger from the rack. Withdraw the rack from the tube and recover the sliding member.

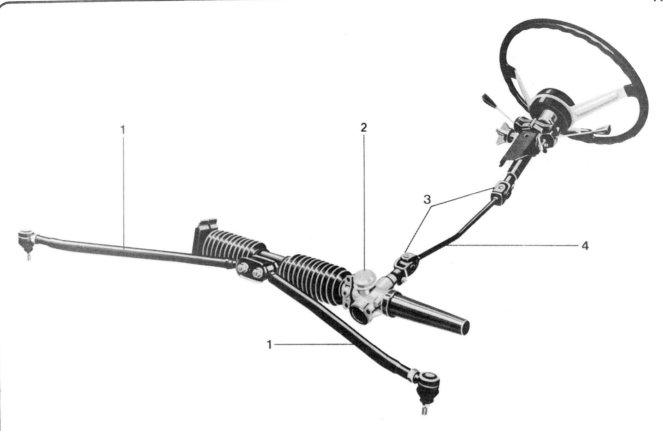

Fig. 10.3. Steering mechanism - components assembled with a breakdown of individual parts

1 Track rods   2 Steering rack   3 Universal joints   4 Steering column

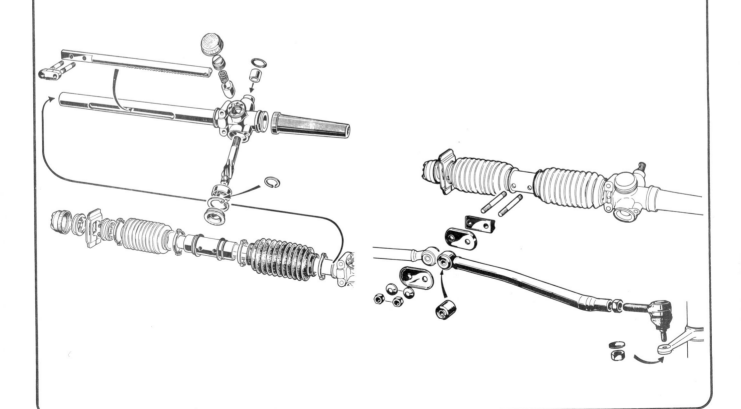

4 Remove the lower cap, protecting the rack pinion. Remove the spring ring and the pinion shaft with the bearing, using a special tool.
5 Remove the circlip and bearing from the pinion shaft, using two special tools. Remove the circlip from the steering box, and extract the bush from the pinion shaft, using a special tool.
6 Remove the rubber bushes from the steering rack rods, using special tools.
7 Where the gaiters are in need of replacement, cut the retaining clips and separate the gaiter from the sliding coupling.
8 Replace damaged or cracked gaiters. Check that the steering rack and pinion do not show any signs of seizure and scoring. Check that the pre-lubricated bushes for the steering housing and the sliding member do not show signs of excessive wear. Excessive wear is indicated by the base metal showing through. Ensure that the bearing surfaces of the pinion and steering guide tube are smooth and free from wear. Check that the sliding member has a slight push fit in the steering tube. The maximum clearance between sliding member and tube should not exceed 0.1 mm (0.004 in). Measure clearance with a feeler gauge. Where the above condition is not fulfilled, select a sliding member of the correct dimension from the range of available spare parts. In this case the clearance should not exceed 0.044 mm (0.001 in). Check that

the new part slides smoothly. Where this condition cannot be obtained, replace steering tube and sliding member. Pair components with identical colour code.
9 Reassembly is a reverse procedure of disassembly. Grease the components as mentioned in paragraph 8.
10 Adjust the steering geometry. See Section 21.

21 Steering geometry and ride height

1 Six measurements are necessary to achieve proper steering and suspension control. None can be done by the d-i-y mechanic. In total seven special tools are necessary. Have each of the following checked if major suspension components have been changed; front suspension ride height, rear suspension ride height, toe-in, swivel pin inclination, castor angle and maximum steering lock of outer wheel. Also if any crash damage has occured, have the appropriate checks done. An Alfa Romeo agent should be able to carry all those out.
2 Diagrams are given to show the various measures. Rest assured your Alfasud will work efficiently if all of the measures are correct.

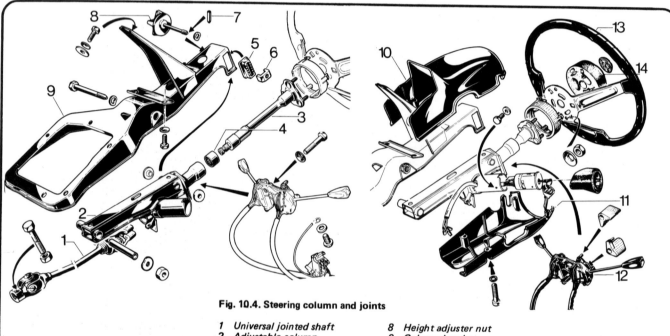

Fig. 10.4. Steering column and joints

1	Universal jointed shaft	8	Height adjuster nut
2	Adjustable column	9	Column bracket
3	Top column	10	Top cowl
4	Bearing	11	Bottom cowl
5	Ratchet	12	Switch gear
6	Ratchet stop	13	Steering wheel
7	Roll pin	14	Plastic bars

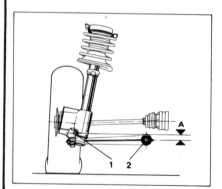

Fig. 10.5. Front suspension height measurement

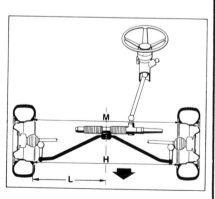

Fig. 10.6. Rear suspension height measurement

Fig. 10.7. Toe-out measurement

A	=	20 ± 7.5 mm	B	=	66.5 ± 5.5 mm
1	Pinch bolt	2 Trailing link bolt	1	Centre watts linkage bolt	

2 Hub watts linkage bolt

$H - M = 2 \pm 1$ mm $(L = \frac{1}{2}M + 1 \pm 1$ mm$)$

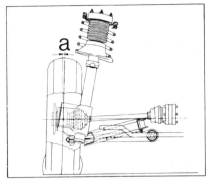

Fig. 10.8. Swivel pin inclination

$a = 2^{o} 12' \pm 30'$

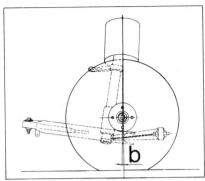

Fig. 10.9. Castor angle

$b = 0^{o} 30' \pm 30'$

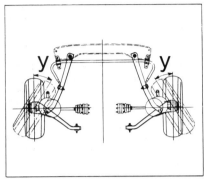

Fig. 10.10. Maximum steering lock of outer wheel

$Y = 30^{o} 30'$

22 Fault diagnosis - suspension and steering

Symptom	Cause	Remedy
Front suspension		
Steering vague, vehicle wanders	Uneven tyre pressures	Inflate tyres.
	Faulty shock absorbers	Renew.
	Broken coil spring	Renew (as pair).
	Worn balljoints	Adjust or renew.
Stiff or heavy steering	Low tyre pressures	Inflate.
	Balljoints dry	Lubricate.
Wheel wobble and vibration	Wheel nuts loose	Tighten.
	Wheels out of balance	Re-balance.
	Weak coil springs	Renew (as pair).
	Faulty shock absorbers	Renew.
	Worn bearings in outer driveshaft carrier	Renew (also oil seals).
Rear suspension		
Vibration or knocking	Worn rear hub bearings	Renew.
	Loose hub nuts	Tighten to torque.
	Worn shock absorber bushes	Renew.
	Worn axle mounting bushes	Renew.
Uneven tyre wear on rear wheels	Worn hub bearings	Renew.
	Worn or loose axle mountings	Renew or tighten.
Rolling on corners or pitching	Weak road spring	Renew.
	Faulty shock absorber	Renew.

Steering
Before diagnosing faults from this chart, check that any irregularities are not caused by:

1 *Binding brakes*
2 *Incorrect 'mix' of radial or crossply tyres*
3 *Incorrect tyre pressures*
4 *Misalignment of bodyframe*

Steering vague, car wanders	Steering angles incorrect	Check and adjust.
	Steering wheel free play excessive	Adjust or renew linkage and gear.
Steering stiff and heavy	Lack of lubrication in steering gear or suspension swivels	Grease.
	Front wheel toe-in incorrect	Check and adjust.
	Steering angles incorrect	Check and adjust.
	Steering gear pinion or rack adjustments too tight	Release and re-adjust.
	Steering column bent	Renew.
Wheel wobble and vibration	Excessive freeplay in steering gear or linkage	Adjust or renew as necessary.

Chapter 11 Bodywork and fittings

Contents

Specifications

Bodyshell ... ... Monocoque construction, of welded and bolted steel panels. 4-door for Alfasud and 2-door for Alfasud TI

For all dimensions see the front of the book

---

1 General description

The bodywork of the Alfasud saloons is a welded, monocoque construction of reasonably conventional design engineering principles. It was styled by Guigiaro and the Italdesign team to fit into the standard European design theme for a 'peoples car'. Its competition lies with those 'fastbacked' saloons such as the Citroen GS and the VW Golf.

The two and four-door saloons differ only in detail. The TI has some extra trim to aid it aerodynamically, a front spoiler and a boot spoiler. These are tacked on and not special integral mouldings.

Design construction tends to be simple and functional following the manner of the engine and gearbox.

---

2 Maintenance - bodywork and underframe

1 The general condition of the vehicle's bodywork is the one thing that significantly affects its value. Maintenance is easy but needs to be regular and particular. Neglect, particularly after minor damage, can lead quickly to further deterioration and costly repair bills. It is important also to keep watch on those parts of the car not immediately visible, for instance, the underside and inside all the wheel arches.

2 The basic maintenance routine for the bodywork is washing - preferably with a lot of water, from a hose. This will remove all the solids which may have stuck to the car. It is important to flush these off in such a way to prevent grit from scratching the finish. The wheel arches and underbody need washing in the same way to remove any accumulated mud which will retain moisture and tend to encourage rust. Paradoxically enough, the best time to clean the underbody and wheel arches is in wet weather when the mud is thoroughly wet and soft. In very wet weather, the underbody is usually cleaned of large accumulations automatically and this is a good time for inspection.

3 Periodically it is a good idea to have the whole of the underside of the vehicle steam cleaned, so that a thorough inspection can be carried out to see what minor repairs and renovations are necessary. Steam cleaning is available at commercial vehicle garages but if not, there are one or two excellent grease solvents available which can be brush applied. The dirt can then be hosed off.

4 After washing paintwork, wipe it with a chamois leather to give an unspotted clear finish. A coat of clear protective wax polish will give added protection against chemical pollutants in the air. If the paintwork sheen has dulled or oxidised, this requires a little more effort, but is usually caused because regular washing has been neglected. Always check that drain holes are completely clear so that water can drain out. Brightwork should be treated the same way as paintwork. Windscreens and windows can be kept clear of the smeary film which often appears if a little ammonia is added to the water. If they are scratched, a good rub with a proprietary metal polish will often clear them. Do not use any form of wax or chromium cleaner on glass.

---

3 Maintenance- upholstery and floor coverings

1 Mats and carpets should be brushed or vacuum cleaned regularly to keep them free of grit. If they are badly stained remove them for scrubbing or sponging and make sure they are dry before replacement. Seats and interior trim panels can be kept clean by a wipe over with a damp cloth. If they do become stained (which can be more apparent on light coloured upholstery) use a little liquid detergent and a soft nailbrush to scour the grime out of the grain of the material. Do not forget to keep the head lining clean in the same way as the upholstery. When using liquid cleaners inside the car do not over wet the surfaces being cleaned. Excessive damp could get into the seams and padded interior causing stains, offensive odours or even rot. If the inside of the car gets wet accidently, it is worthwhile taking some trouble to dry it out properly, particularly where carpets are involved. **Do not** leave heaters inside for this purpose.

4 Minor body damage - repair

See also the photo sequence on pages 122, 123 and 124.

Repair of minor scratches in the bodywork

If the scratch is very superficial and does not penetrate to the metal of the bodywork, repair is very simple. Lightly rub the area of the scratch with a paintwork renovator (eg; T-Cut), or a very fine cutting paste, to remove loose paint from the scratch and to clear the surrounding bodywork of wax polish. Rinse the area with clean water.

Apply touch-up paint to the scratch using a thin paint brush, continue to apply thin layers of paint until the surface of the paint in the scratch is level with the surrounding paintwork. Allow the new paint at least two weeks to harden, then blend it into the surrounding paintwork by rubbing the paintwork in the scratch area with a paintwork renovator (eg; T-Cut), or a very fine cutting paste. Finally apply wax polish.

An alternative to painting over the scratch is to use Holts 'scratch patch'. Use the same preparation for the affected area; then simply pick a patch of suitable size to cover the scratch completely. Hold the patch against the scratch and burnish its backing paper; the patch will adhere to the paintwork, freeing itself from the backing paper at the same time. Polish the affected area to blend the patch into the surrounding paintwork. Where a scratch has penetrated right through to the metal of the bodywork causing the metal to rust, a different repair technique is required. Remove any loose rust from the bottom of the scratch with a penknife, then apply rust inhibiting paint (eg; Kurust) to prevent the formation of rust in the future. Using a rubber or nylon applicator fill the scratch with bodystopper paste. If required, this paste can be mixed with cellulose thinners to provide a very thin paste which is ideal for filling narrow scratches. Before the stopperpaste in the scratch hardens, wrap a piece of smooth cotton rag around the tip of a finger. Dip the finger in cellulose thinners and then quickly sweep it across the surface of the stopperpaste in the scratch; this will ensure that the surface of the stopper paste is slightly hollowed. The scratch can now be painted over as described earlier in this Section.

Repair of dents in the bodywork

When deep denting of the car's bodywork has taken place, the first task is to pull the dent out, until the affected bodywork almost attains its original shape. There is little point in trying to restore the original shape completely, as the metal in the damaged area will have stretched on impact and cannot be reshaped fully to its original contour. It is better to bring the level of the dent up to a point which is about 3 mm (0.125 in) below the level of the surrounding bodywork. In cases where the dent is very shallow, it is not worth trying to pull it out at all.

If the underside of the dent is accessible, it can he hammered out gently from behind, using a mallet with a wooden or plastic head. Whilst doing this, hold a suitable block of wood firmly against the impact from the hammer blows and thus prevent a large area of bodywork from being 'belled-out'.

Should the dent be in a section of the bodywork which has a double skin or some other factor making it inaccessible from behind, a different technique is called for. Drill several small holes through the metal inside the dent area - particularly in the deeper sections. Then screw long self-tapping screws into the holes just sufficiently for them to gain a purchase in the metal. Now the dent can be pulled out by pulling on the protuding heads of the screws with a pair of pliers.

The next stage of the repair is the removal of the paint from the damaged area, and from an inch or so from the surrounding 'sound' bodywork. This is accomplished most easily by using a wire brush or abrasive pad on a power drill, although it can be done just as effectively by hand using sheets of abrasive paper. To complete the preparations for filling, score the surfaces of the bare metal with a screwdriver or the tang of a file, or alternatively drill small holes in the affected areas. This will provide a really good key for the filler paste.

To complete the repair see the Section on filling and respraying.

Repair of rust holes or gashes in the bodywork

Remove all paint from the affected area and from an inch or so of the surrounding 'sound' bodywork, using an abrasive pad or wire brush on a power drill. If these are not available a few sheets of abrasive paper will do the job just as effectively. With the paint removed you will be able to gauge the severity of the corrosion and therefore decide whether to replace the whole panel (if this is possible) or to repair the affected area. Replacement body panels are not as expensive as most people think and it is often quicker and more satisfactory to fit a new panel than to attempt to repair large areas of corrosion.

Remove all fittings from the affected areas except those which will act as a guide to the original shape of the damaged body work (eg; headlamp shells etc.,). Then, using tin snips or a hacksaw blade, remove all loose metal and any other metal badly affected by corrosion. Hammer the edges of the hole inwards in order to create a slight depression for the filler paste.

Wire brush the affected area to remove the powdery rust from the surface of the remaining metal. Paint the affected area with rust inhibiting paint (eg; Kurust). If the back of the rusted area is accessible treat this also.

Before filling can take place it will be necessary to block the hole in some way. This can be achieved by the use of one of the following materials: Zinc gauze, Aluminium tape or Polyurethane foam.

Zinc gauze is probably the best material to use for the large hole. Cut a piece to the approximate size and shape of the hole to be fitted, then position it in the hole so that its edges are below the level of the surrounding bodywork. It can be retained in position by several blobs of filler paste around its periphery.

Aluminium tape should be used for small or very narrow holes. Pull a piece off the roll and trim it to the appropriate size and shape required, then pull off the backing paper (if used) and stick the tape over the hole; it can be overlapped if the thickness of one piece is insufficient. Burnish down the edges of the tape with the handle of a screwdriver or similar to ensure that the tape is securely attached to the metal underneath.

Polyurethane foam is best used where the hole is situated in a section of bodywork of complex shape backed by a small box section (eg; where the sill panel meets the rear wheel arch - most cars.) The unusual mixing procedure for this foam is as follows. Put equal amounts of fluid from each of the two cans provided into one container. Stir until the mixture begins to thicken, then quickly pour this mixture into the hole, and hold a piece of cardboard over the larger apertures. Almost immediately the polyurethane will begine to expand, squirting out of any holes left unblocked. When the foam hardens it can be cut back to just below the level of the surrounding bodywork with a hacksaw blade.

Bodywork repairs - filling and re-spraying

Before using this Section, see the Sections on dent, deep scratch, rust hole and gash repairs.

Many types of bodyfiller are available, but generally speaking those proprietary kits which contain a tin of filler paste and a tube of resin hardener (eg; Holts Cataloy) are best for this type of repair. A wide, flexible plastic or nylon applicator will be found invaluable for imparting a smooth and well contoured finish to the surface of the filler.

Mix a little filler on a piece of card or board - use the hardener sparingly (follow the maker's instructions on the packet), otherwise the filler will set very rapidly.

Using the applicator, apply the filler paste to the prepared area; draw the applicator across the surface of the filler to achieve the correct contour and to level the filler surface. As soon as a contour that approximates the correct one is achieved, stop working the paste - if you carry on too long the paste will become sticky and begin to 'pick up' on the applicator. Continue to add thin layers of filler paste at twenty-minute intervals until the level of the filler is just 'proud' of the surrounding bodywork.

Once the filler has hardened, excess can be removed using a Surform plane or Dreadnought file. From then on, progressively finer grades of abrasive paper should be used, starting with a 40 grade production paper and finishing with 400 grade 'wet-or-dry' paper. Always wrap the abrasive paper around a flat rubber, cork or wooden block - otherwise the surface of the filler will not be completely flat. During the smoothing of the filler surface the 'wet-or-dry' paper should be periodically rinsed in water. This will ensure that a very smooth finish is imparted to the filler at the final stage.

At this stage the 'dent' should be surrounded by a ring of bare metal, which in turn should be encircled by the finely 'feathered' edge of the good paintwork. Rinse the repair area with clean water, until all of the dust produced by the rubbing-down operation is gone.

Spray the whole repair area with a light coat of grey primer - this

Typical example of rust damage to a body panel. Before starting ensure that you have all of the materials required to hand. The first task is to ...

... remove body fittings from effected area, except those which can act as a guide to the original shape of the damaged bodywork - the headlamp shell in this case.

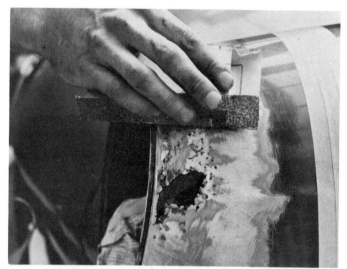

Remove all paint from the rusted area and from an inch or so of the adjoining 'sound' bodywork - use coarse abrasive paper or a power drill fitted with a wire brush or abrasive pad. Gently hammer in the edges of the hole to provide a hollow for the filler.

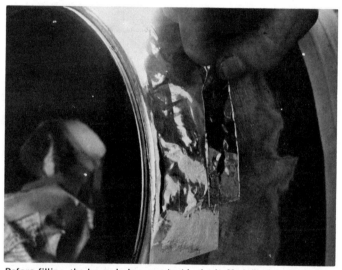

Before filling, the larger holes must be blocked off. Adhesive aluminium tape is one method; cut the tape to the required shape and size, peel off the backing strip (where used), position the tape over the hole and burnish to ensure adhesion.

Alternatively, zinc gauze can be used. Cut a piece of the gauze to the required shape and size; position it in the hole below the level of the surrounding bodywork; then ...

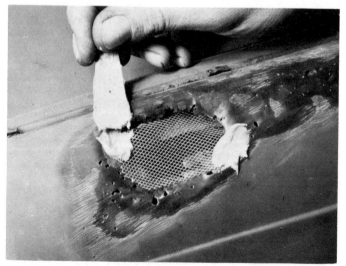

... secure in position by placing a few blobs of filler paste around its periphery. Alternatively, pop rivets or self-tapping screws can be used. Preparation for filling is now complete.

Mix filler and hardener according to manufacturer's instructions - avoid using too much hardener otherwise the filler will harden before you have a chance to work it.

Apply the filler to the affected area with a flexible applicator - this will ensure a smooth finish. Apply thin layers of filler at 20 minute intervals, until the surface of the filler is just 'proud' of the surrounding bodywork. Then ...

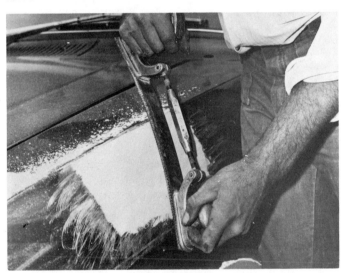

... remove excess filler and start shaping with a Surform plane or a dreadnought file. Once an approximate contour has been obtained and the surface is relatively smooth, start using ...

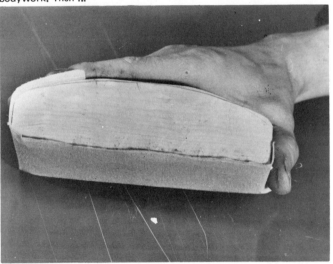

... abrasive paper. The paper should be wrapped around a flat wood, cork or rubber block - this will ensure that it imparts a smooth surface to the filler.

40 grit production paper is best to start with, then use progressively finer abrasive paper, finishing with 400 grade 'wet-and-dry'. When using 'wet-and-dry' paper, periodically rinse it in water ensuring also, that the work area is kept wet continuously.

Rubbing-down is complete when the surface of the filler is really smooth and flat, and the edges of the surrounding paintwork are finely 'feathered'. Wash the area thoroughly with clean water and allow to dry before commencing re-spray.

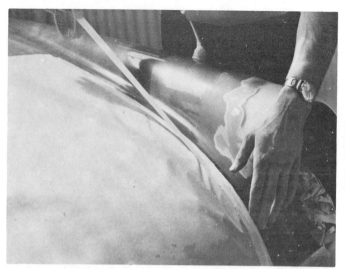

Firstly, mask off all adjoining panels and the fittings in the spray area. Ensure that the area to be sprayed is completely free of dust. Practice using an aerosol on a piece of waste metal sheet until the technique is mastered.

Spray the affected area with primer - apply several thin coats rather than one thick one. Start spraying in the centre of the repair area and then work outwards using a circular motion - in this way the paint will be evenly distributed.

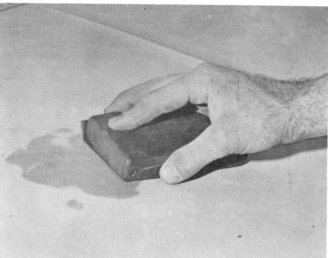

When the primer has dried inspect its surface for imperfections. Holes can be filled with filler paste or body-stopper, and lumps can be sanded smooth. Apply a further coat of primer, then 'flat' its surface with 400 grade 'wet-and-dry' paper.

Spray on the top coat, again building up the thickness with several thin coats of paint. Overspray onto the surrounding original paintwork to a depth of about five inches, applying a very thin coat at the outer edges.

Allow the paint two weeks, at least, to harden fully, then blend it into the surrounding original paintwork with a paint restorative compound or very fine cutting paste. Use wax polish to finish off.

The finished job should look like this. Remember, the quality of the completed work is directly proportional to the amount of time and effort expended at each stage of the preparation.

will show up any imperfections in the surface of the filler. Repair these imperfections with fresh filler paste or bodystopper, and once more smooth the surface with abrasive paper. If bodystopper is used, it can be mixed with cellulose thinners to form a really thin paste which is ideal for filling small holes. Repeat this spray and repair procedure until you are satisfied that the surface of the filler, and the feathered edge of the paintwork are perfect. Clean the repair area with clean water and allow to dry fully.

The repair area is now ready for spraying. Paint spraying must be carried out in a warm, dry, windless and dust free atmosphere. This condition can be created artifically if you have access to a large indoor working area, but if you are forced to work in the open, you will have to pick your day very carefully. If you are working indoors, dousing the floor in the work area with water will 'lay' the dust which would otherwise be in the atmosphere. If the repair area is confined to one body panel, mask off the surrounding panels; this will help to minimise the effect of a slight mis-match in colours. Bodywork fittings (eg; chrome strips, door handles etc) will also need to be masked off. Use a genuine masking tape and several thicknesses of newspaper for the masking operation.

Before commencing to spray, agitate the aerosol can thoroughly, then spray a test area (an old tin or similar) until the technique is mastered. Cover the repair area with a thick coat of primer; the thickness should be built up using several thin layers of paint rather than one thick one. Using 400 grade 'wet-or-dry' paper, rub down the surface of the primer until it is really smooth. While doing this, the work area should be thoroughly doused with water, and the 'wet-or-dry' paper periodically rinsed in water. Allow to dry before spraying on more paint.

Spray on the top coat, again building up the thickness by using several thin layers of paint. Start spraying in the centre of the repair area and then, using a circular motion, work outwards until the whole repair area and about 2 inches of the surrounding original paintwork is covered. Remove all masking material 10 to 15 minutes after spraying on the final coat of paint.

Allow the new paint at least 2 weeks to harden fully; then using a paintwork renovator (eg; T-Cut) or a very fine cutting paste, blend the edges of the new paint into the existing paintwork. Finally apply wax polish.

5 Major body damage - repair

1 Where serious damage has occurred or large areas need renewal due to neglect it means certainly that completely new sections or panels will need welding in and this is best left to professionals. If the damage is due to impact it will also be necessary to check the alignment of the body structure. In such instances the services of an agent with specialist checking jigs are essential. If the body is left misaligned it is first of all dangerous as the car will not handle properly - and secondly, uneven stresses will be imposed on the steering, engine and transmission, causing abnormal wear or complete failure. Tyre wear will also be excessive.

6 Maintenance - hinges and locks

1 Oil the hinges of the bonnet, boot and doors with a drop or two of light oil periodically. A good time is after the car has been washed.
2 Oil the bonnet release, the catch pivot pin and the safety catch pivot pin periodically.
3 Do not over lubricate door latches and strikers. Normally a little oil on the rotary cam spindle alone is sufficient.

7 Door rattles - tracing and rectification

1 Check first that the door is not loose at the hinges and that the latch is holding the door firmly in position. Check also that the door lines up with the aperture in the body.
2 If the hinges are loose or the door is out of alignment it will be necessary to reset the hinge positions, as described later in this Chapter.

3 If the latch is holding the door properly it should hold the door tightly when fully latched and the door should line up with the body. If it is out of alignment it needs adjustment as described in Section 14. If loose, some part of the lock mechanism must be worn out and requires renewal.
4 Other rattles from the door would be caused by wear or looseness in the window winder, the glass channels and sill strips or the door buttons and interior latch release mechanism.

8 Wings - removal and refitting

1 The front wings are strictly the only removable body panels although these are welded and bolted into place.
2 To remove, remove the front bumper, see Section 10 and then unscrew the nine spike nuts which locate the front wing to the inner wing pressing. Inside the wheel arch are two bracing brackets which stop the wing from vibrating. These are bolted to the pressing and the wing and should be removed. Then lift off the wing.
3 To replace, simply clean up the area and replace any sealing and progressively install the wing. Do not forget the two braces. Once installed loose, gradually tighten it, evenly and in alignment. Check for proper sealing and straightness.

9 Window glass - removal and refitting

1 The front and rear screens are glued into place. Their fitting is a job for brave men. Such is the skill with which they have to be installed, firstly to keep the glass in place and secondly to stop them leaking when it rains, it is recommended that their fitting is entrusted to an Alfa Romeo agent or a very skilled windscreen glass fitter.
2 When removal or fitting is necessary for a front or rear screen have the job done properly by a skilled fitter. Success will not be achieved at home.
3 The front and rear side windows in the 4-door saloon are conventional rubber surrounded glass which can be removed and fitted easily in the conventional manner. The same goes for the front side windows of the 2-door TI. The usual 'string' and screwdriver method can be used whereby the lip of the rubber sealing groove is pulled over the glass by the string and it is pressed into place.
4 The 2-door TI rear side windows open in a conventional manner by hanging at their fore edge. The hinge bolts to the pillar with two set-screws, access to which is gained by pulling off the pillar inner trim. The catch at the trailing edge is pinned to the glass with a circlip and rivet whilst it is screwed to the bodyshell. Removal and replacement is straightforward.

10 Bumpers and body fittings

1 The front and rear bumpers are fitted in the same way. Basically the bumper bar is fixed by two front bolts, one to each of the two pieces of the L-shaped bracket. A rubber faced overrider covering a 'square' headed bolt, fixes them. These are easy to remove and replace. The L-shaped bracket bolts to the bodyshell, access comes from below the wheel arch, by two through bolts with captive nuts. At each end of the bumper a bolt passes through the bumper, a rubber cushion and into the wing and through the L-shaped brackets, thereby provided a rigid fixing. Their removal is straightforward.
2 The rear bumper will have the number plate light affixed to it. See Chapter 9. The front bumper of the TI houses the flasher lights, again see Chapter 9.
3 All the external body fittings for the Alfasuds either bolt, screw or press in. Fig. 11.3 will tell you which it is. Basically, badges push-in, grilles, mud flaps and mirrors bolt in with the use of some setscrews and sheet metal screws, whilst the spoilers of the TI bolt-in. The excellent Figs. 11.4A and 11.4B will show all the permutations.

11 Heated rear window

The heated rear window fitted to some models provides added complication to an already difficult one. Leave the repair fitting of this type of window to an experienced glass fitter. Care should always be taken with the electrical side.

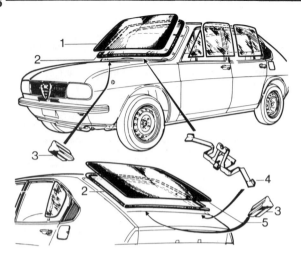

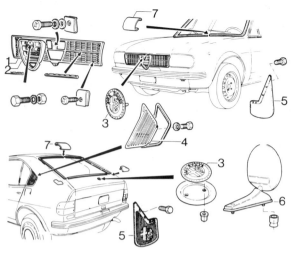

Fig. 11.1. Windscreen with sealing

1 Front screen
2 Sealing
3 Locator
4 Clip
5 Rear screen

Fig. 11.3. Alfasud body fittings

1 Grille
2 Shield
3 Badge
4 Grille
5 Mudflap
6 Mirror
7 Screen clip

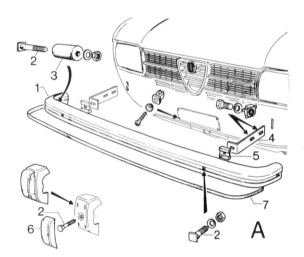

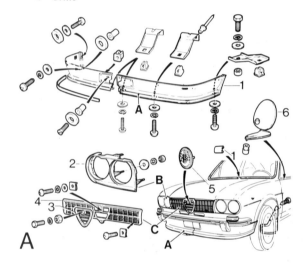

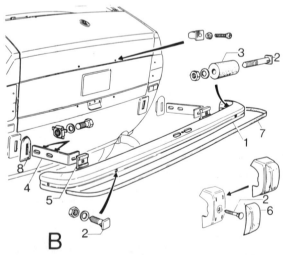

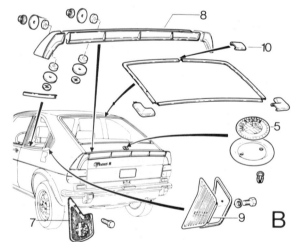

Fig. 11.2A and 11.2B. Front and rear bumpers and fittings

1 Bumper
2 Bolt
3 Spacer rubber
4 Bracket
5 Spacer
6 Overrider rubber
7 Tape
8 Grommet

Fig. 11.4A and 11.4B. Alfasud TI body fittings

1 Front spoiler
2 Headlamp cowl
3 Shield
4 Grille
5 Badge
6 Mirror
7 Mudflap
8 Rear spoiler
9 Grille
10 Screen clip

12 Door lock - removal, refitting and adjustment

1   The door striker plate fixes, by two set screws, to the door pillar. It has a spacer behind it. It is easily removed and provides a certain measure of adjustment, providing movement for the door both up and down and in and out.

2   The door lock is not easily removed without the inner trim panel being removed first. Remove the window winder handle (it has a centre axis screw hidden behind a flat plastic clip plate) and the door release (fixed by two screws, one of which is hidden by the lever itself). When this is removed with its plastic plate, the other screw is exposed. Remove the door pull.

3   Now unscrew the interior push-down door plunger. This plastic cap comes off easily.

4   Now unscrew the trim panel fixing screws, always visible, and lift off the panel.

5   Pull away the polythene cover stuck to the door.

6   On the trailing edge of the door undo the screw which holds the door catch.

7   Now using a socket, release the door lock to the outer handle fixing.

It is now possible to juggle out the lock and push down the door plunger complete with rods when the junction is released from the inner door panel. It has a nut and stud fixing.

8   The outer door handle can be finally removed by releasing the other nut inside the door.

9   Replacement is a direct reverse procedure.

10 Adjust the locks.

13 Door window glass and regulator - removal and refitting

1   Strip the door down as described in Section 12 up to and including paragraph 4.

2   Undo the six setscrews shown in the photographs plus two more at the bottom of each channel down which the glass slides.

3   Unclip the inner transverse channel across the window.

4   The regulator mechanism can now be removed.

5   It is also possible to extract the glass from its grip on its lower edge and the locating channels either side.

6   Replacement of both glass and regulator is a straightforward reverse procedure.

12.2a The plastic strip is removed here

12.2b The door pull fixing plate

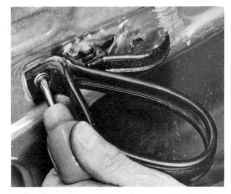
12.2c The pull/catch lever is exposed behind the panel

12.5 The bare door panel with polythene sheet

12.7a The first outer handle fixing nut

12.7b The inner workings of the door mechanism

13.2a The window winder boss with its two setscrews

13.2b The four setscrews just beneath the window glass

13.3 The channel clips should be unclipped

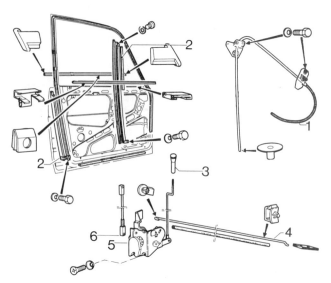

Fig. 11.5. Front door lock and window fittings

1 *Window winder*   4 *Interlink rod*
2 *Channel*   5 *Door lock*
3 *Push button*   6 *Connecting link*

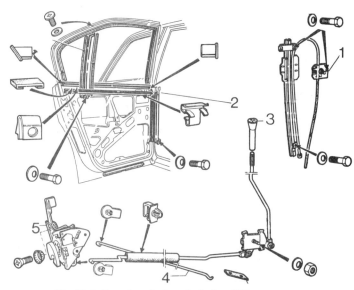

Fig. 11.6. Rear door lock and window fittings

1 *Window*   4 *Interlink rod*
2 *Channel*   5 *Door lock*
3 *Push button*

14 Doors - removal, refitting and adjustment

1 Doors are heavy, have help if you wish to remove one.
2 First release the check strap. The lever arm is fixed to the door pillar by a roll pin. Punch that out.
3 Door removal is easy if you hold the door and punch out the two hinge pins. They have a plug on top of them which can be picked out.
4 It is best to punch out the hinge pins even if you wish to replace the hinges. Once the door is removed the hinges to the pillar can be unscrewed with an impact screwdriver. The hinge half on the door is welded.
5 Replacement is a straight reverse procedure.
6 Door hinge adjustment is not available. Only lock/catch adjustment is available. Read Section 12.

15 Luggage boot lid and bonnet - removal and refitting

1 The boot lid handle is rivetted to the trailing edge. It hinges at its top edge. These hinges are bolted into setscrews to the tail boot lid, visible once the lid is open. The hinges are rivetted to the bodyshell. Remove the four hinge setscrews and the lid will come away. Adjustment takes place on the catch.
2 Fitting is a reverse procedure from the removal sequence.
3 The bonnet hinges on the front edge. The two hinges are welded to the bonnet and bolted to the front of the grill cross member. Open the bonnet, hold it on the catch and remove the setscrews. Retain any shims. Have someone hold the bonnet and then disconnect the spring stop and catch.
4 Replacement is straightforward with adjustment on the catch.

16 Luggage boot lock and bonnet catch - dismantling and reassembly

1 The boot lid uses a cable catch operated from the left-hand seat, just

on the floor front in front of the rear door pillar. The lever is a simple trigger mechanism bolted to the floor with a single setscrew and captive nut.
2 The operating cable, inner and outer, is led round to the centre of the rear of the bolt. A spring loaded catch is used, bolted by two setscrews to the boot floor. A catch is welded to the inside of the boot lid.
3 Replacement is very straightforward. The inner cable which may break has a soldered ferrule at its lever end and is bolted to the spring catch. Access to the boot is available through the back seat panel.
4 The bonnet catch is just as simple as the boot lid. A cable pull under the left-hand dashboard operates a spring catch in the centre of the front screen/bulkhead bolted to it by two setscrews. An emergency nylon pull is also fitted should failure occur of the main pull.
5 Replacement is straightforward with the cable pull end located by a ferrule and the catch end by a soldered loop. It does not have an inner and an outer but only utilises a single cable.

17 Windscreen washers

1 Two windscreen washer jets are fitted to the bonnet. A plunger, manually operated, pumps water from the plastic reservoir bag fixed to the inner wing under the bonnet. (Some cars do have electric pumps).
2 The jets are push-in fit with nothing remotely unconventional concerning the whole system. The length of feed to the jets is rather long, however, to accomodate the bonnet line.

18 Instrument panel and parcel shelf

1 The instrument panel, once the instruments are removed, see Chapter 9, is simple to remove and refit. It is fixed to the bulkhead below the front screen by a number of setscrews and bolts. Their exact position is given in Fig. 11.11. All the fittings in the panel are press fit only.
2 The front panel shelf is bolted and screwed beneath the instrument panel. Its removal is simple and quick as nothing appears below it. See Fig. 11.12.

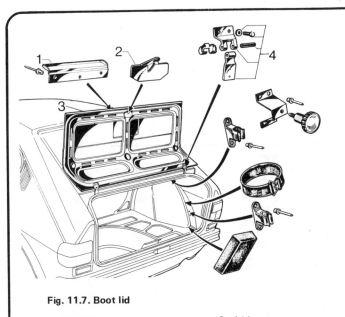

Fig. 11.7. Boot lid

1 Handle   3 Lid
2 Catch   4 Hinge

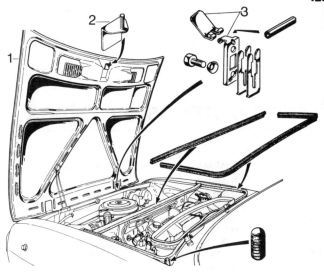

Fig. 11.8. Bonnet

1 Bonnet   3 Hinge
2 Catch

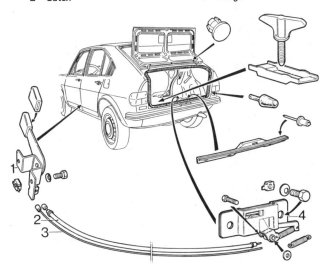

Fig. 11.9. Boot lid catch release

1 Lever   3 Inner cable
2 Outer/inner cable 4 Catch

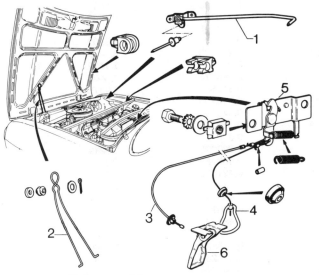

Fig. 11.10. Bonnet catch

1 Prop   4 Emergency release
2 Check strap   5 Catch
3 Release cable   6 Lever

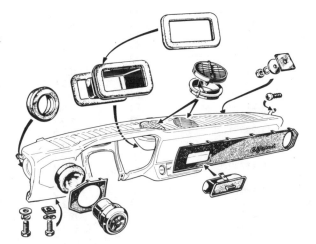

Fig. 11.11. Instrument panel

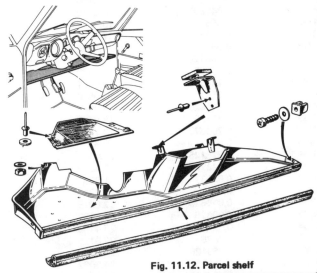

Fig. 11.12. Parcel shelf

Metric conversion tables

Inches	Decimals	Millimetres
1/64	0.015625	0.3969
1/32	0.03125	0.7937
3/64	0.046875	1.1906
1/16	0.0625	1.5875
5/64	0.078125	1.9844
3/32	0.09375	2.3812
7/64	0.109375	2.7781
1/8	0.125	3.1750
9/64	0.140625	3.5719
5/32	0.15625	3.9687
11/64	0.171875	4.3656
3/16	0.1875	4.7625
13/64	0.203125	5.1594
7/32	0.21875	5.5562
15/64	0.234275	5.9531
1/4	0.25	6.3500
17/64	0.265625	6.7469
9/32	0.28125	7.1437
19/64	0.296875	7.5406
5/16	0.3125	7.9375
21/64	0.328125	8.3344
11/32	0.34375	8.7312
23/64	0.359375	9.1281
3/8	0.375	9.5250
25/64	0.390625	9.9219
13/32	0.40625	10.3187
27/64	0.421875	10.7156
7/16	0.4375	11.1125
29/64	0.453125	11.5094
15/32	0.46875	11.9062
31/64	0.484375	12.3031
1/2	0.5	12.7000
33/64	0.515625	13.0969
17/32	0.53125	13.4937
35/64	0.546875	13.8906
9/16	0.5625	14.2875
37/64	0.578125	14.6844
19/32	0.59375	15.0812
39/64	0.609375	15.4781
5/8	0.625	15.8750
41/64	0.640625	16.2719
21/32	0.65625	16.6687
43/64	0.671875	17.0656
11/16	0.6875	17.4625
45/64	0.703125	17.8594
23/32	0.71875	18.2562
47/64	0.734375	18.6531
3/4	0.75	19.0500
49/64	0.765625	19.4469
25/32	0.78125	19.8437
51/64	0.796875	20.2406
13/16	0.8125	20.6375
53/64	0.828125	21.0344
27/32	0.84375	21.4312
55/64	0.859375	21.8281
7/8	0.875	22.2250
57/64	0.890625	22.6219
29/32	0.90625	23.0187
59/64	0.921875	23.4156
15/16	0.9375	23.8125
61/64	0.953125	24.2094
31/32	0.96875	24.6062
63/64	0.984375	25.0031

Millimetres to Inches

mm	Inches
0.01	0.00039
0.02	0.00079
0.03	0.00118
0.04	0.00157
0.05	0.00197
0.06	0.00236
0.07	0.00276
0.08	0.00315
0.09	0.00354
0.1	0.00394
0.2	0.00787
0.3	0.1181
0.4	0.01575
0.5	0.01969
0.6	0.02362
0.7	0.02756
0.8	0.3150
0.9	0.03543
1	0.03937
2	0.07874
3	0.11811
4	0.15748
5	0.19685
6	0.23622
7	0.27559
8	0.31496
9	0.35433
10	0.39270
11	0.43307
12	0.47244
13	0.51181
14	0.55118
15	0.59055
16	0.62992
17	0.66929
18	0.70866
19	0.74803
20	0.78740
21	0.82677
22	0.86614
23	0.90551
24	0.94488
25	0.98425
26	1.02362
27	1.06299
28	1.10236
29	1.14173
30	1.18110
31	1.22047
32	1.25984
33	1.29921
34	1.33858
35	1.37795
36	1.41732
37	1.4567
38	1.4961
39	1.5354
40	1.5748
41	1.6142
42	1.6535
43	1.6929
44	1.7323
45	1.7717

Inches to Millimetres

Inches	mm
0.001	0.0254
0.002	0.0508
0.003	0.0762
0.004	0.1016
0.005	0.1270
0.006	0.1524
0.007	0.1778
0.008	0.2032
0.009	0.2286
0.01	0.254
0.02	0.508
0.03	0.762
0.04	1.016
0.05	1.270
0.06	1.524
0.07	1.778
0.08	2.032
0.09	2.286
0.1	2.54
0.2	5.08
0.3	7.62
0.4	10.16
0.5	12.70
0.6	15.24
0.7	17.78
0.8	20.32
0.9	22.86
1	25.4
2	50.8
3	76.2
4	101.6
5	127.0
6	152.4
7	177.8
8	203.2
9	228.6
10	254.0
11	279.4
12	304.8
13	330.2
14	355.6
15	381.0
16	406.4
17	431.8
18	457.2
19	482.6
20	508.0
21	533.4
22	558.8
23	584.2
24	609.6
25	635.0
26	660.4
27	685.8
28	711.2
29	736.6
30	762.0
31	787.4
32	812.8
33	838.2
34	863.6
35	889.0
46	914.4

1   Imperial gallon = 8 Imp pints = 1.16 US gallons = 277.42 cu in = 4.5459 litres

1   US gallon = 4 US quarts = 0.862 Imp gallon = 231 cu in = 3.785 litres

1   Litre = 0.2199 Imp gallon = 0.2642 US gallon = 61.0253 cu in = 1000 cc

Miles to Kilometres		Kilometres to Miles	
1	1.61	1	0.62
2	3.22	2	1.24
3	4.83	3	1.86
4	6.44	4	2.49
5	8.05	5	3.11
6	9.66	6	3.73
7	11.27	7	4.35
8	12.88	8	4.97
9	14.48	9	5.59
10	16.09	10	6.21
20	32.19	20	12.43
30	48.28	30	18.64
40	64.37	40	24.85
50	80.47	50	31.07
60	96.56	60	37.28
70	112.65	70	43.50
80	128.75	80	49.71
90	144.84	90	55.92
100	160.93	100	62.14

lb f ft to Kg f m		Kg f m to lb f ft		lb f/in^2 : Kg f/cm^2		Kg f/cm^2 : lb f/in^2	
1	0.138	1	7.233	1	0.07	1	14.22
2	0.276	2	14.466	2	0.14	2	28.50
3	0.414	3	21.699	3	0.21	3	42.67
4	0.553	4	28.932	4	0.28	4	56.89
5	0.691	5	36.165	5	0.35	5	71.12
6	0.829	6	43.398	6	0.42	6	85.34
7	0.967	7	50.631	7	0.49	7	99.56
8	1.106	8	57.864	8	0.56	8	113.79
9	1.244	9	65.097	9	0.63	9	128.00
10	1.382	10	62.330	10	0.70	10	142.23
20	2.765	20	144.660	20	1.41	20	284.47
30	4.147	30	216.990	30	2.11	30	426.70

Index

Printed by
Haynes Publishing Group
Sparkford Yeovil Somerset
England